New Perspectives on
Microsoft®
Access 97

INTRODUCTORY

The New Perspectives Series

The New Perspectives Series consists of texts and technology that teach computer concepts and microcomputer applications (listed below). You can order these New Perspectives texts in many different lengths, software releases, custom-bound combinations, CourseKits™ and Custom Editions®. Contact your Course Technology sales representative or customer service representative for the most up-to-date details.

The New Perspectives Series

Computer Concepts

Borland® dBASE®

Borland® Paradox®

Corel® Presentations™

Corel® Quattro Pro®

Corel® WordPerfect®

DOS

HTML

Lotus® 1-2-3®

Microsoft® Access

Microsoft® Excel

Microsoft® Internet Explorer

Microsoft® Office Professional

Microsoft® PowerPoint®

Microsoft® Windows® 3.1

Microsoft® Windows® 95

Microsoft® Windows NT® Server 4.0

Microsoft® Windows NT® Workstation 4.0

Microsoft® Word

Microsoft® Works

Netscape Navigator™

Netscape Navigator™ Gold

Microsoft® Visual Basic® 4 and 5

New Perspectives on
Microsoft®
Access 97

Joseph J. Adamski
Grand Valley State University

Charles Hommel
University of Puget Sound

Kathleen T. Finnegan

COURSE
TECHNOLOGY

ONE MAIN STREET, CAMBRIDGE, MA 02142

an International Thomson Publishing company I(T)P®

Cambridge • Albany • Bonn • Boston • Cincinnati • London • Madrid • Melbourne • Mexico City
New York • Paris • San Francisco • Singapore • Tokyo • Toronto • Washington

New Perspectives on Microsoft® Access 97 — Introductory is published by Course Technology.

Associate Publisher	Mac Mendelsohn
Series Consulting Editor	Susan Solomon
Product Manager	Donna Gridley
Developmental Editor	Kathy Finnegan
Production Editor	Roxanne Alexander
Text and Cover Designer	Ella Hanna
Cover Illustrator	Douglas Goodman

© 1997 by Course Technology—I(T)P®

For more information contact:

Course Technology
One Main Street
Cambridge, MA 02142

ITP Europe
Berkshire House 168-173
High Holborn
London WCIV 7AA
England

Nelson ITP, Australia
102 Dodds Street
South Melbourne, 3205
Victoria, Australia

ITP Nelson Canada
1120 Birchmount Road
Scarborough, Ontario
Canada M1K 5G4

International Thomson Editores
Seneca, 53
Colonia Polanco
11560 Mexico D.F. Mexico

ITP GmbH
Königswinterer Strasse 418
53227 Bonn
Germany

ITP Asia
60 Albert Street, #15-01
Albert Complex
Singapore 189969

ITP Japan
Hirakawacho Kyowa Building, 3F
2-2-1 Hirakawacho
Chiyoda-ku, Tokyo 102
Japan

Trademarks
Course Technology and the Open Book logo are registered trademarks and CourseKits is a trademark of Course Technology. Custom Editions and the ITP logo are registered trademarks of International Thomson Publishing Inc.

Some of the product names and company names used in this book have been used for identification purposes only and may be trademarks or registered trademarks of their respective manufacturers and sellers.

Credits
Course Technology gratefully acknowledges Lexus Corporation and Team One Advertising for allowing the use of the three Model Gallery illustrations created by Jay Malloy and Michael Gaw from the Lexus Corporate Web site that appear on the Student Disk in Tutorial 6.

Disclaimer
Course Technology reserves the right to revise this publication and make changes from time to time in its content without notice.

ISBN 0-7600-5253-0

Printed in the United States of America

7 8 9   BM   01 00 99

At Course Technology we have one foot in education and the other in technology. We believe that technology is transforming the way people teach and learn, and we are excited about providing instructors and students with materials that use technology to teach about technology.

Our development process is unparalleled in the higher education publishing industry. Every product we create goes through an exacting process of design, development, review, and testing.

Reviewers give us direction and insight that shape our manuscripts and bring them up to the latest standards. Every manuscript is quality tested. Students whose backgrounds match the intended audience work through every keystroke, carefully checking for clarity and pointing out errors in logic and sequence. Together with our own technical reviewers, these testers help us ensure that everything that carries our name is error-free and easy to use.

We show both how and why technology is critical to solving problems in college and in whatever field you choose to teach or pursue. Our time-tested, step-by-step instructions provide unparalleled clarity. Examples and applications are chosen and crafted to motivate students.

As the New Perspectives Series team at Course Technology, our goal is to produce the most timely, accurate, creative, and technologically sound product in the entire college publishing industry. We strive for consistent high quality. This takes a lot of communication, coordination, and hard work. But we love what we do. We are determined to be the best. Write to us and let us know what you think. You can also e-mail us at *NewPerspectives@course.com*.

The New Perspectives Series Team

Joseph J. Adamski	Jessica Evans	Dan Oja
Judy Adamski	Marilyn Freedman	David Paradice
Roy Ageloff	Kathy Finnegan	June Parsons
David Auer	Robin Geller	Harry Phillips
Dirk Baldwin	Donna Gridley	Sandra Poindexter
Daphne Barbas	Roger Hayen	Mark Reimold
Rachel Bunin	Charles Hommel	Ann Shaffer
Joan Carey	Janice Jutras	Susan Solomon
Patrick Carey	Chris Kelly	Susanne Walker
Sharon Caswell	Mary Kemper	John Zeanchock
Barbara Clemens	Terry Ann Kremer	Beverly Zimmerman
Rachel Crapser	John Leschke	Scott Zimmerman
Kim Crowley	Mac Mendelsohn	
Michael Ekedahl	William Newman	

Preface The New Perspectives Series

What is the New Perspectives Series?

Course Technology's **New Perspectives Series** is an integrated system of instruction that combines text and technology products to teach computer concepts and microcomputer applications. Users consistently praise this series for innovative pedagogy, creativity, supportive and engaging style, accuracy, and use of interactive technology. The first New Perspectives text was published in January of 1993. Since then, the series has grown to more than 100 titles and has become the best-selling series on computer concepts and microcomputer applications. Others have imitated the New Perspectives features, design, and technologies, but none have replicated its quality and its ability to consistently anticipate and meet the needs of instructors and students.

What is the Integrated System of Instruction?

New Perspectives textbooks are part of a truly Integrated System of Instruction: text, graphics, video, sound, animation, and simulations that are linked and that provide a flexible, unified, and interactive system to help you teach and help your students learn. Specifically, the *New Perspectives Integrated System of Instruction* includes a Course Technology textbook in addition to some or all of the following items: Course Labs, Course Test Manager, Online Companions, and Course Presenter. These components—shown in the graphic on the back cover of this book—have been developed to work together to provide a complete, integrative teaching and learning experience.

How is the New Perspectives Series different from other microcomputer concepts and applications series?

The **New Perspectives Series** distinguishes itself from other series in at least four substantial ways: sound instructional design, consistent quality, innovative technology, and proven pedagogy. The applications texts in this series consist of two or more tutorials, which are based on sound instructional design. Each tutorial is motivated by a realistic case that is meaningful to students. Rather than learn a laundry list of features, students learn the features in the context of solving a problem. This process motivates all concepts and skills by demonstrating to students *why* they would want to know them.

Instructors and students have come to rely on the high quality of the **New Perspectives Series** and to consistently praise its accuracy. This accuracy is a result of Course Technology's unique multi-step quality assurance process that incorporates student testing at at least two stages of development, using hardware and software configurations appropriate to the product. All solutions, test questions, and other supplements are tested using similar procedures. Instructors who adopt this series report that students can work through the tutorials independently with minimum intervention or "damage control" by instructors or staff. This consistent quality has meant that if instructors are pleased with one product from the series, they can rely on the same quality with any other New Perspectives product.

The **New Perspectives Series** also distinguishes itself by its innovative technology. This series innovated Course Labs, truly *interactive* learning applications. These have set the standard for interactive learning.

How do I know that the New Perspectives Series will work?

Some instructors who use this series report a significant difference between how much their students learn and retain with this series as compared to other series. With other series, instructors often find that students can work through the book and do well on homework and tests, but still not demonstrate competency when asked to perform particular tasks outside the context of the text's sample case or project. With the **New Perspectives Series**, however, instructors report that students have a complete, integrative learning experience that stays with them. They credit this high retention and competency to the fact that this series incorporates critical thinking and problem-solving with computer skills mastery.

How does this book I'm holding fit into the New Perspectives Series?

New Perspectives applications books are available in the following categories:

Brief books are typically about 150 pages long, contain two to four tutorials, and are intended to teach the basics of an application.

Introductory books are typically about 300 pages long and consist of four to seven tutorials that go beyond the basics. These books often build out of the Brief editions by providing two or three additional tutorials. The book you are holding is an Introductory book.

Comprehensive books are typically about 600 pages long and consist of all of the tutorials in the Introductory books, plus three to five additional tutorials covering higher-level topics. Comprehensive books also include two Windows tutorials and three or four Additional Cases.

Advanced books cover topics similar to those in the Comprehensive books, but go into more depth. Advanced books present the most high-level coverage in the series.

Custom Books The New Perspectives Series offers you two ways to customize a New Perspectives text to fit your course exactly: *CourseKits*™, two or more texts packaged together in a box, and *Custom Editions*®, your choice of books bound together. Custom Editions offer you unparalleled flexibility in designing your concepts and applications courses. You can build your own book by ordering a combination of titles bound together to cover only the topics you want. Your students save because they buy only the materials they need. There is no minimum order, and books are spiral bound. Both CourseKits and Custom Editions offer significant price discounts. Contact your Course Technology sales representative for more information.

New Perspectives Series Microcomputer Applications

■ Brief Titles or Modules	■ Introductory Titles or Modules	■ Intermediate Tutorials	■ Advanced Titles or Modules	□ Other Modules

Brief	**Introductory**	**Comprehensive**	**Advanced**	**Custom Editions**
2 to 4 tutorials	6 or 7 tutorials, or Brief + 2 or 3 more tutorials	Introductory + 4 or 5 more tutorials. Includes Brief Windows tutorials and Additional Cases	Quick Review of basics + in-depth, high-level coverage	Choose from any of the above to build your own Custom Editions® or CourseKits™

In what kind of course could I use this book?

This book can be used in any course in which you want students to learn all the most important topics of Microsoft Access, including creating and maintaining database tables; defining table relationships; creating, running, and saving queries; sorting and filtering records; creating and customizing forms and reports; and publishing Access objects to the World Wide Web. It is ideal as part of a microcomputer applications course or a short course on Microsoft Access 97. This book assumes that students have learned basic Windows 95 navigation and file management skills from Course Technology's *New Perspectives on Microsoft Windows 95—Brief* or an *equivalent* book.

How do the Windows 95 editions differ from the Windows 3.1 editions?

Sessions We've divided the tutorials into sessions. Each session is designed to be completed in about 45 minutes to an hour (depending, of course, upon student needs and the speed of your lab equipment). With sessions, learning is broken up into more easily assimilated portions. You can more accurately allocate time in your syllabus, and students can better manage the available lab time. Each session begins with a "session box," which quickly describes the skills students will learn in the session. Furthermore, each session is numbered, which makes it easier for you and your students to navigate and communicate about the tutorial. Look on page A 1.5 for the session box that opens Session 1.1.

Quick Checks Each session concludes with meaningful, conceptual Quick Check questions that test students' understanding of what they learned in the session. Answers to all of the Quick Check questions in this book are provided on pages A 4.35 through A 4.36 and A 7.35 through A 7.36.

New Design We have retained the best of the old design to help students differentiate between what they are to *do* and what they are to *read*. The steps are clearly identified by their shaded background and numbered steps. Furthermore, this new design presents steps and screen shots in a larger, easier to read format. Some good examples of our new design are pages A 1.14 and A 1.15.

What features are retained in the Windows 95 editions of the New Perspectives Series?

"Read This Before You Begin" Page This page is consistent with Course Technology's unequaled commitment to helping instructors introduce technology into the classroom. Technical considerations and assumptions about software are listed to help instructors save time and eliminate unnecessary aggravation. See pages A 1.2, and A 5.2 for the "Read This Before You Begin" pages in this book.

Tutorial Case Each tutorial begins with a problem presented in a case that is meaningful to students. The problem turns the task of learning how to use an application into a problem-solving process. The problems increase in complexity with each tutorial. These cases touch on multicultural, international, and ethical issues—so important to today's business curriculum. See page A 1.3 for the case that begins Tutorial 1.

1.
2.
3.

Step-by-Step Methodology This unique Course Technology methodology keeps students on track. They enter data, click buttons, or press keys always within the context of solving the problem posed in the tutorial case. The text constantly guides students, letting them know where they are in the course of solving the problem. In addition, the numerous screen shots include labels that direct students' attention to what they should look at on the screen. On almost every page in this book, you can find an example of how steps, screen shots, and labels work together.

TROUBLE?

TROUBLE? Paragraphs These paragraphs anticipate the mistakes or problems that students are likely to have and help them recover and continue with the tutorial. By putting these paragraphs in the book, rather than in the Instructor's Manual, we facilitate independent learning and free the instructor to focus on substantive conceptual issues rather than on common procedural errors. Some representative examples of TROUBLE? paragraphs appear on pages A 1.7 and A1.10.

Reference Windows Reference Windows appear throughout the text. They are succinct summaries of the most important tasks covered in the tutorials. Reference Windows are specially designed and written so students can refer to them when doing the Tutorial Assignments and Case Problems, and after completing the course. Page A 1.18 contains the Reference Window for Using the Office Assistant.

Task Reference The Task Reference contains a summary of how to perform common tasks using the most efficient method, as well as references to pages where the task is discussed in more detail. It appears as a table at the end of the book.

Tutorial Assignments, Case Problems, and Lab Assignments Each tutorial concludes with Tutorial Assignments, which provide students with additional hands-on practice of the skills they learned in the tutorial. See page A 1.23 for examples of Tutorial Assignments. The Tutorial Assignments are followed by four Case Problems that have approximately the same scope as the tutorial case. See page A 1.24 for examples of Case Problems. Finally, if a Course Lab accompanies a tutorial, Lab Assignments are included after the Case Problems. See page A 1.27 for examples of Lab Assignments.

Exploration Exercises The Windows environment allows students to learn by exploring and discovering what they can do. Exploration Exercises can be Tutorial Assignments or Case Problems that challenge students, encourage them to explore the capabilities of the program they are using, and extend their knowledge using the Help facility and other reference materials. Page A 1.23 contains Exploration Exercises for Tutorial 1.

What supplements are available with this textbook?

Course Labs: Now, Concepts Come to Life Computer skills and concepts come to life with the New Perspectives Course Labs—highly-interactive tutorials that combine illustrations, animations, digital images, and simulations. The Labs guide students step-by-step, present them with Quick Check questions, let them explore on their own, test their comprehension, and provide printed feedback. Lab icons at the beginning of the tutorial and in the tutorial margins indicate when a topic has a corresponding Lab. Lab Assignments are included at the end of each relevant tutorial. The Lab available with this book and the tutorial in which it appears is:

TUTORIAL 1

Databases

Course Test Manager: Testing and Practice at the Computer or on Paper Course Test Manager is cutting-edge, Windows-based testing software that helps instructors design and administer practice tests and actual examinations. This full-featured program allows students to randomly generate practice tests that provide immediate on-screen feedback and detailed study guides. Instructors can also use Course Test Manager to produce printed tests. Course Test Manager can automatically grade the tests students take at the computer and can generate statistical information on individual as well as group performance.

Course Presenter: This lecture presentation tool allows instructors to create electronic slide shows or traditional overhead transparencies using the figure files from the book. Instructors can customize, edit, save, and display the figures from the text in order to illustrate key topics or concepts in class.

Online Companions: Dedicated to Keeping You and Your Students Up-To-Date When you use a New Perspectives product, you can access Course Technology's faculty sites and student sites on the World Wide Web. You can browse the password-protected Faculty Online Companions to obtain online Instructor's Manuals, Solution Files, Student Files, and more. Please see your Instructor's Manual or call your Course Technology customer service representative for more information. Student and Faculty Online Companions are accessible by clicking the appropriate links on the Course Technology home page at http://www.course.com.

Student Files Student Files contain all of the data that students will use to complete the tutorials, Tutorial Assignments, and Case Problems. A Readme file includes technical tips for lab management. See the inside covers of this book and the "Read This Before You Begin" pages for more information on Student Files.

Instructor's Manual New Perspectives Series Instructor's Manuals contain instructor's notes and printed solutions for each tutorial. Instructor's notes provide tutorial overviews and outlines, technical notes, lecture notes, and extra Case Problems. Printed solutions include solutions to Tutorial Assignments, Case Problems, Additional Cases, and Lab Assignments.

Solution Files Solution Files contain every file students are asked to create or modify in the tutorials, Tutorial Assignments, and Case Problems.

The following supplements are included in the Instructor's Resource Kit that accompanies this textbook:

- Instructor's Manual
- Solution Files
- Student Files
- Databases Course Lab

- Course Test Manager Release 1.1 Test Bank
- Course Test Manager Release 1.1 Engine
- Course Presenter

Some of the supplements listed above are also available over the World Wide Web through Course Technology's password-protected Faculty Online Companions. Please see your Instructor's Manual or call your Course Technology customer service representative for more information.

Acknowledgments

I would like to thank the dedicated and enthusiastic Course Technology staff, including Joe Dougherty, Mac Mendelsohn, Susan Solomon, and Mark Reimold. Thanks as well to all the Production staff, including everyone from GEX who worked hard to produce this book. And a special thanks to Kathy Finnegan for her talents, verve, and long hours of dedicated work.

Joseph J. Adamski

I want to thank all those who helped in completing this book, including Nancy Acree of University of Puget Sound, and Joyce Strain of Green River Community College, who reviewed the first draft; Course Technology's great team, including Mark Reimold, Donna Gridley, Roxanne Alexander, Jane Pedicini, Greg Bigelow, John McCarthy, and all the others involved in creating this book. Also, my thanks to Kathy Finnegan, whose keen eye greatly improved the book and whose good humor made deadlines seem almost fun. Finally, special thanks to Joan, who tolerated many late nights and lost weekends while I worked, and Anna, who helped with paste-ups and backups when she would have preferred a good game of checkers.

Charles Hommel

I would like to thank the following reviewers for their excellent feedback: Cynthia J. Kachik, Jean Smelewicz of Quinsigamond Community College, and Patricia A. Smith, Ph.D., of Temple Junior College. My thanks to all the Course Technology staff, including Mac Mendelsohn, Mark Reimold, Donna Gridley, and Rachel Crapser for their support; Roxanne Alexander for her outstanding management of the production process; Jane Pedicini for her superior copy-editing skills; and Greg Bigelow and Brian McCooey for ensuring the accuracy of the text. Thanks, too, to everyone at GEX for their efforts in the composition of this book. Special thanks to Sasha Vodnik for his contributions in developing this text, and to Joe Adamski for his invaluable guidance and encouragement. Finally, thanks to Joe, Connor, and Devon for their support and for interrupting me just enough so that I remembered what the outside of my office looked like.

Kathleen T. Finnegan

Brief **Contents**

Table of **Contents**

NEW
PERSPECTIVES
S E R I E S

Microsoft®
Access 97

LEVEL I

TUTORIALS

Read This **Before You Begin**

STUDENT DISKS

To complete Access 97 Tutorials 1-4, you need three Student Disks. Your instructor will either provide you with the Student Disks or ask you to make your own.

If you are supposed to make your own Student Disks, you will need three blank, formatted, high-density disks. You will need to copy a set of folders from a file server or standalone computer onto your disks. Your instructor will tell you which computer, drive letter, and folders contain the files you need. The following table shows you which folders go on each of your disks, so that you will have enough disk space to complete all the tutorials, Tutorial Assignments, and Case Problems:

Student Disk	Write this on the disk label	Put these folders on the disk
1	Student Disk 1: Access 97 Tutorials 1-4 Tutorials and Tutorial Assignments	Tutorial and TAssign from Disk 1 folder
2	Student Disk 2: Access 97 Tutorials 1-4 Case Problems 1 and 2	Cases from Disk 2 folder
3	Student Disk 3: Access 97 Tutorials 1-4 Case Problems 3 and 4	Cases from Disk 3 folder

When you begin each tutorial, be sure you are using the correct Student Disk. See the inside front or inside back cover of this book for more information on Student Disk files, or ask your instructor or technical support person for assistance.

COURSE LAB

Tutorial 1 features an interactive Course Lab to help you understand database concepts. There are Lab Assignments at the end of the tutorial that relate to this Lab. To start the Lab, click the Start button on the Windows 95 taskbar, point to Programs, point to Course Labs, point to New Perspectives Applications, and click Databases.

USING YOUR OWN COMPUTER

If you are going to work through Tutorials 1-4 using your own computer, you need:

■ **Computer System** Microsoft Windows 95 or Microsoft Windows NT Workstation 4.0 and Microsoft Access 97 must be installed on your computer. Tutorials 1-4 assume a typical installation of Microsoft Access 97.

■ **Student Disks** Ask your instructor or lab manager for details on how to get the Student Disks. You will not be able to complete the tutorials or end-of-tutorial assignments in this book using your own computer until you have the Student Disks. The Student Files may also be obtained electronically over the Internet. See the inside front or inside back cover of this book for more details.

■ **Course Lab** See your instructor or technical support person to obtain the Course Lab software for use on your own computer.

To complete Access 97 Tutorials 1-4, your students must use a set of files on three Student Disks. These files are included in the Instructor's Resource Kit, and they may also be obtained electronically over the Internet. See the inside front or inside back cover of this book for more details. Follow the instructions in the Readme file to copy the files to your server or standalone computer. You can view the Readme file using WordPad. Once the files are copied, you can make Student Disks for the students yourself, or you can tell students where to find the files so they can make their own Student Disks.

COURSE LAB SOFTWARE

The Course Lab software is distributed on a CD-ROM included in the Instructor's Resource Kit. To install the Course Lab software, follow the setup instructions in the Readme file on the CD-ROM. Refer also to the Readme file for essential technical notes related to running the Lab in a multi-user environment. Once you have installed the Course Lab software, your students can start the Lab from the Windows 95 desktop by following the instructions in the Course Lab section above.

COURSE TECHNOLOGY STUDENT FILES AND LAB SOFTWARE

You are granted a license to copy the Student Files and Lab software to any computer or computer network used by students who have purchased this book.

Introduction to Microsoft Access 97

Viewing and Working with a Table Containing Customer Data

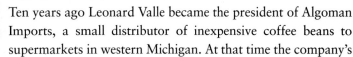

Access

OBJECTIVES

In this tutorial you will:

- Define the terms field, record, table, relational database, primary key, and foreign key
- Start and exit Access
- Open an existing database
- Identify the components of the Access and Database windows
- Open, navigate, and print a table
- Create, run, and print a query
- Create and print a form
- Use the Access Help system
- Create, preview, and print a report

LAB

Databases

Valle Coffee

CASE

Ten years ago Leonard Valle became the president of Algoman Imports, a small distributor of inexpensive coffee beans to supermarkets in western Michigan. At that time the company's growth had leveled off, so during his first three years Leonard took several dramatic, risky steps in an attempt to increase sales and profits. First, he changed the inexpensive coffee bean varieties that Algoman Imports had been distributing to a selection of gourmet varieties from Central and South America, Africa, and several island nations. Second, he purchased facilities and equipment so that the company could roast, grind, flavor, and package the coffee beans instead of buying them already roasted and packaged whole. Because the company could now control the quality of the finest gourmet coffees, Leonard stopped distributing to supermarkets and shifted sales to restaurants and offices throughout the area.

Within two years, company sales and profits soared; consequently, Leonard took over ownership of the company. He changed the company name to Valle Coffee, continued expanding into other markets and geographic areas (specifically, Ohio and Indiana), and expanded the company's line of coffee flavors and blends.

Part of Valle Coffee's success can be credited to its use of computers in all aspects of its business, including financial management, inventory control, shipping, receiving, production, and sales. Several months ago the company upgraded to Microsoft Windows 95 and **Microsoft Access 97** (or simply **Access**), a computer program used to enter, maintain, and retrieve related data in a format known as a database. Barbara Hennessey, office manager at Valle Coffee, and her staff use Access to maintain company data such as customer orders and billing, coffee supplier orders and payments, and advertising placements and payments. Barbara recently created a database named Restaurant to track the company's restaurant customers, their orders, and related data such as the products they order. She asks for your help in completing and maintaining this database.

Using the Tutorials Effectively

These tutorials are designed to be used at a computer. Each tutorial is divided into sessions. Watch for the session headings, such as "Session 1.1" and "Session 1.2." Each session is designed to be completed in about 45 minutes, but take as much time as you need. When you've completed a session, it's a good idea to exit the program and take a break. You can exit Microsoft Access by clicking the Close button in the top-right corner of the program window.

Before you begin, read the following questions and answers. They are designed to help you use the tutorials effectively.

Where do I start?

Each tutorial begins with a case, which sets the scene for the tutorial and gives you background information to help you understand what you will be doing in the tutorial. Read the case before you go to the lab. In the lab, begin with the first session of the tutorial.

How do I know what to do on the computer?

Each session contains steps that you will perform on the computer to learn how to use Microsoft Access. The steps are numbered and are set against a colored background. Read the text that introduces each series of steps, and read each step carefully and completely before you try it.

How do I know if I did the step correctly?

As you work, compare your computer screen with the corresponding figure in the tutorial. Don't worry if your screen display is somewhat different from the figure. The important parts of the screen display are labeled in each figure. Check to make sure these parts are on your screen.

What if I make a mistake?

Don't worry about making mistakes—they are part of the learning process. Paragraphs labeled **"TROUBLE?"** identify common problems and explain how to get back on track. Follow the steps in a **"TROUBLE?"** paragraph *only* if you are having the problem described. If you run into other problems, carefully consider the current state of your system, the position of the pointer, and any messages on the screen.

How do I use the Reference Windows?

Reference Windows summarize the procedures you learn in the tutorial steps. Do not complete the actions in the Reference Windows when you are working through the tutorial. Instead, refer to the Reference Windows while you are working on the assignments at the end of the tutorial.

How can I test my understanding of the material I learned in the tutorial?

At the end of each session, you can answer the Quick Check questions. If necessary, refer to the Answers to Quick Check Questions to check your work.

After you have completed the entire tutorial, you should complete the Tutorial Assignments and Case Problems. These exercises are carefully structured so you will review what you have learned and then apply your knowledge to new situations.

What if I can't remember how to do something?

You should refer to the Task Reference at the end of the book; it summarizes how to accomplish commonly performed tasks.

What is the Databases Course Lab, and how should I use it?

This interactive Lab helps you review database concepts and practice skills that you learn in Tutorial 1. The Lab Assignments section at the end of Tutorial 1 includes instructions for using the Lab.

Now that you've seen how to use the tutorials effectively, you are ready to begin.

SESSION

1.1

In this session you will define key database terms and concepts, start Access and open an existing database, identify components of the Access and Database windows, open and navigate a table, print a table, and exit Access.

Databases

Introduction to Database Concepts

Before you begin working on Barbara's database and using Access, you need to understand a few key terms and concepts associated with databases.

Organizing Data

Data is a valuable resource to any business. At Valle Coffee, for example, important data includes customers' names and addresses, and order dates and amounts. Organizing, storing, maintaining, retrieving, and sorting this type of data are critical activities that enable a business to find and use information effectively. Before storing data on a computer, however, you first must organize the data.

Your first step in organizing data is to identify the individual fields. A **field** is a single characteristic or attribute of a person, place, object, event, or idea. For example, some of the many fields that Valle Coffee tracks are customer number, customer name, customer address, customer phone number, order number, billing date, and invoice amount.

Next, you group related fields together into tables. A **table** is a collection of fields that describe a person, place, object, event, or idea. Figure 1-1 shows an example of a Customer table consisting of four fields: Customer Number, Customer Name, Customer Address, and Phone Number.

Figure 1-1 ◀

Data organization for a table of customers

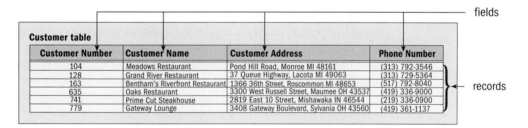

The specific value, or content, of a field is called the **field value**. In Figure 1-1, the first set of field values for Customer Number, Customer Name, Customer Address, and Phone Number are, respectively, 104; Meadows Restaurant; Pond Hill Road, Monroe MI 48161; and (313) 792-3546. This set of field values is called a **record**. In the Customer table, the data for each customer is stored as a separate record. Six records are shown in Figure 1-1; each row of field values is a record.

Databases and Relationships

A collection of related tables is called a **database**, or **relational database**. Valle Coffee's Restaurant database will contain two related tables: the Customer table, which Barbara has already created, and the Order table, which you will create in Tutorial 2. Sometimes you might want information about customers and the orders they placed. To obtain this information you must have a way to connect records in the Customer table to records in the Order table. You connect the records in the separate tables through a **common field** that appears in both tables. In the sample database shown in Figure 1-2, each record in the Customer table has a field named Customer Number, which is also a field in the Order table. For example, Oaks Restaurant is the fourth customer in the Customer table and has a Customer Number of 635. This same Customer Number field value, 635, appears in three records in the Order table. Therefore, Oaks Restaurant is the customer that placed these three orders.

Figure 1-2 ◀
Database
relationship
between tables
for customers
and orders

primary keys

Each Customer Number in the Customer table must be unique, so that you can distinguish one customer from another and identify the customer's specific orders in the Order table. The Customer Number field is referred to as the primary key of the Customer table. A **primary key** is a field, or a collection of fields, whose values uniquely identify each record in a table. In the Order table, Order Number is the primary key.

When you include the primary key from one table as a field in a second table to form a relationship between the two tables, it is called a **foreign key** in the second table, as shown in Figure 1-2. For example, Customer Number is the primary key in the Customer table and a foreign key in the Order table. Although the primary key Customer Number has unique values in the Customer table, the same field as a foreign key in the Order table does not have unique values. The Customer Number value 635, for example, appears three times in the Order table, because the Oaks Restaurant placed three orders. Each foreign key value, however, must match one of the field values for the primary key in the other table. In the example in Figure 1-2, each Customer Number value in the Order table must match a Customer Number value in the Customer table. The two tables are related, enabling users to tie together the facts about customers with the facts about orders.

Relational Database Management Systems

To manage its databases, a company purchases a database management system. A **database management system** (**DBMS**) is a software program that lets you create databases and then manipulate data in the databases. Most of today's database management systems, including Access, are called relational database management systems. In a **relational database management system**, data is organized as a collection of tables. As stated earlier, a relationship between two tables in a relational DBMS is formed through a common field.

A relational DBMS controls the storage of databases on disk by carrying out data creation and manipulation requests. Specifically, a relational DBMS provides the following functions, which are illustrated in Figure 1-3:

■ It allows you to create database structures containing fields, tables, and table relationships.

■ It lets you easily add new records, change field values in existing records, and delete records.

■ It contains a built-in query language, which lets you obtain immediate answers to the questions you ask about your data.

■ It contains a built-in report generator, which lets you produce professional-looking, formatted reports from your data.

■ It provides protection of databases through security, control, and recovery facilities.

Figure 1-3 ◀
A relational
database
management
system

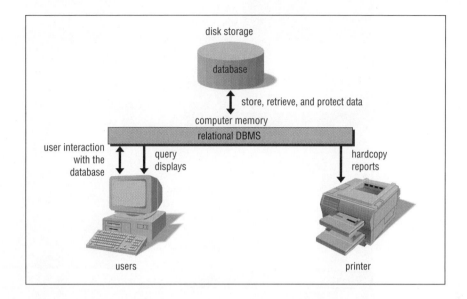

A company like Valle Coffee benefits from a relational DBMS because it allows several users working in different departments to share the same data. More than one user can enter data into a database, and more than one user can retrieve and analyze data that was entered by others. For example, Valle Coffee will keep only one copy of the Customer table, and all employees will be able to use it to meet their specific needs for customer information.

Finally, unlike other software programs, such as spreadsheets, a DBMS can handle massive amounts of data and can easily form relationships among multiple tables. Each Access database, for example, can be up to 1 gigabyte in size and can contain up to 32,768 objects (tables, queries, and so on).

Now that you've learned some database terms and concepts, you're ready to start Access and open the Restaurant database.

Starting Access

You start Access in the same way that you start other Windows 95 programs—using the Start button on the taskbar.

To start Access:

1. Make sure Windows 95 is running on your computer and the Windows 95 desktop appears on your screen.

   TROUBLE? If you're running Windows NT Workstation 4.0 (or a later version) on your computer or network, don't worry. Although the figures in this book were created while running Windows 95, Windows NT 4.0 and Windows 95 share the same interface, and Access 97 runs equally well under either operating system.

2. Click the **Start** button on the taskbar to display the Start menu, and then point to **Programs** to display the Programs menu.

3. Point to **Microsoft Access** on the Programs menu. See Figure 1-4.

Figure 1-4 ◀
Starting
Microsoft
Access

Programs menu
option

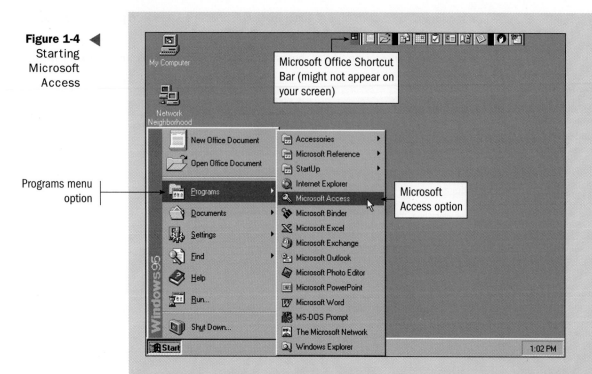

TROUBLE? If you don't see the Microsoft Access option on the Programs menu, ask your instructor or technical support person for help.

TROUBLE? The Office Shortcut Bar, which appears along the top of the desktop in Figure 1-4, might look different on your screen or it might not appear at all, depending on how your system is set up. The steps in these tutorials do not require that you use the Office Shortcut Bar; therefore, the remaining figures do not display the Office Shortcut Bar.

4. Click **Microsoft Access** to start Access. After a short pause, the Access copyright information appears in a message box and remains on the screen until the Access window is displayed. See Figure 1-5.

Figure 1-5 ◀
The Microsoft
Access window

toolbar

initial dialog box

status bar

> **TROUBLE?** Depending on how your system is set up, the Office Assistant (see Figure 1-5) might open when you start Access. For now, click the Close button ☒ on the Office Assistant window to close it; you'll learn more about this feature later in this tutorial. If you've started Access immediately after installing it, you'll need to click the Start Using Microsoft Access option, which the Office Assistant displays, before closing the Office Assistant window.

When you start Access, the Access window contains a dialog box that allows you to create a new database or open an existing database. You can choose either the Blank Database option to create a new database on your own, or you can choose the Database Wizard option and let the wizard guide you through the steps for creating a database. In this case, you need to open an existing database.

Opening an Existing Database

To open an existing database, you can select the name of a database in the list of recently opened databases (if the list appears), or you can choose the More Files option to open a database not listed. You need to open an existing database—the Restaurant database on your Student Disk.

To open the Restaurant database:

1. Make sure you have created your copy of the Access Student Disk, and then place your Student Disk in the appropriate disk drive.

   TROUBLE? If you don't have a Student Disk, you need to get one before you can proceed. Your instructor will either give you one or ask you to make your own. (See your instructor for information.) In either case, be sure you have made a copy of your Student Disk before you begin; in this way, the original Student Disk files will be available on the copied disk in case you need to start over because of an error or problem.

2. In the Microsoft Access dialog box, make sure the **Open an Existing Database** option button is selected. Also, if your dialog box contains a list of files, make sure the **More Files** option is selected.

3. Click the **OK** button to display the Open dialog box. See Figure 1-6.

Figure 1-6 ◀
Open dialog box

Look in list box

list of folders and
database files in
current folder

click to display the list
of available drives
and folders

> **TROUBLE?** The list of folders and files on your screen might be different from the list in Figure 1-6.

4. Click the **Look in** list arrow, and then click the drive that contains your Student Disk.

5. Click **Tutorial** in the list box (if necessary), and then click the **Open** button to display a list of the files in the Tutorial folder.

6. Click **Restaurant** in the list box, and then click the **Open** button. The Restaurant database is displayed in the Access window. See Figure 1-7.

Figure 1-7 ◀
Access and
Database
windows

Access window
title bar

Database window
menu bar

Database toolbar

Tables list box

Database window

TROUBLE? The filename on your screen might be Restaurant.mdb instead of Restaurant, depending on the default settings on your computer. The extension "mdb" identifies the file as an Access database.

TROUBLE? If the Tables tab is not selected in the Database window, click it to display the list of tables in the database.

Before you can begin working with the database, you need to become familiar with the components of the Access and Database windows.

The Access and Database Windows

The **Access window** is the program window that appears when you start the program. The **Database window** appears when you open a database; this window is the main control center for working with an open Access database. Except for the Access window title bar, all screen components now on your screen are associated with the Database window (see Figure 1-7). Most of these screen components—including the title bars, window sizing buttons, menu bar, toolbar, and status bar—are the same as the components in other Windows 95 programs.

The Database window contains six object tabs. Each **object tab** controls one of the six major object groups, such as tables, in an Access database. (In addition to tables, you'll work with queries, forms, and reports later in this book; macros and modules are used for more complex database design and programming and, therefore, are outside the scope of this text.)

Barbara has already created the Customer table in the Restaurant database. She suggests that you open the Customer table and view its contents.

Opening an Access Table

As noted earlier, tables contain all the data in a database. Tables are the fundamental objects for your work in Access. To view, add, change, or delete data in a table, you first must open the table. You can open any Access object by using the Open button in the Database window.

REFERENCE window

OPENING AN ACCESS OBJECT

- Click the tab in the Database window for the type of object you want to open.
- Scroll the object list box until the object name appears, and then click the object name.
- Click the Open button in the Database window.

You need to open the Customer table, which is the only table currently in the Restaurant database.

To open the Customer table:

1. If the Customer table is not highlighted, click **Customer** to select it.

2. Click the **Open** button in the Database window. The Customer table opens in Datasheet view on top of the Database and Access windows. See Figure 1-8.

Figure 1-8 ◀
Table displayed in Datasheet view

field selector for CustomerName field

table name

current record symbol

record selector for second record

field name

total number of records in the table

Specific Record box

navigation buttons

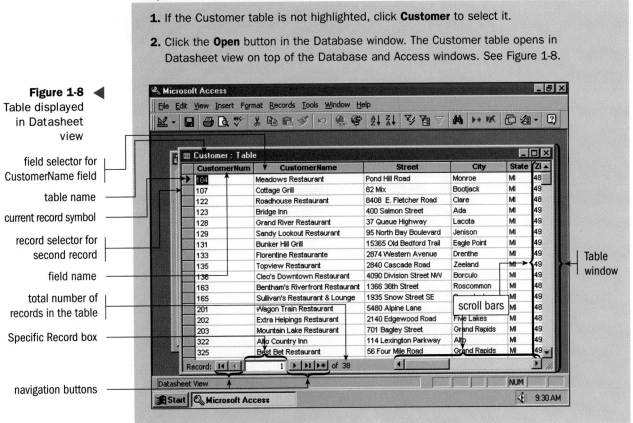

Table window

scroll bars

Datasheet view shows a table's contents as a **datasheet** in rows and columns, similar to a table or spreadsheet. Each row is a separate record in the table, and each column contains the field values for one field in the table. Each column is headed by a field name inside a field selector, and each row has a record selector to its left. Clicking a **field selector** or a **record selector** selects that entire column or row (respectively), which you can then manipulate. A field selector is also called a **column selector**, and a record selector is also called a **row selector**.

Navigating an Access Datasheet

When you first open a datasheet, Access selects the first field value in the first record. Notice that this field value is highlighted and that a darkened triangle symbol, called the current record symbol, appears in the record selector to the left of the first record. The **current record symbol** identifies the currently selected record. Clicking a record selector or field value in another row moves the current record symbol to that row. You can also move the pointer over the data on the screen and click one of the field values to position the insertion point.

The Customer table currently has nine fields and 38 records. To view fields or records not currently visible in the datasheet, you can use the horizontal and vertical scroll bars shown in Figure 1-8 to navigate through the data. The **navigation buttons**, also shown in Figure 1-8, provide another way to move vertically through the records. Figure 1-9 shows which record becomes the current record when you click each navigation button. The **Specific Record box**, which appears between the two sets of navigation buttons, displays the current record number; and the total number of records in the table appears to the right of the navigation buttons.

Figure 1-9 ◀
Navigation
buttons

Navigation Button	Record Selected	Navigation Button	Record Selected
⏮	First Record	⏭	Last Record
◀	Previous Record	▶✱	New Record
▶	Next Record		

Barbara suggests that you use the various navigation techniques to move through the Customer table and become familiar with its contents.

To navigate the Customer datasheet:

1. Click the right arrow button in the horizontal scroll bar a few times to scroll to the right and view the remaining fields in the Customer table.

2. Drag the scroll box in the horizontal scroll bar back to the left to return to the previous display of the datasheet.

3. Click the **Next Record** navigation button ▶. The second record is now the current record, as indicated by the current record symbol in the second record selector. Also, notice that the second record's value for the CustomerNum field is highlighted, and "2" (for record number 2) appears in the Specific Record box.

4. Click the **Last Record** navigation button ⏭. The last record in the table, record 38, is now the current record.

5. Click the **Previous Record** navigation button ◀. Record 37 is now the current record.

6. Click the **First Record** navigation button ⏮. The first record is now the current record.

Next, Barbara asks you to print the Customer table so that you can refer to it as you continue working with the Restaurant database.

Printing a Table

In Access you can print a table using either the Print command on the File menu or the Print button on the toolbar. The Print command displays a dialog box in which you can specify print settings. The Print button prints the table using the current settings. You'll use the Print button to print the Customer table.

To print the Customer table:

1. Click the **Print** button 🖼 on the Table Datasheet toolbar. Because all of the fields can't fit across one page, the table prints on two pages. You'll learn how to specify different print settings in later tutorials.

Now that you've viewed and printed the Customer table, you can exit Access.

Exiting Access

To exit Access, you simply click the Close button on the Access window title bar. When exiting, Access closes any open tables and the open database before closing the program.

To exit Access:

1. Click the **Close** button ⊠ on the Access window title bar. The Customer table and the Restaurant database close, Access closes, and you return to the Windows 95 desktop.

Quick Check

1. A(n) _____ is a single characteristic of a person, place, object, event, or idea.

2. You connect the records in two separate tables through a(n) _____ that appears in both tables.

3. The _____, whose values uniquely identify each record in a table, is called a _____ when it is placed in a second table to form a relationship between the two tables.

4. In a table, the rows are called _____ and the columns are called _____.

5. The _____ identifies the selected record in an Access table.

6. Describe the two methods for navigating through a table.

Now that you've become familiar with Access and the Restaurant database, you're ready to work with the data stored in the database.

SESSION

1.2

In this session you will create and print a query; create and print a form; use the Help system; and create, preview, and print a report.

Kim Carpenter, the director of marketing at Valle Coffee, wants a list of all restaurant customers so that her staff can call customers to check on their satisfaction with Valle

Coffee's services and products. She doesn't want the list to include all the fields in the Customer table (such as Street and ZipCode). To produce this list for Kim, you need to create a query using the Customer table.

Creating and Printing a Query

A **query** is a question you ask about the data stored in a database. In response to a query, Access displays the specific records and fields that answer your question. When you create a query, you tell Access which fields you need and what criteria Access should use to select the records. Access then displays only the information you want, so you don't have to scan through the entire database for the information.

You can design your own queries or use an Access **Query Wizard**, which guides you through the steps to create a query. The Simple Query Wizard allows you to select records and fields quickly, and is an appropriate choice for producing the customer list Kim wants.

To start the Simple Query Wizard:

1. Insert your Student Disk in the appropriate disk drive.

2. Start Access, make sure the **Open an Existing Database** option button is selected and the **More Files** option is selected, and then click the **OK** button to display the Open dialog box.

3. Click the **Look in** list arrow, click the drive that contains your Student Disk, click **Tutorial** in the list box, and then click the **Open** button to display the list of files in the Tutorial folder.

4. Click **Restaurant** in the list box, and then click the **Open** button.

5. Click the **Queries** tab in the Database window to display the Queries list. The Queries list box is empty because you haven't defined any queries yet.

6. Click the **New** button to open the New Query dialog box.

7. Click **Simple Query Wizard** and then click the **OK** button. The first Simple Query Wizard dialog box opens. See Figure 1-10.

Figure 1-10 ◀
First Simple
Query Wizard
dialog box

selected table —

removes all selected
fields

Because Customer is the only object currently in the Restaurant database, it is listed in the Tables/Queries box. You could click the Tables/Queries list arrow to choose another table or a query on which to base the query you're creating. The Available Fields box lists the fields in the selected table (in this case, Customer). You need to select fields from this list to include them in the query. To select fields one at a time, click a field and then click the [>] button. The selected field moves from the Available Fields list box on the left to the Selected Fields list box on the right. To select all the fields, click the [>>] button. If you change your mind or make a mistake, you can remove a field by clicking it in the Selected Fields list box and then clicking the [<] button. To remove all selected fields, click the [<<] button.

Each wizard dialog box contains buttons on the bottom that allow you to move to the previous dialog box (Back button), the next dialog box (Next button), or to cancel the creation process (Cancel button) and return to the Database window. You can also finish creating the object (Finish button) and accept the wizard's defaults for the remaining options.

Kim wants her list to include data from only the following fields: CustomerNum, CustomerName, City, State, OwnerName, and Phone. You need to select these fields to be included in the query.

To create the query using the Simple Query Wizard:

1. Click **CustomerNum** in the Available Fields list box (if necessary), and then click the [>] button. The CustomerNum field moves to the Selected Fields list box.

2. Repeat Step 1 for the fields **CustomerName**, **City**, **State**, **OwnerName**, and **Phone**, and then click the **Next** button. The second, and final, Simple Query Wizard dialog box opens and asks you to choose a name for your query. This name will appear in the Queries list in the Database window. You'll change the suggested name (Customer Query) to "Customer List."

3. Click at the end of the highlighted name, use the Backspace key to delete the word "Query," and then type **List**. You can now view the query results.

4. Click the **Finish** button to complete the query. Access displays the query results in Datasheet view.

5. Click the **Maximize** button on the Query window to maximize the window. See Figure 1-11.

Figure 1-11
Query results

selected fields
displayed

CustomerNum	CustomerName	City	State	OwnerName	Phone
104	Meadows Restaurant	Monroe	MI	Mr. Ray Suchecki	(313) 792-3546
107	Cottage Grill	Bootjack	MI	Ms. Doris Reaume	(616) 643-8821
122	Roadhouse Restaurant	Clare	MI	Ms. Shirley Woodruff	(517) 966-8651
123	Bridge Inn	Ada	MI	Mr. Wayne Bouwman	(616) 888-9827
128	Grand River Restaurant	Lacota	MI	Mr. John Rohrs	(313) 729-5364
129	Sandy Lookout Restaurant	Jenison	MI	Ms. Michele Yasenak	(616) 111-9148
131	Bunker Hill Grill	Eagle Point	MI	Mr. Ronald Kooienga	(906) 895-2041
133	Florentine Restaurante	Drenthe	MI	Mr. Donald Bench	(616) 111-3260
135	Topview Restaurant	Zeeland	MI	Ms. Janice Stapleton	(616) 643-4635
136	Cleo's Downtown Restaurant	Borculo	MI	Ms. Joan Hoffman	(616) 888-2046
163	Bentham's Riverfront Restaurant	Roscommon	MI	Mr. Joe Markovicz	(517) 792-8040
165	Sullivan's Restaurant & Lounge	Saugatuck	MI	Ms. Dawn Parker	(616) 575-6731
201	Wagon Train Restaurant	Selkirk	MI	Mr. Carl Seaver	(517) 111-5545
202	Extra Helpings Restaurant	Five Lakes	MI	Ms. Deborah Wolfe	(517) 889-6003
203	Mountain Lake Restaurant	Grand Rapids	MI	Mr. Donald MacPherson	(616) 532-4499
322	Alto Country Inn	Alto	MI	Mr. James Cowan	(616) 888-7111
325	Best Bet Restaurant	Grand Rapids	MI	Ms. Rebecca Van Singel	(616) 415-7294
407	Jean's Country Restaurant	Mattawan	MI	Ms. Jean Brooks	(517) 620-4431
423	Bay Pointe Restaurant	Shelbyville	MI	Mr. Janosfi Petofi	(616) 679-5681
515	Cheshire Restaurant	Burlington	MI	Mr. Jeffrey Hersha	(517) 717-9855
507	Around the Clock Restaurant	Copper Harbor	MI	Ms. Jennifer Lewis	(906) 273-0465

Record: I◄ ◄ 1 ► ►I ►* of 38

Datasheet View   NUM

Start Microsoft Access - [C...   9:35 AM

all 38 records are
included in the results

The datasheet displays the six selected fields for each record in the Customer table. The fields are shown in the order you selected them, from left to right.

The records are currently listed in order by the primary key field (CustomerNum). Kim prefers the records to be listed in order by state so that her staff members can focus on all the customers in a particular state. To display the records in the order Kim wants, you need to sort the query results by the State field.

To sort the query results:

1. Click to position the insertion point anywhere in the State column. This establishes the State column as the current field.

2. Click the **Sort Ascending** button ![Sort Ascending] on the Query Datasheet toolbar. The records are now sorted in ascending alphabetical order by the values in the State field. All the records for Indiana are listed first, followed by the records for Michigan and then Ohio.

Kim asks for a printed copy of the query results so that she can bring the customer list to a meeting with her staff members. To print the query results, you can use the Print button on the Query Datasheet toolbar.

To print the query results:

1. Click the **Print** button ![Print] on the Query Datasheet toolbar to print one copy of the query results with the current settings.

2. Click the **Close** button ![Close] on the menu bar to close the query.

   A dialog box opens asking if you want to save changes to the design of the query. This box appears because you changed the sort order of the query results.

3. Click the **Yes** button to save the changed query design and return to the Database window. Notice that the Customer List query is now shown in the Queries list box. In addition, because you had maximized the Query window, the Database window is also now maximized. You need to restore the window.

4. Click the **Restore** button ![Restore] on the menu bar to restore the Database window.

The results of the query are not stored with the database; however, the query design is stored as part of the database with the name you specify. You can then re-create the query results at any time by running the query again. You'll learn more about creating and running queries in Tutorial 3.

After Kim leaves for her staff meeting, Barbara asks you to create a form for the Customer table so that her staff members can use the form to enter and work with data easily in the table.

Creating and Printing a Form

A **form** is an object you use to maintain, view, and print records in a database. Although you can perform these same functions with tables and queries, forms can present data in customized and useful ways.

In Access, you can design your own forms or use a Form Wizard to create forms for you automatically. A **Form Wizard** is an Access tool that asks you a series of questions, then creates a form based on your answers. The quickest way to create a form is to use an **AutoForm Wizard**, which places all the fields from a selected table (or query) on a form automatically, without asking you any questions, and then displays the form on the screen.

Barbara wants a form for the Customer table that will show all the fields for one record at a time, with fields listed one below another. This type of form will make it easier for her staff to focus on all the data for a particular customer. You'll use the AutoForm: Columnar Wizard to create the form.

To create the form using an AutoForm Wizard:

1. Click the **Forms** tab in the Database window to display the Forms list. The Forms list box is currently empty because you haven't created any forms yet.

2. Click the **New** button to open the New Form dialog box. See Figure 1-12.

Figure 1-12 ◄
New Form
dialog box

click to design your
own form

Form Wizards

click to select the
table or query for
the form

The top list box provides options for designing your own form or creating a form using one of the Form Wizards. In the bottom list box, you choose the table or query that will supply the data for the form.

3. Click **AutoForm: Columnar** to select this AutoForm Wizard.

4. Click the list arrow for choosing the table or query on which to base the form, and then click **Customer**.

5. Click the **OK** button. The AutoForm Wizard creates the form and displays it in Form view. See Figure 1-13.

Figure 1-13 ◄
Form created
by the
AutoForm:
Columnar
Wizard

The form displays one record at a time in the Customer table. Access displays the field values for the first record in the table and selects the first field value (CustomerNum). Each field name appears on a separate line and on the same line as its field value, which appears in a box. The widths of the boxes are different to accommodate the different sizes of the displayed field values; for example, compare the small box for the State field's value with the larger box for the CustomerName field's value. The AutoForm: Columnar Wizard automatically placed the field names and values on the form and supplied the background style.

Also, notice that the Form window contains navigation buttons, similar to those available in Datasheet view, which you can use to move to different records in the table.

Barbara asks you to print the data for the Embers Restaurant, which is the last record in the table. After printing this record in the form, you'll save the form with the name "Customer Data" in the Restaurant database. The form will then be available for later use. You'll learn more about creating and customizing forms in Tutorial 4.

To print the form with data for the last record, and then save and close the form:

1. Click the **Last Record** navigation button [▶|]. The last record in the table, record 38 for Embers Restaurant, is now the current record.

2. Click **File** on the menu bar, and then click **Print**. The Print dialog box opens.

3. Click the **Selected Record(s)** option button, and then click the **OK** button to print only the current record in the form.

4. Click the **Save** button [🖫] on the Form View toolbar. The Save As dialog box opens.

5. In the Form Name text box, click at the end of the highlighted word "Customer," press the **spacebar**, type **Data**, and then press the **Enter** key. Access saves the form as Customer Data in your Restaurant database and closes the dialog box.

6. Click the **Close** button [✕] on the Form window title bar to close the form and return to the Database window. Note that the Customer Data form is now listed in the Forms list box.

Kim returns from her staff meeting with another request. She wants the same customer list you produced earlier when you created the Customer List query, but she'd like the information presented in a more readable format. She suggests you use the Access Help system to learn about formatting data in reports.

Getting Help

The Access Help system provides the same options as the Help system in other Windows programs—the Help Contents, the Help Index, and the Find Feature, which are available on the Help menu. The Access Help system also provides additional ways to get help as you work—the Office Assistant and the What's This? command. You'll learn how to use the Office Assistant next in this section. The What's This? [▶?] command provides context-sensitive Help information. When you choose this command from the Help menu, the pointer changes to the Help pointer, which you can then use to click any object or option on the screen to see a description of the object.

Finding Information with the Office Assistant

The Office Assistant is an interactive guide to finding information in the Help system. You can ask the Office Assistant a question, and it will look through the Help system to find an answer.

REFERENCE window

USING THE OFFICE ASSISTANT

- Click the Office Assistant button on any toolbar (or choose Microsoft Access Help from the Help menu).
- Click in the text box, type your question, and then click the Search button.
- Choose a topic from the list of topics displayed by the Office Assistant. Click additional topics, as necessary.
- When finished, close the Help window and the Office Assistant.

You'll use the Office Assistant to get Help about creating reports in Access.

To get Help about reports:

1. Click the **Office Assistant** button [?] on the Database toolbar. The Office Assistant appears and displays a dialog box with several options. See Figure 1-14.

Figure 1-14 ◀
Office
Assistant

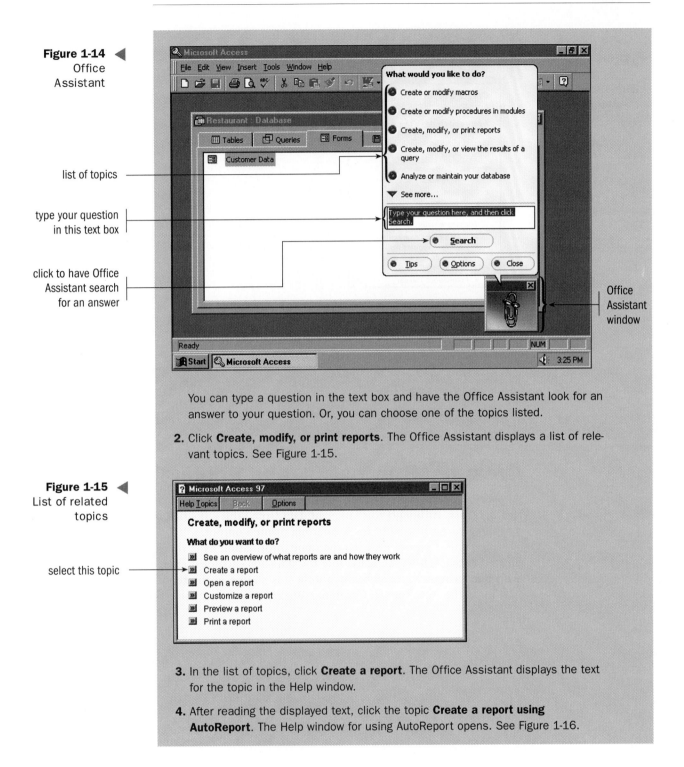

list of topics

type your question
in this text box

click to have Office
Assistant search
for an answer

Office
Assistant
window

You can type a question in the text box and have the Office Assistant look for an answer to your question. Or, you can choose one of the topics listed.

2. Click **Create, modify, or print reports**. The Office Assistant displays a list of relevant topics. See Figure 1-15.

Figure 1-15 ◀
List of related
topics

select this topic

3. In the list of topics, click **Create a report**. The Office Assistant displays the text for the topic in the Help window.

4. After reading the displayed text, click the topic **Create a report using AutoReport**. The Help window for using AutoReport opens. See Figure 1-16.

Figure 1-16 ◀
Help
information on
AutoReport

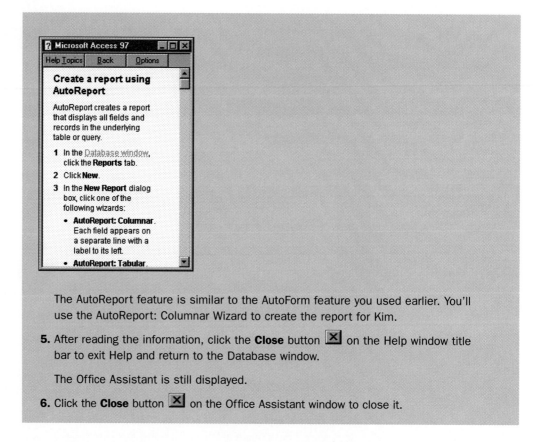

The AutoReport feature is similar to the AutoForm feature you used earlier. You'll use the AutoReport: Columnar Wizard to create the report for Kim.

5. After reading the information, click the **Close** button ☒ on the Help window title bar to exit Help and return to the Database window.

The Office Assistant is still displayed.

6. Click the **Close** button ☒ on the Office Assistant window to close it.

Creating, Previewing, and Printing a Report

A **report** is a formatted printout (or screen display) of the contents of one or more tables in a database. Although you can print data from tables, queries, and forms, reports allow you the greatest flexibility for formatting printed output.

Kim wants a report showing the same information as in the Customer List query you created earlier. However, she'd like the data for each customer to be grouped together, with one customer record below another, as shown in the report sketch in Figure 1-17. You'll use the AutoReport: Columnar Wizard to produce the report for Kim.

Figure 1-17 ◄
Sketch of
Kim's report

Customer List

CustomerNum   _____

CustomerName   _____

City   _____

State   ____

OwnerName   _____

Phone   _____

CustomerNum   _____

CustomerName   _____

City   _____

State   ____

OwnerName   _____

Phone   _____

To create the report using the AutoReport: Columnar Wizard:

1. Click the **Reports** tab in the Database window, and then click the **New** button to open the New Report dialog box. This dialog box is similar to the New Form dialog box you saw earlier.

2. Click **AutoReport: Columnar** to select this wizard for creating the report.

    Because Kim wants the same data as in the Customer List query, you need to choose that query as the basis for the report.

3. Click the list arrow for choosing the table or query on which to base the report, and then click **Customer List**.

4. Click the **OK** button. The AutoReport Wizard creates the report and displays it in Print Preview, which shows exactly how the report will look when printed.

    To better view the report, you'll maximize the window and change the Zoom setting so that you can see the entire page.

5. Click the **Maximize** button ▢ on the Report window, click the **Zoom** list arrow (next to the value 100%) on the Print Preview toolbar, and then click **Fit**. The entire first page of the report is displayed in the window. See Figure 1-18.

Figure 1-18 ◀
First page of
the report in
Print Preview

report title taken from
query name

fields grouped for
each record

lines
separate
records

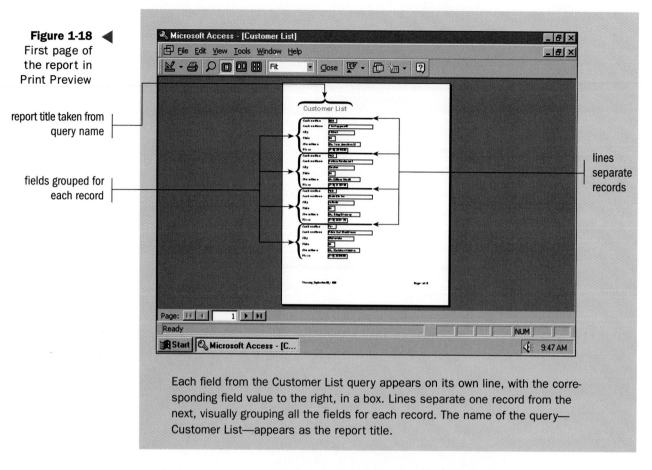

Each field from the Customer List query appears on its own line, with the corresponding field value to the right, in a box. Lines separate one record from the
next, visually grouping all the fields for each record. The name of the query—
Customer List—appears as the report title.

The report spans multiple pages. Kim asks you to print just the first page of the report
so that she can review its format. After printing the report page, you'll close the report
without saving it, because you can easily re-create it at any time. In general, it's best to save
an object—report, form, or query—only if you anticipate using the object frequently or if
it is time-consuming to create, because these objects can take up considerable storage space
on your disk. You'll learn more about creating and customizing reports in Tutorial 4.

To print the first report page, and then close the report and exit Access:

1. Click **File** on the menu bar, and then click **Print**. The Print dialog box opens. You
   need to change the print settings so that only the first page of the report is printed.

2. In the Print Range section, click the **Pages** option button, type **1** in the From text
   box, press the **Tab** key, and then type **1** in the To text box.

3. Click the **OK** button to print the first page of the report. Now you can close the report.

4. Click the **Close** button ☒ on the menu bar. *Do not* click the Close button on the
   Print Preview toolbar.

   TROUBLE? If you clicked the Close button on the Print Preview toolbar, you
   switched to Design view. Simply click the Close button ☒ on the menu bar, and
   then continue with the tutorial.

   A dialog box opens asking if you want to save the changes to the report design.

5. Click the **No** button to close the report without saving it. Now you can exit Access.

6. Click the **Close** button ☒ on the Access window title bar to exit Access.

Quick Check

1. A(n) _____ is a question you ask about the data stored in a database.

2. Unless you specify otherwise, the records resulting from a query are listed in order by the _____.

3. The quickest way to create a form is to use a(n) _____.

4. Describe the form created by the AutoForm: Columnar Wizard.

5. Describe how you use the Office Assistant to get Help.

6. After creating a report, the AutoReport Wizard displays the report in _____.

With the Customer table in place, Barbara can continue to build the Restaurant database and use it to store, manipulate, and retrieve important data for Valle Coffee. In the following tutorials, you'll help Barbara complete and maintain the database, and you'll use it to meet the specific information needs of other Valle Coffee employees.

Tutorial Assignments

In the Tutorial Assignments, you'll work with the Customer database, which is similar to the database you worked with in the tutorial. Complete the following:

1. Make sure your Student Disk is in the disk drive.

2. Start Access and open the Customer database, which is located in the TAssign folder on your Student Disk.

3. Choose the Contents and Index command from the Help menu, and then select the Contents tab. Open the topic "Introduction to Microsoft Access 97" and then open the topic "Databases: What they are and how they work." Read the displayed information, and then click the >> button at the top of the window to move through the remaining screens for the topic. When finished, click the Help Topics button at the top of the window to return to the Contents tab. Repeat this procedure for the similarly worded topics for tables, queries, forms, and reports. On any screen that contains boxed items, click each item and read the information displayed in the pop-up window. When finished reading all the topics, close the Help window.

4. Use the Office Assistant to ask the following question: "How do I rename a table?" Choose the topic "Rename a table, query, form, report, macro, or module" and read the displayed information. Close the Help window and the Office Assistant. Then, in the Customer database, rename the Table1 table as Customers.

5. Open the Customers table.

6. Choose the Contents and Index command from the Help menu, and then select the Index tab. Look up the word "landscape," and then choose the topic "landscape page orientation." Choose the subtopic "Set margins, page orientation, and other page setup options." Read the displayed information, and then close the Help window. Print the Customers table datasheet in landscape orientation. Close the Customers table.

7. Use the Simple Query Wizard to create a query that includes the CustomerName, OwnerName, and Phone fields from the Customers table. Name the query Customer Phone List. Sort the query results in ascending order by CustomerName. Print the query results, and then close and save the query.

8. Use the AutoForm: Columnar Wizard to create a form for the Customers table.

9. Use context-sensitive Help to find out how to move to a particular record and display it in the form. Choose the What's This? command from the Help menu, and then use the Help pointer to click the number 1 in the Specific Record box at the bottom of the form. Read the displayed information. Click to close the Help box, and then use the Specific Record box to move to record 20 (for Cheshire Restaurant) in the Customers table.

10. Print the form for the current record (20), save the form as Customer Info, and then close the form.

11. Use the AutoReport: Tabular Wizard to create a report based on the Customers table. Print the first page of the report, and then close the report without saving it.

12. Exit Access.

Case Problems

1. Ashbrook Mall Information Desk Ashbrook Mall is a large, modern mall located in Phoenix, Arizona. The Mall Operations Office is responsible for everything that happens within the mall and anything that affects the mall's operation. Among the independent operations that report to the Mall Operations Office are the Maintenance Group, the Mall Security Office, and the Information Desk. You will be helping the personnel at the Information Desk.

One important service provided by the Information Desk is to maintain a catalog of current job openings at stores within the mall. Sam Bullard, the director of the Mall Operations Office, recently created an Access database named MallJobs to store this information. You'll help Sam complete and maintain this database. Complete the following:

1. Make sure your Student Disk is in the disk drive.

2. Start Access and open the MallJobs database, which is located in the Cases folder on your Student Disk.

3. Open the Store table, print the table datasheet, and then close the table.

4. Use the Simple Query Wizard to create a query that includes the StoreName, Contact, and Extension fields from the Store table. Name the query Contact Phone List. Print the query results, and then close the query.

5. Use the AutoForm: Tabular Wizard to create a form for the Store table. Print the form, and then close it without saving it.

6. Use the AutoReport: Columnar Wizard to create a report based on the Store table. Maximize the Report window and change the Zoom setting to Fit. Use the Two Pages button on the Print Preview toolbar to view both pages of the report in Print Preview. Print the first page of the report, and then close the report without saving it.

7. Exit Access.

2. Professional Litigation User Services Professional Litigation User Services (PLUS) is a company that creates all types of visual aids for judicial proceedings. Clients are usually private law firms, although the District Attorney's office has occasionally contracted for their services. PLUS creates graphs, maps, timetables, and charts, both for computerized presentations and in large-size form for presentation to juries. PLUS also creates videos, animations, presentation packages, slide shows—in short, anything of a visual nature that can be used in a judicial proceeding to make, clarify, or support a point.

Raj Jawahir, a new employee at PLUS, is responsible for tracking the daily payments received from the firm's clients. He created an Access database named Payments, and needs your help in working with this database. Complete the following:

1. Make sure your Student Disk is in the disk drive.

2. Start Access and open the Payments database, which is located in the Cases folder on your Student Disk.

3. Open the Firm table, print the table datasheet, and then close the table.

4. Use the Simple Query Wizard to create a query that includes the FirmName, PLUSAcctRep, and Extension fields from the Firm table. Name the query Rep List. Sort the results in ascending order by the PLUSAcctRep field.

5. Use the Office Assistant to ask the following question: "How do I select multiple records?" Choose the topic "Selecting fields and records in Datasheet view," read the displayed information, and then close the Help window and the Office Assistant. Then select the first 11 records in the datasheet (all the records with the value "Abelson, David" in the PLUSAcctRep field), and then print just the selected records. Close the query, saving the changes to the design.

6. Use the AutoForm: Columnar Wizard to create a form for the Firm table. Move to record 31, and then print the form for the current record only. Close the form without saving it.

7. Use the AutoReport: Columnar Wizard to create a report based on the Firm table. Maximize the Report window and change the Zoom setting to Fit.

8. Use the View menu to view all eight pages of the report at the same time in Print Preview.

9. Print just the first page of the report, and then close the report without saving it.

10. Exit Access.

3. Best Friends Best Friends is a not-for-profit organization that trains hearing and service dogs for people with disabilities. Established in 1989 in Boise, Idaho, by Noah and Sheila Warnick, Best Friends is modeled after Paws With A Cause®, the original and largest provider of hearing and service dogs in the United States. Like Paws With A Cause® and other such organizations, Best Friends strives to provide "Dignity Through Independence."

To raise funds for Best Friends, Noah and Sheila periodically conduct Walk-A-Thons. The events have become so popular, Noah and Sheila created an Access database named Walks to track walker and pledge data. You'll help them complete and maintain the Walks database. Complete the following:

1. Make sure your Student Disk is in the disk drive.

2. Start Access and open the Walks database, which is located in the Cases folder on your Student Disk.

3. Open the Walker table, print the table datasheet, and then close the table.

4. Use the Simple Query Wizard to create a query that includes all the fields in the Walker table *except* the Phone field. (*Hint:* Use the >> and < buttons to select the necessary fields.) In the second Simple Query Wizard dialog box, make sure the Detail option button is selected. (This second dialog box appears because the table contains numeric values.) Name the query "Walker Distance." Sort the results in ascending order by the LastName field. Print the query results, and then close and save the query.

5. Use the AutoForm: Columnar Wizard to create a form for the Walker table. Move to record 25, and then print the form for the current record only. Close the form without saving it.

6. Use the AutoReport: Columnar Wizard to create a report based on the Walker table. Maximize the Report window and change the Zoom setting to Fit.

7. Use the View menu to view all six pages of the report at the same time in Print Preview.

8. Print just the first page of the report, and then close the report without saving it.

9. Exit Access.

4. Lopez Lexus Dealerships Maria and Hector Lopez own a chain of Lexus dealerships throughout Texas. They have used a computer in their business for several years to handle payroll and typical accounting functions. Because of their phenomenal expansion, both in the number of car locations and the number of cars handled, they created an Access database named Lexus to track their car inventory. You'll help them work with and maintain this database. Complete the following:

1. Make sure your Student Disk is in the disk drive.

2. Start Access and open the Lexus database, which is located in the Cases folder on your Student Disk.

3. Open the Cars table.

4. Print the Cars table datasheet in landscape orientation, and then close the table.

5. Use the Simple Query Wizard to create a query that includes the Model, Year, LocationCode, Cost, and SellingPrice fields from the Cars table. In the second Simple Query Wizard dialog box, make sure the Detail option button is selected. (This second dialog box appears because the table contains numeric values.) Name the query "Cost vs Selling."

6. Sort the query results in descending order by SellingPrice. (*Hint:* Use a toolbar button.)

7. Print the query results, and then close and save the query.

8. Use the AutoForm: Columnar Wizard to create a form for the Cars table. Move to record 11, and then print the form for the current record only. Close the form without saving it.

9. Use the AutoReport: Tabular Wizard to create a report based on the Cars table. Maximize the Report window and change the Zoom setting to Fit. Use the Two Pages button on the Print Preview toolbar to view both pages of the report in Print Preview. Print the first page of the report, and then close the report without saving it.

10. Exit Access.

Lab Assignments

These Lab Assignments are designed to accompany the interactive Course Lab called Databases. To start the Databases Lab, click the Start button on the Windows 95 taskbar, point to Programs, point to Course Labs, point to New Perspectives Applications, and click Databases. If you do not see Course Labs on your Programs menu, see your instructor or technical support person.

Databases

Databases This Databases Lab demonstrates the essential concepts of file and database management systems. You will use the Lab to search, sort, and report the data contained in a file of classic books.

1. Click the Steps button to review basic database terminology and to learn how to manipulate the classic books database. As you proceed through the Steps, answer all of the Quick Check questions that appear. After you complete the Steps, you will see a Quick Check summary report. Follow the instructions on the screen to print this report.

2. Click the Explore button. Make sure you can apply basic database terminology to describe the classic books database by answering the following questions:
   a. How many records does the file contain?
   b. How many fields does each record contain?
   c. What are the contents of the Catalog # field for the book written by Margaret Mitchell?
   d. What are the contents of the Title field for the record with Thoreau in the Author field?
   e. Which field has been used to sort the records?

3. In Explore, manipulate the database as necessary to answer the following questions:
   a. When the books are sorted by title, what is the first record in the file?
   b. Use the Search button to search for all the books in the West location. How many do you find?
   c. Use the Search button to search for all the books in the Main location that are checked in. What do you find?

4. Use the Report button to print out a report that groups the books by Status and sorts them by Title. On your report, circle the four field names. Draw a box around the summary statistics showing which books are currently checked in and which books are currently checked out.

TUTORIAL 2

Maintaining a Database

Creating, Modifying, and Updating an Order Table

OBJECTIVES

In this tutorial you will:

- Learn the guidelines for designing databases and Access tables

- Create and save a table

- Define fields and specify the primary key

- Add records to a table

- Modify the structure of a table

- Delete, move, and add fields

- Change field properties

- Copy records from another Access database

- Delete and change records

Valle Coffee

CASE

The Restaurant database currently contains only one table—the Customer table—which stores data about Valle Coffee's restaurant customers. Barbara also wants to track information about each order placed by each restaurant customer. This information includes the order's billing date and invoice amount. Barbara asks you to create a second table in the Restaurant database, named Order, in which to store the order data.

Some of the order data Barbara needs is already stored in another Valle Coffee database. After creating the Order table and adding some records to it, you'll copy the records from the other database into the Order table. Then you'll maintain the Order table by modifying it and updating it to meet Barbara's specific data requirements.

In this session you will learn the guidelines for designing databases and Access tables. You'll also learn how to create a table, define the fields for a table, select the primary key for a table, save the table structure, and add records to a table datasheet.

Guidelines for Designing Databases

A database management system can be a useful tool, but only if you first carefully design the database so that it meets the needs of those who will use it. In database design, you determine the fields, tables, and relationships needed to satisfy the data and processing requirements. When you design a database, you should follow these guidelines:

- **Identify all the fields needed to produce the required information.** For example, Barbara needs information about customers and orders. Figure 2-1 shows the fields that satisfy those information requirements.

Figure 2-1
Barbara's data
requirements

CustomerName	BillingDate
OrderNum	OwnerName
Street	InvoiceAmt
City	PlacedBy
State	Phone
ZipCode	FirstContact
CustomerNum	

- **Group related fields into tables.** For example, Barbara grouped the fields relating to customers into the Customer table. The other fields are grouped logically into the Order table, which you will create, as shown in Figure 2-2.

Figure 2-2
Barbara's fields
grouped into
Customer and
Order tables

<u>Customer table</u>	<u>Order table</u>
CustomerNum	OrderNum
CustomerName	BillingDate
Street	PlacedBy
City	InvoiceAmt
State	
ZipCode	
OwnerName	
Phone	
FirstContact	

- **Determine each table's primary key.** Recall that a primary key uniquely identifies each record in a table. Although a primary key is not mandatory in Access, it's usually a good idea to include one in each table. Without a primary key, selecting the exact record you want can be a problem. For some tables, one of the fields, such as a Social Security number or credit card number, naturally serves the function of a primary key. For other tables, two or more fields might be needed to function as the primary key. In these cases, the primary key is referred to as a **composite key**. For example, a school grade table would use a combination of student number and course code to serve as the primary key. For a third category of tables, no single field or combination of fields can uniquely identify a record in a table. In these cases, you need to add a field whose sole purpose is to serve as the primary key.

For Barbara's tables, CustomerNum is the primary key for the Customer table, and OrderNum will be the primary key for the Order table.

■ **Include a common field in related tables.** You use the common field to connect one table logically with another table. For example, Barbara's Customer and Order tables will include the CustomerNum field as a common field. Recall that when you include the primary key from one table as a field in a second table to form a relationship, the field is called a foreign key in the second table; therefore, the CustomerNum field will be a foreign key in the Order table. With this common field, Barbara can find all orders placed by a customer; she can use the CustomerNum value for a customer and search the Order table for all orders with that CustomerNum value. Likewise, she can determine which customer placed a particular order by searching the Customer table to find the one record with the same CustomerNum value as the corresponding value in the Order table.

■ **Avoid data redundancy.** Data redundancy occurs when you store the same data in more than one place. With the exception of common fields to connect tables, you should avoid redundancy because it wastes storage space and can cause inconsistencies, if, for instance, you type a field value one way in one table and a different way in the same table or in a second table. Figure 2-3 shows an example of incorrect database design that illustrates data redundancy in the Order table; the Customer Name field is redundant and one value was entered incorrectly, in three different ways.

Figure 2-3 ◄
Incorrect
database
design with
data
redundancy

Customer table

Customer Number	Customer Name	Customer Address	Phone Number
104	Meadows Restaurant	Pond Hill Road, Monroe MI 48161	(313) 792-3546
128	Grand River Restaurant	37 Queue Highway, Lacota MI 49063	(313) 729-5364
163	Bentham's Riverfront Restaurant	1366 36th Street, Roscommon MI 48653	(517) 792-8040
635	Oaks Restaurant	3300 West Russell Street, Maumee OH 43537	(419) 336-9000
741	Prime Cut Steakhouse	2819 East 10 Street, Mishawaka IN 46544	(219) 336-0900
779	Gateway Lounge	3408 Gateway Boulevard, Sylvania OH 43560	(419) 361-1137

data redundancy

Order table

Order Number	Customer Number	Customer Name	Billing Date	Invoice Amount
202	104	Meadows Restaurant	1/15/99	1,280.50
226	635	Oakes Restaurant	1/15/99	1,939.00
231	779	Gateway Lounge	1/15/99	1,392.50
309	741	Prime Cut Steakhouse	2/15/99	1,928.00
313	635	Stokes Inn	2/15/99	1,545.00
377	128	Grand River Restaurant	3/15/99	562.00
359	635	Raks Restaurant	3/15/99	1,939.00
373	779	Gateway Lounge	3/15/99	1,178.00
395	163	Bentham's Riverfront Restaurant	3/15/99	1,348.00

inconsistent data

■ **Determine the properties of each field.** You need to identify the **properties**, or characteristics, of each field so that the DBMS knows how to store, display, and process the field. These properties include the field name, the field's maximum number of characters or digits, the field's description, the field's valid values, and other field characteristics. You will learn more about field properties later in this tutorial.

The Order table you need to create will contain the fields shown in Figure 2-2. Before you create the table, you first need to learn some guidelines for designing Access tables.

Guidelines for Designing Access Tables

As just noted, the last step of database design is to determine the properties, such as the name and data type, of each field. Access has rules for naming fields, choosing data types, and defining other properties for fields.

Naming Fields and Objects

You must name each field, table, and other object in an Access database. Access then stores these items in the database using the names you supply. It's best to choose a field or object name that describes the purpose or contents of the field or object, so that later you can easily remember what the name represents. For example, the two tables in the Restaurant database will be named Customer and Order, because these names suggest their contents.

The following rules apply to naming fields and objects:

- A name can be up to 64 characters long.

- A name can contain letters, numbers, spaces, and special characters except a period (.), exclamation mark (!), accent grave (`), and square brackets ([ ]).

- A name cannot start with a space.

- A table or query name must be unique within a database. A field name must be unique within a table, but it can be used again in another table.

In addition, experienced users of databases have the following tips for naming fields and objects:

- Capitalize the first letter of each word in the name.

- Avoid extremely long names because they are difficult to remember and refer to.

- Use standard abbreviations such as Num for Number, Amt for Amount, and Qty for Quantity.

- Do not use spaces in field names because these names will appear in column headings on datasheets and labels on forms and reports. By not using spaces you'll be able to show more fields on these objects at one time.

Assigning Field Data Types

You must assign a data type for each field. The **data type** determines what field values you can enter for the field and what other properties the field will have. For example, the Order table will include a BillingDate field, so you will assign the date/time data type to this field because it will store date values. Access will allow you to enter only dates or times as values for the field and will allow you to manipulate a value only as a date or time.

Figure 2-4 lists the ten data types available in Access, describes the field values allowed with each data type, explains when each data type should be used, and indicates the field size of each data type.

Figure 2-4 ◀
Data types
for fields

Data Type	Description	Field Size
Text	Allows field values containing letters, digits, spaces, and special characters. Use for names, addresses, descriptions, and fields containing digits that are not used in calculations.	1 to 255 characters; 50 characters default
Memo	Allows field values containing letters, digits, spaces, and special characters. Use for long comments and explanations.	1 to 64,000 characters; exact size is determined by entry
Number	Allows positive and negative numbers as field values. Numbers can contain digits, a decimal point, commas, a plus sign, and a minus sign. Use for fields that you will use in calculations, except calculations involving money.	1 to 15 digits
Date/Time	Allows field values containing valid dates and times from January 1, 100 to December 31, 9999. Dates can be entered in mm/dd/yy (month, day, year) format, several other date formats, or a variety of time formats such as 10:35 PM. You can perform calculations on dates and times and you can sort them. For example, you can determine the number of days between two dates.	8 digits
Currency	Allows field values similar to those for the number data type. Unlike calculations with number data type decimal values, calculations performed using the currency data type are not subject to round-off error.	15 digits
AutoNumber	Consists of integers with values controlled by Access. Access automatically inserts a value in the field as each new record is created. You can specify sequential numbering or random numbering. This guarantees a unique field value, so that such a field can serve as a table's primary key.	9 digits
Yes/No	Limits field values to yes and no, or true and false. Use for fields that indicate the presence or absence of a condition, such as whether an order has been filled, or if an employee is eligible for the company dental plan.	1 character
OLE Object	Allows field values that are created in other programs as objects, such as photographs, video images, graphics, drawings, sound recordings, voice-mail messages, spreadsheets, and word-processing documents. These objects can be linked or embedded.	1 gigabyte maximum; exact size depends on object size
Hyperlink	Consists of text or combinations of text and numbers stored as text and used as a hyperlink address. A hyperlink address can have up to three parts: the text that appears in a field or control; the path to a file or page; and a location within the file or page. Hyperlinks help you to connect your application easily to the Internet or an intranet.	Up to 2048 characters for each of the three parts of a hyperlink data type
Lookup Wizard	Creates a field that lets you look up a value in another table or in a predefined list of values.	Same size as the primary key field used to perform the lookup

Assigning Field Sizes

The **field size** property defines a field value's maximum storage size for text and number fields only. The other data types have no field size property, because their storage size is either a fixed, predetermined amount or is determined automatically by the field value itself, as shown in Figure 2-4. A text field has a default field size of 50 characters. You set its field size by entering a number in the range 1 to 255. For example, the OrderNum and CustomerNum fields in the Order table will be text fields with sizes of 3 each.

Barbara documented the design for the Order table by listing each field's name, data type, size (if applicable), and description, as shown in Figure 2-5. OrderNum, the table's primary key, CustomerNum, a foreign key to the Customer table, and PlacedBy will each be assigned the text data type. BillingDate will have the date/time data type, and InvoiceAmt will have the currency data type.

Figure 2-5 ◀

Design for the
Order table

Field Name	Data Type	Field Size	Description
OrderNum	Text	3	primary key
CustomerNum	Text	3	foreign key
BillingDate	Date/Time		
PlacedBy	Text	25	person who placed order
InvoiceAmt	Currency		

With Barbara's design, you are ready to create the Order table.

Creating a Table

Creating a table consists of naming the fields and defining the properties for the fields, specifying a primary key (and a foreign key, if applicable) for the table, and then saving the table structure. You will use Barbara's design (Figure 2-5) as a guide to creating the Order table. First, you need to open the Restaurant database.

To open the Restaurant database:

1. Place your Student Disk in the appropriate disk drive.

2. Start Access. The Access window opens with the initial dialog box.

3. Make sure the **Open an Existing Database** option button and the **More Files** option are selected, and then click the **OK** button to display the Open dialog box.

4. Click the **Look in** list arrow, and then click the drive that contains your Student Disk.

5. Click **Tutorial** in the list box, and then click the **Open** button to display a list of the files in the Tutorial folder.

6. Click **Restaurant** in the list box, and then click the **Open** button. The Restaurant database is displayed in the Access window.

7. Make sure the Tables tab is selected in the Database window.

The Customer table is listed in the Tables list box. Now you'll create the Order table in the Restaurant database.

To begin creating the Order table:

1. Click the **New** button in the Database window. The New Table dialog box opens. See Figure 2-6.

Figure 2-6 ◄
New Table
dialog box

click to design
your own table

other ways to
define a table

In Access, you can create a table from entered data (Datasheet View), define
your own table (Design View), use a wizard to automate the table creation
process (Table Wizard), or use a wizard to import or link data from another database or other data source (Import Table or Link Table). For the Order table, you
will define your own table.

2. Click **Design View** in the list box, and then click the **OK** button. The Table window
opens in Design view. See Figure 2-7.

default table name

Table window
Maximize button

Figure 2-7 ◄
Table window in
Design view

Table window
menu bar

Table Design toolbar

current row symbol

row selectors

Field Properties

Table Design grid

other field properties
will appear here

help for using the
current property

A field name can be up to 64
characters long, including spaces.
Press F1 for help on field names.

You use Design view to define or modify a table structure or the properties of the fields
in a table. If you create a table without using a wizard, you enter the fields and their properties for your table directly in this window.

Defining Fields

Initially, the default table name, Table1, appears in the Table window title bar, the current row symbol is positioned in the first row selector of the Table Design grid, and the
insertion point is located in the first row's Field Name box. The purpose or characteristics of the current property (Field Name, in this case) appear in the lower-right of the
Table window. You can display more complete information about the current property by
pressing the F1 key.

You enter values for the Field Name, Data Type, and Description field properties in the upper-half of the Table window. You select values for all other field properties, most of which are optional, in the lower-half of the window. These other properties will appear when you move to the first row's Data Type text box.

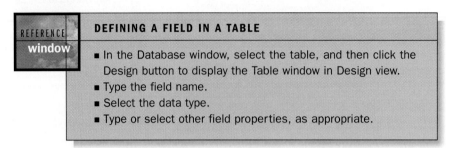

REFERENCE window	**DEFINING A FIELD IN A TABLE**
	■ In the Database window, select the table, and then click the Design button to display the Table window in Design view.
	■ Type the field name.
	■ Select the data type.
	■ Type or select other field properties, as appropriate.

The first field you need to define is OrderNum.

To define the OrderNum field:

1. Type **OrderNum** in the first row's Field Name text box, and then press the **Tab** key (or press the **Enter** key) to advance to the Data Type text box. The default data type, Text, appears highlighted in the Data Type text box, which now also contains a list arrow, and field properties for a text field appear in the lower-half of the window. See Figure 2-8.

Figure 2-8
Table window after entering the first field name

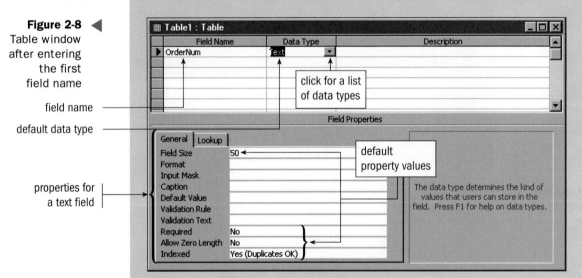

field name

default data type

properties for a text field

Notice that the lower-right of the window now provides an explanation for the current property, Data Type.

TROUBLE? If you make a typing error, you can correct it by clicking the mouse to position the insertion point, and then using either the Backspace key to delete characters to the left of the insertion point or the Delete key to delete characters to the right of the insertion point. Then type the correct text.

Because order numbers will not be used for calculations, you will assign the text data type to it instead of the number data type, and then enter the Description property value as "primary key." You can use the Description property to enter an optional description for a field to explain its purpose or usage. A field's Description property can be up to 255 characters long, and its value appears in the status bar when you view the table datasheet.

2. Press the **Tab** key to accept Text as the field's data type and move to the Description text box, and then type **primary key** in the Description text box.

The Field Size property has a default value of 50, which you will change to a value of 3, because order numbers at Valle Coffee contain 3 digits. The Required property has a default value of No, which means that a value does not need to be entered for the field. Because Barbara doesn't want an order entered without an order number, you will change the Required property to Yes. The Allow Zero Length property has a value of No, meaning that a value *must* be entered for the field, as is appropriate for the OrderNum field. Finally, the Indexed property has a value of "Yes (Duplicates OK)," which means that a list of index entries will be created to speed up operations using the OrderNum field.

3. Select **50** in the Field Size text box either by dragging the pointer or double-clicking the mouse, and then type **3**.

4. Click the **Required** text box to position the insertion point there. A list arrow appears on the right side of the Required text box.

5. Click the **Required** list arrow. Access displays the Required list box. See Figure 2-9.

Figure 2-9 ◀
Defining the
OrderNum field

changed from
default value of 50

Field Name	Data Type	Description
▶ OrderNum	Text	primary key

Field Properties

General | Lookup

Field Size	3
Format	
Input Mask	
Caption	
Default Value	
Validation Rule	
Validation Text	
Required	No
Allow Zero Length	Yes
Indexed	No

Require data entry in this field?

Required
list box

When you position the insertion point or select text in many Access text boxes, Access displays a list arrow, which you can click to display a list box with options. You can display the list arrow *and* the list box simultaneously if you click the text box near its right side.

6. Click **Yes** in the list box. The list box closes, and Yes is now the value for the Required property. The definition of the first field is complete.

Barbara's Order table design shows CustomerNum as the second field. You will define CustomerNum as a text field with a Description of "foreign key" and a Field Size of 3, because customer numbers at Valle Coffee contain 3 digits. Because it's possible that a record for an order might need to be entered for a customer not yet added to the database, Barbara asks you to leave the Required property at its default value of No and to change the Allow Zero Length property value to Yes.

To define the CustomerNum field:

1. Place the insertion point in the second row's Field Name text box, type **CustomerNum** in the text box, and then press the **Tab** key to advance to the Data Type text box.

Customer numbers are not used in calculations, so you'll assign the text data type to the field, and then enter its Description value as "foreign key."

2. Press the **Tab** key to accept Text as the field's data type and move to the Description text box, and then type **foreign key** in the Description text box.

Finally, change the Field Size property to 3 and the Allow Zero Length property to Yes.

3. Select **50** in the Field Size text box, type **3**, click the right side of the Allow Zero Length text box, and then click **Yes**. You have completed the definition of the second field. See Figure 2-10.

Figure 2-10 ◀
Table window after defining the first two fields

current field

property values for the current field

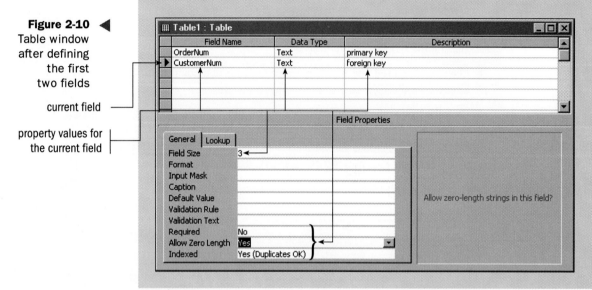

Using Barbara's Order table design in Figure 2-5, you can now complete the remaining field definitions: BillingDate with the date/time data type, PlacedBy with the text data type, and InvoiceAmt with the currency data type.

To define the BillingDate, PlacedBy, and InvoiceAmt fields:

1. Place the insertion point in the third row's Field Name text box, type **BillingDate** in the text box, and then press the **Tab** key to advance to the Data Type text box.

2. Click the **Data Type** list arrow, click **Date/Time** in the list box, and then press the **Tab** key to advance to the Description text box.

If you've assigned a descriptive field name and the field does not fulfill a special function (for example, primary key), you usually do not enter a value for the optional Description property. BillingDate is a field that does not require a value for its Description property.

Barbara does not want to require that a value be entered for the BillingDate field, nor does she want an index for the field. So, you do not need to change any of the default property values for the BillingDate field. Neither do you need to enter any new property values. Because you have finished defining the BillingDate field, you can now define the PlacedBy field.

3. Press the **Tab** key to advance to the fourth row's Field Name text box.

4. Type **PlacedBy** in the Field Name text box, and then press the **Tab** key to advance to the Data Type text box.

This field will contain names, so you'll assign the text data type to it. Also, Barbara wants to include the description "person who placed order" to clarify the contents of the field.

5. Press the **Tab** key to accept Text as the field's data type and move to the Description text box, and then type **person who placed order** in the Description text box.

Next, you'll change the Field Size property's default value of 50 to 25, which should be long enough to accommodate all names. Also, Barbara does not want to require that a value be entered for the field.

6. Select **50** in the Field Size text box, type **25**, click the right side of the Allow Zero Length text box, and then click **Yes**.

The definition of the PlacedBy field is complete. Next, you'll define the fifth and final field, InvoiceAmt. This field will contain dollar amounts so you'll assign the currency data type to it.

7. Place the insertion point in the fifth row's Field Name text box.

8. Type **InvoiceAmt** in the Field Name text box, and then press the **Tab** key to advance to the Data Type text box.

You can select a value from the Data Type list box as you did for the BillingDate field. Alternatively, you can type the property value in the text box or type just the first character of the property value.

9. Type **c**. The value in the fifth row's Data Type text box changes to "currency," with the letters "urrency" highlighted. See Figure 2-11.

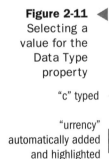

Figure 2-11
Selecting a value for the Data Type property

"c" typed

"urrency" automatically added and highlighted

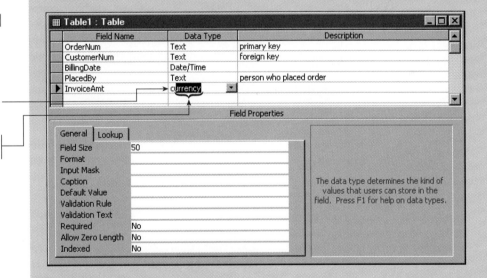

10. Press the **Tab** key to advance to the Description text box. Access changes the value for the Data Type property to Currency.

In the Field Properties section, notice the default values for the Format and Decimal Places properties. For a field with a Format property value of Currency, two decimal places are provided when the Decimal Places property value is Auto. This is the format Barbara wants for the InvoiceAmt field, so you have finished defining the fields for the Order table.

Next, you need to specify the primary key for the Order table.

Specifying the Primary Key

Although Access does not require a table to have a primary key, including a primary key offers several advantages:

- A primary key uniquely identifies each record in a table.

- Access does not allow duplicate values in the primary key field. If a record already exists with an OrderNum value of 143, for example, Access prevents you from adding another record with this same value in the OrderNum field. Preventing duplicate values ensures the uniqueness of the primary key field and helps to avoid data redundancy.

- Access forces you to enter a value for the primary key field in every record in the table. This is known as **entity integrity**. If you do not enter a value for a field, you have actually given the field what is known as a **null value**. You cannot give a null value to the primary key field because entity integrity prevents Access from accepting and processing that record.

- Access stores records on disk in the same order as you enter them but displays them in order by the field values of the primary key. If you enter records in no specific order, you are ensured that you will later be able to work with them in a more meaningful, primary key sequence.

- Access responds faster to your requests for specific records based on the primary key.

REFERENCE window

SPECIFYING A PRIMARY KEY FOR A TABLE

- In the Table window in Design view, click the row selector for the field you've chosen to be the primary key.
- If the primary key will consist of two or more fields, press and hold down the Ctrl key, and then click the row selector for each field.
- Click the Primary Key button on the Table Design toolbar.

According to Barbara's design, you need to specify OrderNum as the primary key for the Order table.

To specify OrderNum as the primary key:

1. Position the pointer on the row selector for the OrderNum field until the pointer changes to ➡. See Figure 2-12.

Figure 2-12 ◀
Specifying
OrderNum as
the primary key

pointer

row selector

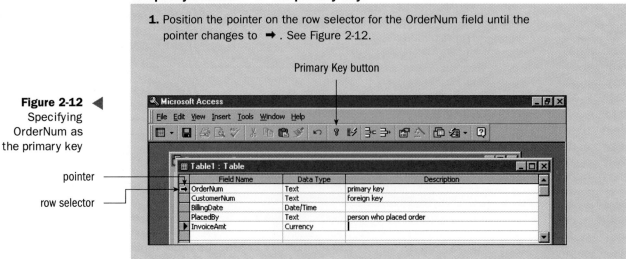

2. Click the mouse button. The entire first row of the Table Design grid is highlighted.

3. Click the **Primary Key** button ⌨ on the Table Design toolbar, and then click to the right of InvoiceAmt in the fifth row's Field Name text box to deselect the first row. A key symbol appears in the row selector for the first row, indicating that the OrderNum field is the table's primary key. See Figure 2-13.

Figure 2-13 ◀
OrderNum selected as the primary key

key symbol indicating the primary key

You've defined the fields for the Order table and specified its primary key, so you can now save the table structure.

Saving the Table Structure

The last step in creating a table is to name the table and save the table's structure on disk. Once the table is saved, you can use it to enter data in the table.

REFERENCE
window

SAVING A TABLE STRUCTURE

- Click the Save button on the Table Design toolbar.
- Type the name of the table in the Table Name text box of the Save As dialog box.
- Click the OK button (or press the Enter key).

You need to save the table you've defined as "Order."

To name and save the Order table:

1. Click the **Save** button 🖫 on the Table Design toolbar. The Save As dialog box opens.

2. Type **Order** in the Table Name text box, and then press the **Enter** key. Access saves the table with the name Order in the Restaurant database on your Student Disk. Notice that Order appears instead of Table1 in the Table window title bar.

Next, Barbara asks you to add two records, shown in Figure 2-14, to the Order table. These two records contain data for orders that were recently placed with Valle Coffee.

Figure 2-14 ◀
Records to be added to the Order table

OrderNum	CustomerNum	BillingDate	PlacedBy	InvoiceAmt
323	624	2/15/99	Isabelle Rouy	$1,986.00
201	107	1/15/99	Matt Gellman	$854.00

Adding Records to a Table

You can add records to an Access table in several ways. A table datasheet provides a simple way for you to add records. As you learned in Tutorial 1, a datasheet shows a table's contents in rows and columns, similar to a table or worksheet. Each row is a separate record in the table, and each column contains the field values for one field in the table. To view a table datasheet, you first must change from Design view to Datasheet view.

You'll switch to Datasheet view and add the two records in the Order table datasheet.

To add the records in the Order table datasheet:

1. Click the **View** button for Datasheet view 🔲 on the Table Design toolbar. The Table window opens in Datasheet view. See Figure 2-15.

Figure 2-15 ◀
Table window in
Datasheet view

current record symbol

field names

Description property
for the current field

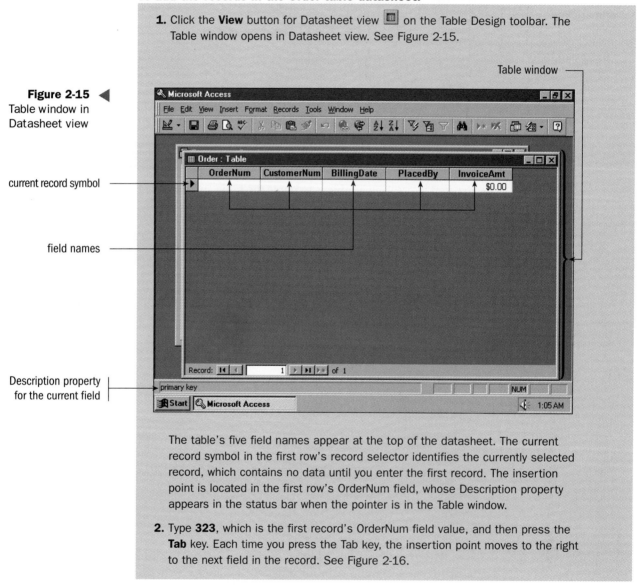

The table's five field names appear at the top of the datasheet. The current record symbol in the first row's record selector identifies the currently selected record, which contains no data until you enter the first record. The insertion point is located in the first row's OrderNum field, whose Description property appears in the status bar when the pointer is in the Table window.

2. Type **323**, which is the first record's OrderNum field value, and then press the **Tab** key. Each time you press the Tab key, the insertion point moves to the right to the next field in the record. See Figure 2-16.

Figure 2-16
Datasheet for
Order table
after entering
the first
field value

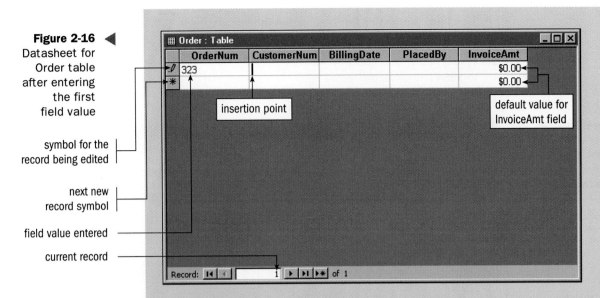

symbol for the
record being edited

next new
record symbol

field value entered

current record

TROUBLE? If you make a mistake when typing a value, use the Backspace key to delete characters to the left of the insertion point or the Delete key to delete characters to the right of the insertion point. Then type the correct text. If you want to correct a value by replacing it entirely, double-click the value to select it, and then type the correct value.

The pencil symbol in the first row's record selector indicates that the record is being edited. The star symbol in the second row's record selector identifies the second row as the next one available for a new record. The InvoiceAmt column displays "$0.00," the default value for the field.

3. Type **624** and then press the **Tab** key. The insertion point moves to the right side of the BillingDate field.

4. Type **2/15/99** and then press the **Tab** key. The insertion point moves to the PlacedBy field.

5. Type **Isabelle Rouy** and then press the **Tab** key. The insertion point moves to the InvoiceAmt field, whose field value is highlighted.

Notice that field values for text fields are left-aligned in their boxes and field values for date/time and currency fields are right-aligned in their boxes. If the default value of $0.00 is correct for the InvoiceAmt field, you can press the Tab key to accept the value and advance to the beginning of the next record. Otherwise, type the field value for the InvoiceAmt field. You do not need to type the dollar sign, commas, or decimal point (for whole dollar amounts) because Access adds these symbols automatically for you.

6. Type **1986** and then press the **Tab** key. Access displays $1,986.00 for the InvoiceAmt field, stores the first completed record in the Order table, removes the pencil symbol from the first row's record selector, advances the insertion point to the second row's OrderNum text box, and places the current record symbol in the second row's record selector.

Now you can enter the values for the second record.

7. Type **201** in the OrderNum field, press the **Tab** key to move to the CustomerNum field, type **107** in the CustomerNum field, and then press the **Tab** key. The insertion point moves to the right side of the BillingDate field.

8. Type **1/15/99** and then press the **Tab** key. The insertion point moves to the PlacedBy field.

9. Type **Matt Gellman** and then press the **Tab** key. The value in the InvoiceAmt field is now highlighted.

10. Type **854** and then press the **Tab** key. Access changes the InvoiceAmt field value to $854.00, saves the record in the Order table, and moves the insertion point to the beginning of the third row. See Figure 2-17.

Figure 2-17 ◄
Order table
datasheet after
entering the
second record

two added records ────

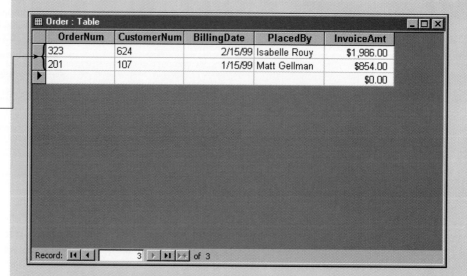

Notice that "Record 3 of 3" appears around the navigation buttons even though the table contains only two records. Access is anticipating that you will enter a new record, which would be the third of three records in the table. If you move the insertion point to the second record, the display would change to "Record 2 of 2."

Even though the Order table contains only two records, Barbara asks you to print the table datasheet so that she can bring it with her to a staff meeting. She wants to show the table design to her staff members to make sure that it will meet their needs for tracking order data.

You'll use the Print button on the Table Datasheet toolbar to print one copy of the Order table with the current settings.

To print the Order table:

1. Click the **Print** button 🖨 on the Table Datasheet toolbar.

Notice that the two records are currently listed in the order in which you entered them. However, once you close the table or change to another view, and then redisplay the table datasheet, the records will be listed in primary key order by the values in the OrderNum field.

You have created the Order table in the Restaurant database and added two records to the table, which Access saved automatically to the database on your Student Disk.

Saving a Database

Notice the Save button on the Table Datasheet toolbar. This Save button, unlike the Save buttons in other Windows programs, does not save the active document (database) to your disk. Instead, you use the Save button to save the design of a table, query, form, or report, or to save datasheet format changes. Access does not have a button or option you can use to save the active database.

Access saves the active database to your disk automatically, both on a periodic basis and whenever you close the database. This means that if your database is stored on a disk in drive A or drive B, you should never remove the disk while the database file is open. If you do remove the disk, Access will encounter problems when it tries to save the database; this might damage the database.

Quick Check

1. What guidelines should you follow when you design a database?

2. What is the purpose of the data type property for a field?

3. For which two types of fields do you assign a field size?

4. Why did you define the OrderNum field as a text field instead of a number field?

5. A(n) _____ value, which results when you do not enter a value for a field, is not permitted for a primary key.

6. What does a pencil symbol in a datasheet's row selector represent? A star symbol?

The Order table is now complete. In Session 2.2, you'll continue to work with the Order table by modifying its structure and entering and maintaining data in the table.

SESSION 2.2

In this session you will modify the structure of a table by deleting, moving, and adding fields and changing field properties; copy records from another Access database; and update a database by deleting and changing records.

Modifying the Structure of an Access Table

Even a well-designed table might need to be modified. For example, the government at all levels and the competition place demands on a company to track more data and to modify the data it already tracks. Access allows you to modify a table's structure in Design view: you can add and delete fields, change the order of fields, and change the properties of the fields.

After meeting with her staff members and reviewing the structure of the Order table and the format of the field values in the datasheet, Barbara has several changes she wants you to make to the table. First, she has decided that it's not necessary to keep track of the name of the person who placed a particular order, so she wants you to delete the PlacedBy field. Also, she thinks that the InvoiceAmt field should remain a currency field, but she wants the dollar signs removed from the displayed field values in the datasheet. She also wants the BillingDate field moved to the end of the table. Finally, she wants you to add a yes/no field, named Paid, to the table to indicate whether the invoice has been paid for the order. The Paid field will be inserted between the CustomerNum and InvoiceAmt fields. Figure 2-18 shows Barbara's modified design for the Order table.

Figure 2-18 ◀
Modified design for the Order table

Field Name	Data Type	Field Size	Description
OrderNum	Text	3	primary key
CustomerNum	Text	3	foreign key
Paid	Yes/No		
InvoiceAmt	Currency		
BillingDate	Date/Time		

You'll begin modifying the table by deleting the PlacedBy field.

Deleting a Field

After you've defined a table structure and added records to the table, you can delete a field from the table structure. When you delete a field, you also delete all the values for the field from the table. Therefore, you should make sure that you need to delete a field and that you delete the correct field.

REFERENCE window	**DELETING A FIELD FROM A TABLE STRUCTURE**
	■ In the Table window in Design view, right-click the row selector for the field you want to delete to select the field and display the shortcut menu.
	■ Click Delete Rows on the shortcut menu.

You need to delete the PlacedBy field from the Order table structure.

To delete the PlacedBy field:

1. If you took a break after the previous session, make sure that Access is running and that the Order table of the Restaurant database is open.

2. Click the **View** button for Design view ![icon] on the Table Datasheet toolbar. The Table window for the Order table opens in Design view.

3. Position the pointer on the row selector for the PlacedBy field until the pointer changes to ➡ .

4. Right-click to select the entire row for the field and display the shortcut menu, and then click **Delete Rows**.

A dialog box opens asking you to confirm the deletion.

5. Click the **Yes** button to close the dialog box and to delete the field and its values from the table. See Figure 2-19.

Figure 2-19 ◀
Table structure
after deleting
PlacedBy field

field deleted here ───

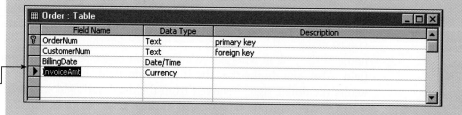

You have deleted the PlacedBy field in the Table window, but the change doesn't take place in the table on disk until you save the table structure. Because you have other modifications to make to the table, you'll wait until you finish them all before saving the modified table structure to disk.

Moving a Field

To move a field, you use the mouse to drag it to a new location in the Table window in Design view. Your next modification to the Order table structure is to move the BillingDate field to the end of the table, as Barbara requested.

Access

To move the BillingDate field:

1. Click the **row selector** for the BillingDate field to select the entire row.

2. Place the pointer in the row selector for the BillingDate field, click the pointer ↖ , and then drag the pointer 🖑 to the row selector below the InvoiceAmt row selector. See Figure 2-20.

Figure 2-20 ◀
Moving a field in the table structure

selected field

position the move pointer in this row selector

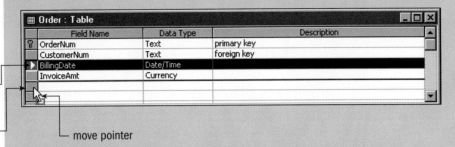

move pointer

3. Release the mouse button. Access moves the BillingDate field below the InvoiceAmt field in the table structure.

TROUBLE? If the BillingDate field did not move, repeat Steps 1 through 3, making sure you firmly hold down the mouse button during the drag operation.

Adding a Field

Next, you need to add the Paid field to the table structure between the CustomerNum and InvoiceAmt fields. To add a new field between existing fields, you must insert a row. You begin by selecting the field that will be below the new field you want to insert.

REFERENCE window

ADDING A FIELD BETWEEN TWO EXISTING FIELDS

■ In the Table window in Design view, right-click the row selector for the row above which you want to add a new field to select the field and display the shortcut menu.
■ Click Insert Rows on the shortcut menu.
■ Define the new field by entering the field name, data type, description (optional), and any property specifications.

To add the Paid field to the Order table:

1. Right-click the **row selector** for the InvoiceAmt field to select this field and display the shortcut menu, and then click **Insert Rows**. Access adds a new, blank row between the CustomerNum and InvoiceAmt fields. See Figure 2-21.

Figure 2-21 ◀
After inserting a row in the table structure

You'll define the Paid field in the new row for the Order table. Access will add this new field to the Order table structure between the CustomerNum and InvoiceAmt fields.

2. Click the **Field Name** text box for the new row, type **Paid**, and then press the **Tab** key.

The Paid field will be a yes/no field that will specify whether an invoice has been paid.

3. Type **y**. Access completes the data type as "yes/No."

4. Press the **Tab** key to select the yes/no data type and move to the Description text box.

Notice that Access changes the value in the Data Type text box from "yes/No" to "Yes/No." Barbara wants the Paid field to have a Default Value property value of "no." When you select or enter a value for a property, you *set* the property.

5. In the Field Properties section, click the **Default Value** text box, type **no**, and then click the **Description** text box for the Paid field. Notice that Access changes the Default Value property value from "no" to "No." See Figure 2-22.

Figure 2-22 ◄
Paid field
added to the
Order table

new field —

Default Value —
property set to "No"

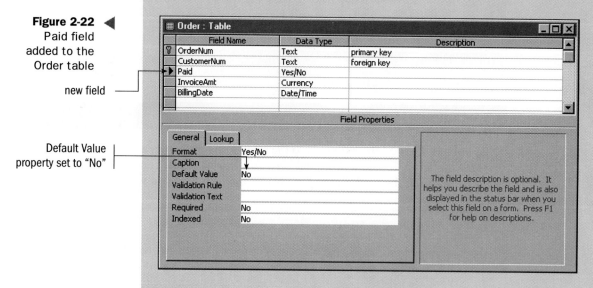

Because its field name clearly indicates its purpose, you do not need to enter a description for the Paid field.

You've completed adding the Paid field to the Order table in Design view. As with the other changes you've made, however, the Paid field is not added to the Order table in the Restaurant database until you save the changes to the table structure.

Changing Field Properties

Barbara's last modification to the table structure is to remove the dollar signs from the InvoiceAmt field values displayed in the datasheet, because repeated dollar signs are unnecessary and clutter the datasheet. You use the **Format property** to control the display of a field value.

To change the Format property of the InvoiceAmt field:

1. Click the **Description** text box for the InvoiceAmt field. The InvoiceAmt field is now the current field.

2. Click the **Format** text box in the Field Properties section, and then click the **Format** list arrow to display the Format list box. See Figure 2-23.

Figure 2-23 ◀
Format list box

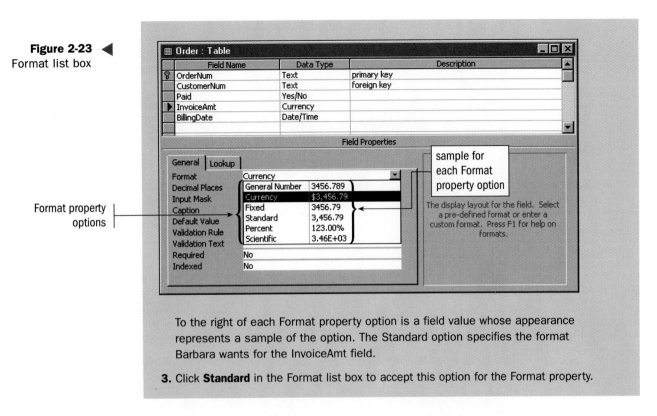

Format property
options

To the right of each Format property option is a field value whose appearance represents a sample of the option. The Standard option specifies the format Barbara wants for the InvoiceAmt field.

3. Click **Standard** in the Format list box to accept this option for the Format property.

Barbara wants you to add a third record to the Order table datasheet. Before you can add the record, you must save the modified table structure, and then switch to the Order table datasheet.

To save the modified table structure, and then switch to the datasheet:

1. Click the **Save** button 🖫 on the Table Design toolbar. The modified table structure for the Order table is stored in the Restaurant database.

2. Click the **View** button for Datasheet view 🔲 on the Table Design toolbar. The Order table datasheet opens. See Figure 2-24.

Figure 2-24 ◀
Datasheet for
the modified
Order table

records in primary
key order

field added

check box for
a yes/no field

dollar signs removed

field moved

Notice that the PlacedBy field no longer appears in the datasheet, the BillingDate field is now the rightmost column, the InvoiceAmt field values do not contain dollar signs, and the Paid field appears between the CustomerNum and InvoiceAmt fields. The Paid column contains check boxes to represent the yes/no field values. Empty check boxes signify "No," which is the default value you assigned to the Paid field. A "Yes" value is indicated by a check mark in the check box. Also notice that the records appear in ascending order based on the value in the OrderNum field, the Order table's primary key, even though you did not enter the records in this order.

Barbara asks you to add a third record to the table. This record is for an order that has been paid.

To add the record to the modified Order table:

1. Click the **New Record** button [▶*] on the Table Datasheet toolbar. The insertion point is located in the OrderNum field for the third row, which is the next row available for a new record.

2. Type **211**. The pencil symbol appears in the row selector for the third row, and the star appears in the row selector for the fourth row. Recall that these symbols represent a record being edited and the next available record, respectively.

3. Press the **Tab** key. The insertion point moves to the CustomerNum field.

4. Type **201** and then press the **Tab** key. The insertion point moves to the Paid field.

   Recall that the default value for this field is "No," which means the check box is initially empty. For yes/no fields with check boxes, you press the Tab key to leave the check box unchecked; you press the spacebar or click the check box to add or remove a check mark in the check box. Because the invoice for this order has been paid, you need to insert a check mark in the check box.

5. Press the **spacebar**. A check mark appears in the check box.

6. Press the **Tab** key. The value in the InvoiceAmt field is now highlighted.

7. Type **703.5** and then press the **Tab** key. The insertion point moves to the BillingDate field.

8. Type **1/15/99** and then press the **Tab** key. Access saves the record in the Order table and moves the insertion point to the beginning of the fourth row. See Figure 2-25.

Figure 2-25 ◀
Order table datasheet with third record added

record added

"Yes" value

"No" values

	OrderNum	CustomerNum	Paid	InvoiceAmt	BillingDate
	201	107	☐	854.00	1/15/99
	323	624	☐	1,986.00	2/15/99
▶	211	201	☑	703.50	1/15/99
▶			☐	0.00	

Order : Table

As you add records, Access places them at the end of the datasheet. If you switch to Design view then return to the datasheet or if you close the table then open the datasheet, Access will display the records in primary key sequence.

You have modified the Order table structure and added one record. Instead of typing the remaining records in the Order table, Barbara suggests that you copy them from a table that already exists in another database, and then paste them into the Order table.

Copying Records from Another Access Database

You can copy and paste records from a table in the same database or in a different database, but only if the tables have the same table structure. Barbara's Valle database in the Tutorial folder on your Student Disk has a table named Restaurant Order, which has the same table structure as the Order table. The records in the Restaurant Order table are the records Barbara wants you to copy into the Order table.

Other programs, such as Microsoft Word and Microsoft Excel, allow you to have two or more documents open at a time. However, you can have only one Access database open at a time. Therefore, you need to close the Restaurant database, open the Restaurant Order table in the Valle database, select and copy the table records, close the Valle database, reopen the Order table in the Restaurant database, and then paste the copied records.

To copy the records from the Restaurant Order table:

1. Click the **Close** button ☒ on the Table window title bar to close the Order table, and then click the **Close** button ☒ on the Database window title bar to close the Restaurant database.

2. Click the **Open Database** button 🗁 on the Database toolbar. The Open dialog box opens.

3. If necessary, display the list of files on your Student Disk, and then open the **Tutorial** folder.

4. Open the file named **Valle**. The Database window opens, showing the tables for the Valle database.

   Notice that the Valle database contains two tables: the Restaurant Customer table and the Restaurant Order table. The Restaurant Order table contains the records you need to copy.

5. Click **Restaurant Order** in the Tables list box, and then click the **Open** button. The datasheet for the Restaurant Order table opens. See Figure 2-26. Note that this table contains a total of 102 records.

Figure 2-26
Datasheet for the Valle database's Restaurant Order table

click here to select all records

total number of records in the table

OrderNum	CustomerNum	Paid	InvoiceAmt	BillingDate
200	135	☑	871.35	1/15/99
202	104	☑	1,280.50	1/15/99
203	122	☑	1,190.00	1/15/99
204	123	☑	1,055.00	1/15/99
205	128	☑	654.50	1/15/99
206	129	☑	1,392.50	1/15/99
207	131	☑	1,604.50	1/15/99
208	133	☑	1,784.00	1/15/99
209	136	☐	1,106.00	1/15/99
210	163	☑	1,223.00	1/15/99
212	203	☑	1,220.50	1/15/99
213	325	☑	1,426.50	1/15/99
214	407	☐	1,070.50	1/15/99
215	741	☑	1,852.00	1/15/99
216	515	☑	1,309.50	1/15/99

Record: 1 of 102

Barbara wants you to copy all the records in the Restaurant Order table. You can select all records by clicking the row selector for the field name row.

6. Click the **row selector** for the field name row (see Figure 2-26). All the records in the table are now highlighted, which means that Access has selected all of them.

7. Click the **Copy** button 🗐 on the Table Datasheet toolbar. All the records are copied to the Clipboard.

8. Click the **Close** button ☒ on the Table window title bar. A dialog box opens asking if you want to save the data you copied on the Clipboard.

9. Click the **Yes** button in the dialog box. The dialog box closes and then the table closes.

10. Click the **Close** button ☒ on the Database window title bar to close the Valle database.

To finish copying and pasting the records, you must open the Order table and paste the copied records into the table.

To paste the copied records into the Order table:

1. Click **File** on the menu bar, and then click **Restaurant** in the list of recently opened databases. The Database window opens, showing the tables for the Restaurant database.

2. In the Tables list box, click **Order** and then click the **Open** button. The datasheet for the Order table opens.

You must paste the records at the end of the table.

3. Click the **row selector** for row four, which is the next row available for a new record.

4. Click the **Paste** button 🖺 on the Table Datasheet toolbar. All the records are pasted from the Clipboard, and a dialog box appears, asking if you are sure you want to paste the records.

5. Click the **Yes** button. The pasted records remain highlighted. See Figure 2-27. Notice that the table now contains a total of 105 records—the three original records plus the 102 copied records.

Figure 2-27 ◀
Table after copying and pasting records

original records (3)

pasted records (102)

table now contains a total of 105 records

You've completed copying and pasting the records between the two tables. Now that you have all the records in the Order table, Barbara examines the records to make sure they are correct. She finds one record that she wants you to delete and another record that needs changes to its field values.

Updating a Database

Updating, or **maintaining,** a database is the process of adding, changing, and deleting records in database tables to keep them current and accurate. You've already added records to the Order table. Now Barbara wants you to delete and change records.

Deleting Records

To delete a record, you need to select the record in Datasheet view, and then delete it using the Delete Record button on the Table Datasheet toolbar or the Delete Record option on the shortcut menu.

REFERENCE window	DELETING A RECORD
	■ In the Table window in Datasheet view, click the row selector for the record you want to delete and then click the Delete Record button on the Table Datasheet toolbar (or right-click the row selector for the record, and then click Delete Record on the shortcut menu).
	■ In the dialog box asking you to confirm the deletion, click the Yes button.

Barbara asks you to delete the record whose OrderNum is 200 because this record was entered in error; it represents an order from an office customer, not a restaurant customer, and therefore does not belong in the Restaurant database. The fourth record in the table has an OrderNum value of 200. This is the record you need to delete.

To delete the record:

1. Right-click the **row selector** for row four. Access selects the fourth record and displays the shortcut menu. See Figure 2-28.

Figure 2-28 ◀
Deleting
a record

selected record ───

click to delete the
selected record |

OrderNum	CustomerNum	Paid	InvoiceAmt	BillingDate
201	107	☐	854.00	1/15/99
211	201	☑	703.50	1/15/99
323	624	☐	1,986.00	2/15/99
200	435	☑	871.35	1/15/99
	04	☑	1,280.50	1/15/99
	22	☑	1,190.00	1/15/99
	23	☑	1,055.00	1/15/99
	28	☑	654.50	1/15/99
	29	☑	1,392.50	1/15/99
	31	☑	1,604.50	1/15/99
	33	☑	1,784.00	1/15/99
209	136	☐	1,106.00	1/15/99
210	163	☑	1,223.00	1/15/99
212	203	☑	1,220.50	1/15/99
213	325	☑	1,426.50	1/15/99

(shortcut menu items: New Record, Delete Record, Cut, Copy, Paste, Row Height...)

Order : Table

Record: 14 ◀ 4 ▶ ▶I ▶✱ of 105

2. Click **Delete Record** on the shortcut menu. Access deletes the record and opens a dialog box asking you to confirm the deletion.

TROUBLE? If you selected the wrong record for deletion, click the No button. Access ends the deletion process and redisplays the deleted record. Repeat Steps 1 and 2 to delete the correct record.

3. Click the **Yes** button to confirm the deletion and close the dialog box.

Barbara's final update to the Order table involves changes to field values in one of the records.

Changing Records

To change the field values in a record, you first must make the record the current record. Then you position the insertion point in the field value to make minor changes or select the field value to replace it entirely. In Tutorial 1, you used the mouse with the scroll bars and the navigation buttons to navigate through the records in a datasheet. You can also use keystroke combinations and the F2 key to navigate a datasheet and to select field values.

The **F2 key** is a toggle that you use to switch between navigation mode and editing mode:

- In **navigation mode**, Access selects an entire field value. If you type while you are in navigation mode, your typed entry replaces the highlighted field value.

- In **editing mode**, you can insert or delete characters in a field value based on the location of the insertion point.

The navigation mode and editing mode keystroke techniques are shown in Figure 2-29.

Figure 2-29 ◀
Navigation mode and editing mode keystroke techniques

Press	To Move the Selection in Navigation Mode	To Move the Insertion Point in Editing Mode
←	Left one field value at a time	Left one character at a time
→	Right one field value at a time	Right one character at a time
Home	Left to the first field value in the record	To the left of the first character in the field value
End	Right to the last field value in the record	To the right of the last character in the field value
↑ or ↓	Up or down one record at a time	Up or down one record at a time and switch to navigation mode
Tab or Enter	Right one field value at a time	Right one field value at a time and switch to navigation mode
Ctrl + Home	To the first field value in the first record	To the left of the first character in the field value
Ctrl + End	To the last field value in the last record	To the right of the last character in the field value

The record Barbara wants you to change has an OrderNum field value of 397. Some of the values were entered incorrectly for this record, and you need to enter the correct values.

To modify the record:

1. Make sure the OrderNum field value for the fourth record is still highlighted, indicating that the table is in navigation mode.

2. Press **Ctrl + End**. Access displays records from the end of the table and selects the last field value in the last record. This field value is for the BillingDate field.

3. Press the **Home** key. The first field value in the record is now selected. This field value is for the OrderNum field.

4. Press the ↑ key. The OrderNum field value for the previous record is selected. This is the record you need to change.

Barbara wants you to change these field values in the record: OrderNum to 398, CustomerNum to 165, Paid to "Yes" (checked), and InvoiceAmt to 1426.50. The BillingDate does not need to be changed.

5. Type **398**, press the **Tab** key, type **165**, press the **Tab** key, press the **spacebar** to insert a check mark in the Paid check box, press the **Tab** key, and then type **1426.5**. This completes the changes to the record.

6. Press the ↓ key to save the changes to the record and make the next record the current record. See Figure 2-30.

Figure 2-30 ◀
Table after changing field values in a record

field values changed ———

You've completed all of Barbara's updates to the Order table. Barbara asks you to print just the first page of data from the Order table datasheet so that she can show the revised table structure to her staff members. After you print the page, you can exit Access.

To print the first page of Order table data, and then exit Access:

1. Click **File** on the menu bar, and then click **Print** to display the Print dialog box.

2. In the Print Range section, click the **Pages** option button, type **1** in the From text box, press the **Tab** key, and then type **1** in the To text box.

3. Click the **OK** button to print the first page of data.

   Now you can exit Access.

4. Click the **Close** button ☒ on the Access window title bar to close the Order table and the Restaurant database and to exit Access.

Quick Check

1 What is the effect of deleting a field from a table structure?

2 How do you insert a field between existing fields in a table structure?

3 A field with the _____ data type can appear in the table datasheet as a check box.

4 Which property do you use to control the display appearance of a field value?

5 Why must you close an open database when you want to copy records to it from a table in another database?

6 What is the difference between navigation mode and editing mode?

Barbara and her staff members approve of the revised table structure for the Order table. They are confident that the table will allow them to easily track order data for Valle Coffee's restaurant customers.

Tutorial Assignments

Barbara needs a database to track the coffee products offered by Valle Coffee. She asks you to create the database by completing the following:

1. Make sure your Student Disk is in the disk drive, and then start Access.

 2. In the initial Access dialog box, click the Blank Database option button, and then click the OK button. In the File New Database dialog box, select the TAssign folder on your Student Disk, and then enter the filename Valle Products for the database. Click the Create button to create the new database.

3. Create a table using the table design shown in Figure 2-31.

Figure 2-31 ◀

Field Name	Data Type	Description	Field Size	Other Properties
ProductCode	Text	primary key	4	
CoffeeCode	Text	foreign key	4	
Price	Currency	price for this product		Format: Fixed Decimal Places: 2
Decaf	Text	D if decaf, Null if regular	1	Default Value: D
BackOrdered	Yes/No	back-ordered from supplier?		

4. Specify ProductCode as the primary key, and then save the table as Product.

5. Add the product records shown in Figure 2-32 to the Product table.

Figure 2-32 ◀

ProductCode	CoffeeCode	Price	Decaf	BackOrdered
2316	JRUM	8.99		Yes
9754	HAZL	40.00	D	No
9309	COCO	9.99	D	No

6. Make the following changes to the structure of the Product table:
   a. Add a new field between the CoffeeCode and Price fields, using these properties:
      Field Name: WeightCode
      Data Type: Text
      Description: foreign key
      Field Size: 1
   b. Move the BackOrdered field so that it appears between the WeightCode and Price fields.
   c. Save the revised table structure.

7. Use the Product datasheet to update the database as follows:
   a. Enter these WeightCode values for the three records: A for ProductCode 2316, A for ProductCode 9309, and E for ProductCode 9754.

b. Add a record to the Product datasheet with these field values:

ProductCode:	9729
CoffeeCode:	COLS
WeightCode:	E
BackOrdered:	No
Price:	37.50
Decaf:	D

8. Barbara created a database with her name as the database name. The Coffee Product table in that database has the same format as the Product table you created. Copy all the records from the Coffee Product table in the Barbara database (located in the TAssign folder on your Student Disk) to the end of your Product table.

9. Close the Product table, and then reopen it so that the records are displayed in primary key order by ProductCode. Then delete the record with the ProductCode 2333 from the Product table.

10. Delete the BackOrdered field from the Product table structure.

11. Use the Access Help system to learn how to resize datasheet columns to fit the data, and then resize all columns in the datasheet for the Product table so that each column fits its data. Scroll the datasheet to make sure all field values are fully displayed. For any field values that are not fully displayed, make sure the field values are visible on the screen, and then resize the appropriate columns again.

12. Print the first page of data from the Product table datasheet, and then save and close the table.

Figure 2-33 ◀

13. Create a table named Weight based on the data shown in Figure 2-33.

WeightCode	Weight/Size
A	1 lb pkg
B	6 lb case
C	24 ct 1.5 oz pkg
D	44 ct 1.25 oz pkg
E	44 ct 1.5 oz pkg
F	88 ct 1.25 oz pkg
G	88 ct 1.5 oz pkg

a. Select the Datasheet View option in the New Table dialog box.
b. Enter the seven records shown in Figure 2-33. (Do *not* enter the field names at this point.)
c. Switch to Design view, supply the table name, and then answer No if asked if you want to create a primary key.
d. Type the following field names and set the following properties:
WeightCode
Description: primary key
Field Size: 1

Weight/Size
Description: weight in pounds or size in packages
                 (number and weight) per case
Field Size: 17
e. Specify the primary key, save the table structure changes, and then switch back to Datasheet view. If you receive any warning messages, answer Yes to continue.

f. Resize both datasheet columns to fit the data (use Access Help to learn how to resize datasheet columns, if necessary); then save, print, and close the datasheet.

14. Create a table named Coffee using the Import Table Wizard. The table you need to import is named Coffee.dbf and is located in the TAssign folder on your Student Disk. This table has a dBASE 5 file type. (You'll need to change the entry in the Files of type list box to display the file in the list.) After importing the table, complete the following:
   a. Change all field names to use the Valle Coffee convention of uppercase and lowercase letters, and then enter the following Description property values:
   CoffeeCode: primary key
   Decaf: Is decaf available for this coffee?
   b. Change the Format property of the Decaf field to Yes/No.
   c. Specify the primary key, and then save the table structure changes.
   d. Switch to Datasheet view, and then resize all columns in the datasheet to fit the data. (Use Access Help to learn how to resize datasheet columns, if necessary.) Be sure to scroll through the table to make sure that all field values are fully displayed.
   e. Save, print, and then close the datasheet. Close the Valle Products database.

Case Problems

1. Ashbrook Mall Information Desk Sam Bullard, the director of the Mall Operations Office at Ashbrook Mall, uses the MallJobs database to maintain information about current job openings at stores in the mall. Sam asks you to help him maintain the database by completing the following:

1. Make sure your Student Disk is in the disk drive.

2. Start Access and open the MallJobs database located in the Cases folder on your Student Disk.

3. Create a table using the table design shown in Figure 2-34.

Figure 2-34 ◀

Field Name	Data Type	Description	Field Size
Job	Text	primary key	5
Store	Text	foreign key	3
Hours/Week	Text		20
Position	Text		35
ExperienceReq	Yes/No		

4. Specify Job as the primary key, and then save the table as Job.

5. Add the job records shown in Figure 2-35 to the Job table.

Figure 2-35 ◀

Job	Store	Hours/Week	Position	ExperienceReq
10037	WT	negotiable	Salesclerk	No
10053	BR	14-24	Server Assistant	No
10022	JP	35-45	Assistant Manager	Yes

6. Sam created a database named Openings that contains a table with job data named Current Jobs. The Job table you created has the same format as the Current Jobs table. Copy all the records from the Current Jobs table in the Openings database (located in the Cases folder on your Student Disk) to the end of your Job table.

Access

7. Modify the structure of the Job table by completing the following:
   a. Delete the ExperienceReq field.
   b. Move the Hours/Week field so that it follows the Position field.

8. Use the Access Help system to learn how to resize datasheet columns to fit the data, and then switch to Datasheet view and resize all columns in the datasheet for the Job table.

9. Use the Job datasheet to update the database as follows:
   a. For Job 10046, change the Position value to Clerk, and change the Hours/Week value to 20-30.
   b. Add a record to the Job datasheet with the following field values:
      Job: 10034
      Store: JP
      Position: Salesclerk
      Hours/Week: negotiable
   c. Delete the record for Job 10029.

10. Switch to Design view, and then switch back to Datasheet view so that the records are displayed in primary key sequence by Job.

11. Print the Job table datasheet, and then save and close the table. Close the MallJobs database.

2. Professional Litigation User Services Raj Jawahir is responsible for tracking the daily payments received from PLUS clients. You'll help him maintain the Payments database by completing the following:

1. Make sure your Student Disk is in the disk drive.

2. Start Access and open the Payments database located in the Cases folder on your Student Disk.

3. Create a table named Payment using the table design shown in Figure 2-36.

Figure 2-36 ◀

Field Name	Data Type	Description	Field Size	Other Properties
Payment#	Text	primary key	5	
Firm#	Text	foreign key	4	
DatePaid	Date/Time			Format: Medium Date
AmtPaid	Currency			Format: Standard
				Decimal Places: 2
				Default Value: 0

4. Add the payment records shown in Figure 2-37 to the Payment table.

Figure 2-37 ◀

Payment#	Firm#	DatePaid	AmtPaid
10031	1147	6/3/99	2435.00
10002	1100	6/1/99	1300.00
10015	1142	6/1/99	2000.00

5. Modify the structure of the Payment table by completing the following:
   a. Add a new field between the Payment# and Firm# fields, using these properties:
      Field Name: Deposit#
      Data Type: Text
      Field Size: 3
   b. Move the DatePaid field so that it follows the AmtPaid field.

6. Use the Payment datasheet to update the database as follows:
   a. Enter these Deposit# values for the three records: 100 for Payment# 10002, 101 for Payment# 10015, and 103 for Payment# 10031.
   b. Add a record to the Payment datasheet with these field values:
   Payment#:   10105
   Deposit#:   117
   Firm#:   1103
   AmtPaid: 2,500.00
   DatePaid: 6/20/99

7. Raj created a database named PlusPays that contains recent payments in the Payment Records table. The Payment table you created has the same format as the Payment Records table. Copy all the records from the Payment Records table in the PlusPays database (located in the Cases folder on your Student Disk) to the end of your Payment table.

8. Use the Access Help system to learn how to resize datasheet columns to fit the data, and then resize all columns in the datasheet for the Payment table.

9. For Payment# 10002, change the AmtPaid value to 1100.00.

10. Delete the record for Payment# 10101.

11. Print the first page of data from the Payment table datasheet, and then save and close the table. Close the Payments database.

3. Best Friends Noah and Sheila Warnick continue to track information about participants in the Walk-A-Thons held to benefit Best Friends. Help them maintain the Walks database by completing the following:

1. Make sure your Student Disk is in the disk drive.

2. Start Access and open the Walks database located in the Cases folder on your Student Disk.

3. Create a table named Pledge using the Import Table Wizard. The table you need to import is named Pledge.dbf and is located in the Cases folder on your Student Disk. This table has a Microsoft FoxPro file type. (You'll need to change the entry in the Files of type list box to display the file in the list. Make sure you choose the Microsoft FoxPro file type, not the Microsoft FoxPro 3.0 file type.) After importing the table, complete the following:
   a. Change all field names to use uppercase and lowercase letters, as appropriate, and then enter the following Description property values:
   PledgeNo: primary key
   WalkerID: foreign key
   PerMile: amount pledged per mile
   b. Specify the primary key, and then save the table structure changes.
   c. Switch to Datasheet view, and then resize all columns in the datasheet to fit the data. (Use Access Help to learn how to resize datasheet columns, if necessary.)

4. Modify the structure of the Pledge table by completing the following:
   a. Add a new field between the PaidAmt and PerMile fields, using these properties:
   Field Name: DatePaid
   Data Type: Date/Time
   Format: Medium Date
   b. Change the Data Type of both the PledgeAmt field and the PaidAmt field to Currency. For each of these fields, choose the Fixed format.

5. Use the Pledge datasheet to update the database as follows:
    a. Enter these DatePaid values for the five records: 9/15/99 for PledgeNo 1, 9/1/99 for PledgeNo 2, 8/27/99 for PledgeNo 3, 9/20/99 for PledgeNo 4, and 8/30/99 for PledgeNo 5. Resize the DataPaid column to fit the data.
    b. Add a record to the Pledge datasheet with these field values:

        PledgeNo: 6
        Pledger: Fernando Carazana
        WalkerID: 138
        PledgeAmt: 25
        PaidAmt: 25
        DatePaid: 9/18/99
        PerMile: 0
    c. Enter the value 183 in the WalkerID field for PledgeNo 1.
    d. Change both the PledgeAmt value and the PaidAmt value for PledgeNo 3 to 10.00.
    e. Change the WalkerID value for PledgeNo 5 to 187.

6. Print the Pledge table datasheet, and then save and close the table. Close the Walks database.

4. Lopez Lexus Dealerships Maria and Hector Lopez use the Lexus database to track the car inventory in the chain of Lexus dealerships they own. You'll help them maintain the Lexus database by completing the following:

1. Make sure your Student Disk is in the disk drive.

2. Start Access and open the Lexus database located in the Cases folder on your Student Disk.

3. Use the Import Spreadsheet Wizard to create a new table named Locations. The data you need to import is contained in the Lopez workbook, which is a Microsoft Excel file located in the Cases folder on your Student Disk.
    a. Select the Import Table option in the New Table dialog box.
    b. Change the entry in the Files of type list box to display the list of Excel workbook files in the Cases folder.
    c. Select the Lopez file and then click the Import button.
    d. In the Import Spreadsheet Wizard dialog boxes, choose the option for using column headings as field names; select the option for choosing your own primary key and specify LocationCode as the primary key; and enter the table name (Locations). Otherwise, accept the wizard's choices for all other options for the imported data.

4. Use the Access Help system to learn how to resize datasheet columns to fit the data, and then open the Locations table and resize all columns in the datasheet.

5. Modify the structure of the Locations table by completing the following:
    a. For the LocationCode field, enter a Description property of "primary key," change the Field Size to 2, and change the Required property to Yes.
    b. For the LocationName field, change the Field Size to 20.
    c. For the ManagerName field, change the Field Size to 30.
    d. Save the table. If you receive any warning messages about lost data or integrity rules, click the Yes button.

6. Use the Locations datasheet to update the database as follows:
   a. For LocationCode A2, change the ManagerName value to Curran, Leo.
   b. Add a record to the Locations datasheet with these field values:
      LocationCode: H2
      LocationName: Houston
      ManagerName: Cohen, Sandra
   c. Delete the record for LocationCode L2.

7. Print the Locations table datasheet, and then close the table and the Lexus database.

Querying a Database

Retrieving Information About Restaurant Customers and Their Orders

Access

CASE

Valle Coffee

At a recent company meeting, Leonard Valle and other Valle Coffee employees discussed the importance of regularly monitoring the business activity of the company's restaurant customers. For example, Kim Carpenter and her marketing staff track customer activity to develop new strategies for promoting Valle Coffee products. Barbara Hennessey and her office staff need to track information about all the orders for which bills were sent out on a specific date so that they can determine whether the bills have been paid. In addition, Leonard is interested in analyzing the payment history of restaurant customers to determine which customers pay their invoices in a timely manner, which customers have higher invoice amounts, and so on. All of these informational needs can be satisfied by queries that retrieve information from the Restaurant database.

SESSION

3.1

In this session you will use the Query window in Design view to create, run, and save queries; define a one-to-many relationship between two tables; sort data with a toolbar button and in Design view; and filter data in a query datasheet.

Introduction to Queries

As you learned in Tutorial 1, a query is a question you ask about data stored in a database. For example, Kim might create a query to find records in the Customer table for only those customers in a specific state. When you create a query, you tell Access which fields you need and what criteria Access should use to select the records.

Access provides powerful query capabilities that allow you to:

- display selected fields and records from a table

- sort records

- perform calculations

- generate data for forms, reports, and other queries

- update data in the tables in a database

- find and display data from two or more tables

Most questions about data are generalized queries in which you specify the fields and records you want Access to select. These common requests for information, such as "Which customers have unpaid bills?" or "Which type of coffee sells best in Ohio?" are called **select queries**. The answer to a select query is returned in the form of a datasheet.

More specialized, technical queries, such as finding duplicate records in a table, are best formulated through a Query Wizard. A Query Wizard prompts you for information through a set of questions and then creates the appropriate query based on your answers. In Tutorial 1, you used the Simple Query Wizard to display only some of the fields in the Customer table; Access provides other Query Wizards for more complex queries. For common, informational queries, it is easier for you to design your own query rather than use a Query Wizard.

Kim wants you to create a query to display the customer number, customer name, city, owner name, and first contact information for each record in the Customer table. She needs this information for a market analysis her staff is completing on Valle Coffee's restaurant customers. You'll open the Query window to create the query for Kim.

The Query Window

You use the Query window in Design view to create a query. In Design view you specify the data you want to view by constructing a query by example. Using **query by example (QBE)**, you give Access an example of the information you are requesting. Access then retrieves the information that precisely matches your example.

For Kim's query, you need to display data from the Customer table. You'll begin by starting Access, opening the Restaurant database, and displaying the Query window in Design view.

To start Access, open the Restaurant database, and open the Query window in Design view:

1. Place your Student Disk in the appropriate disk drive.

2. Start Access and open the Restaurant database located in the Tutorial folder on your Student Disk. The Restaurant database is displayed in the Access window.

3. Click the **Queries** tab in the Database window, and then click the **New** button. The New Query dialog box opens. See Figure 3-1.

Figure 3-1 ◀
New Query
dialog box

option to design your own query

Query Wizards

You'll design your own query instead of using a Query Wizard.

4. If necessary, click **Design View** in the list box.

5. Click the **OK** button. Access opens the Show Table dialog box on top of the Query window. Notice that the title bar of the window shows that you are creating a select query.

The query you are creating will retrieve data from the Customer table, so you need to add this table to the Select Query window.

6. Click **Customer** in the Tables list box (if necessary), click the **Add** button, and then click the **Close** button. Access places the Customer table field list in the Select Query window and closes the dialog box.

To display more of the fields you'll be using for creating queries, you'll maximize the Select Query window.

7. Click the **Maximize** button ☐ on the Select Query window title bar. See Figure 3-2.

Query Type button shows select query   Run button

Figure 3-2 ◀
Select Query
window in
Design view

View button for
Datasheet view

field list

design grid

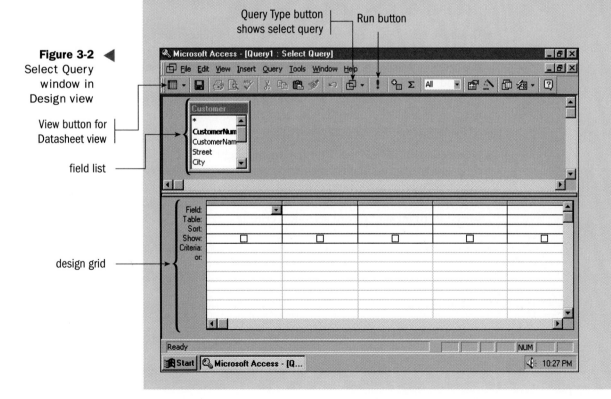

In Design view, the Select Query window contains the standard title bar, menu bar, toolbar, and status bar. On the toolbar, the Query Type button shows a select query; the icon on this button changes according to the type of query you are creating. The title bar on the Select Query window displays the query type, Select Query, and the default query name, Query1. You'll change the default query name to a more meaningful one later when you save the query.

The Select Query window in Design view contains a field list and the design grid. The **field list**, which appears in the upper-left area of the window, contains the fields for the table you are querying. The table name appears at the top of the list box, and the fields are listed in the order in which they appear in the table.

In the **design grid**, you include the fields and record selection criteria for the information you want to see. Each column in the design grid contains specifications about a field you will use in the query. You can choose a single field for your query by dragging its name from the field list to the design grid in the lower portion of the window. Alternatively, you can double-click a field name to place it in the next available column in the design grid.

When you are constructing a query, you can see the query results at any time by clicking the View button or the Run button on the Query Design toolbar. In response, Access displays the datasheet, which contains the set of fields and records that result from answering, or **running**, the query. The order of the fields in the datasheet is the same as the order of the fields in the design grid. Although the datasheet looks just like a table datasheet and appears in Datasheet view, a query datasheet is temporary and its contents are based on the criteria you establish in the design grid. In contrast, a table datasheet shows the permanent data in a table. However, you can update data while viewing a query datasheet, just as you can when working in a table datasheet or a form.

If the query you are creating includes all the fields from the specified table, you could use one of the following three methods to transfer all the fields from the field list to the design grid:

- Click and drag each field individually from the field list to the design grid. Use this method if you want the fields in your query to appear in an order that is different from the order in the field list.

- Double-click the asterisk in the field list. Access places the table name followed by a period and an asterisk (as in "Customer.*") in the design grid. This signifies that the order of the fields will be the same in the query as it is in the field list. Use this method if the query does not need to be sorted or to have conditions for the records you want to select. The advantage of using this method is that you do not need to change the query if you add or delete fields from the underlying table structure. They will all appear automatically in the query.

- Double-click the field list title bar to highlight all the fields, and then click and drag one of the highlighted fields to the design grid. Access places each field in a separate column and arranges the fields in the order in which they appear in the field list. Use this method rather than the previous one if your query needs to be sorted or to include record selection criteria.

Now you'll create and run Kim's query to display selected fields from the Customer table.

Creating and Running a Query

A table datasheet displays all the fields in the table, in the same order as they appear in the table. In contrast, a query datasheet can display selected fields from a table, and the order of the fields can be different from that of the table.

Kim wants the CustomerNum, CustomerName, City, OwnerName, and FirstContact fields to appear in the query results. You'll add each of these fields to the design grid.

To select the fields for the query, and then run the query:

1. Drag **CustomerNum** from the Customer field list to the design grid's first column Field text box, and then release the mouse button. See Figure 3-3.

Figure 3-3 ◀
Field added to
the design grid

drag field from here ─────

release mouse
button here |

indicates that the
field will appear
in the datasheet |

In the design grid's first column, the field name CustomerNum appears in the Field text box, the table name Customer appears in the Table text box, and the check mark in the Show check box indicates that the field will be displayed in the datasheet when you run the query. There are times when you might choose not to display a field and its values in the query results. For example, if you are creating a query to show all the customers located in Michigan, and you assign the name "Customers in Michigan" to the query, you would not need to include the State field value for each record in the query results. Even if you choose not to include a field in the display of the query results, you can still use the field as part of the query to select specific records or to specify a particular sequence for the records in the datasheet.

2. Double-click **CustomerName** in the Customer field list. Access adds this field to the second column of the design grid.

3. Scrolling the Customer field list as necessary, repeat Step 2 for the **City**, **OwnerName**, and **FirstContact** fields to add these fields to the design grid in that order.

Having selected the fields for Kim's query, you can now run the query.

4. Click the **Run** button ⊡ on the Query Design toolbar. Access runs the query and displays the results in Datasheet view. See Figure 3-4.

Figure 3-4
Datasheet
displayed
after running
the query

selected
fields displayed

38 records selected

The five fields appear in the datasheet, and the records are displayed in primary key sequence, by customer number. Access selected a total of 38 records for display in the datasheet.

Kim asks you to save the query as "Customer Analysis" so that she can easily retrieve the same data again.

5. Click the **Save** button ◻ on the Query Datasheet toolbar. The Save As dialog box opens.

6. Type **Customer Analysis** in the Query Name text box, and then press the **Enter** key. Access saves the query with the specified name in the Restaurant database on your Student Disk and displays the name in the title bar.

7. Click the **Close** button ☒ on the menu bar to close the query and return to the Database window.

8. Click the **Restore** button ◻ on the menu bar to return the Database window to its original size.

Barbara also wants to view specific information in the Restaurant database. However, she needs to see data from both the Customer table and the Order table at the same time. To accomplish this, you need to define a relationship between the two tables.

Defining Table Relationships

One of the most powerful features of a relational database management system is its ability to define relationships between tables. You use a common field to relate one table to another. The process of relating tables is often called performing a **join**. When you join tables that have a common field, you can extract data from them as if they were one larger table. For example, you can join the Customer and Order tables by using the CustomerNum field in both tables as the common field. You then can use a query, form, or report to extract selected data from each table, even though the data is contained in two separate tables, as shown in Figure 3-5. In the Orders query shown in Figure 3-5, the OrderNum, Paid, and InvoiceAmt columns are fields from the Order table; and the CustomerName and State columns are fields from the Customer table. The joining of records is based on the common field of CustomerNum. The Customer and Order tables have a type of relationship called a one-to-many relationship.

Figure 3-5 ◀
One-to-many
relationship
and sample
query

primary table

fields from Order
table

query that joins fields
from the Customer
and Order tables

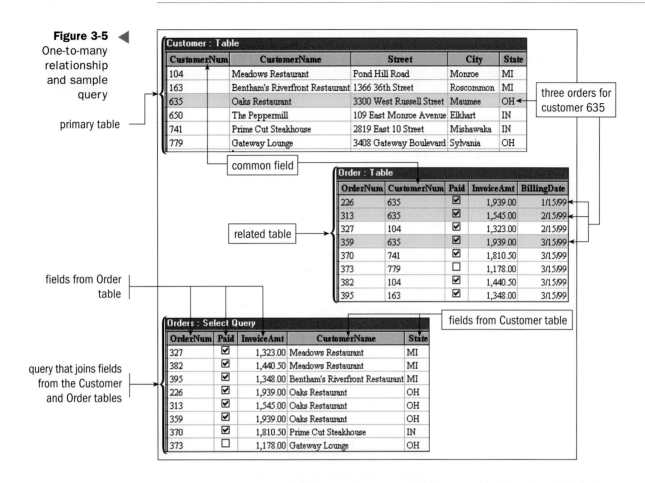

One-to-Many Relationships

A **one-to-many relationship** exists between two tables when one record in the first table matches zero, one, or many records in the second table, and when one record in the second table matches exactly one record in the first table. For example, as shown in Figure 3-5, customer 635 has three orders, customer 650 has zero orders, customers 163, 741, and 779 each have one order, and customer 104 has two orders. Every order has a single matching customer.

Access refers to the two tables that form a relationship as the primary table and the related table. The **primary table** is the "one" table in a one-to-many relationship; in Figure 3-5, the Customer table is the primary table because there is only one customer for each order. The **related table** is the "many" table; in Figure 3-5, the Order table is the related table because there can be many orders for each customer.

Because related data is stored in two tables, inconsistencies between the tables can occur. Consider the following scenarios:

- Barbara adds an order to the Order table for customer 107, Cottage Grill. This order does not have a matching record in the Customer table. The data is inconsistent, and the order record is considered to be an **orphaned** record.

- Barbara changes Oaks Restaurant from customer number 635 to 997 in the Customer table. Three orphaned records for customer 635 now exist in the Order table, and the database is inconsistent.

- Barbara deletes the record for Meadows Restaurant, customer 104, in the Customer table because this customer is no longer a Valle Coffee customer. The database is again inconsistent; two records for customer 104 in the Order table have no matching record in the Customer table.

You can avoid these problems by specifying referential integrity between tables when you define their relationships.

Referential Integrity

Referential integrity is a set of rules that Access enforces to maintain consistency between related tables when you update data in a database. Specifically, the referential integrity rules are as follows:

- When you add a record to a related table, a matching record must already exist in the primary table.

- If you attempt to change the value of the primary key in the primary table, Access prevents this change if matching records exist in a related table. However, if you choose the **cascade updates** option, Access permits the change in value to the primary key and changes the appropriate foreign key values in the related table.

- When you delete a record in the primary table, Access prevents the deletion if matching records exist in a related table. However, if you choose the **cascade deletes** option, Access deletes the record in the primary table and all records in related tables that have matching foreign key values.

Now you'll define a one-to-many relationship between the Customer and Order tables so that you can use fields from both tables to create a query that will retrieve the information Barbara wants.

Defining a Relationship Between Two Tables

When two tables have a common field, you can define a relationship between them in the Relationships window. The **Relationships window** illustrates the relationships among a database's tables. In this window you can view or change existing relationships, define new relationships between tables, and rearrange the layout of the tables.

You need to open the Relationships window and define the relationship between the Customer and Order tables. You'll define a one-to-many relationship between the two tables, with Customer as the primary table and Order as the related table, and with CustomerNum as the common field (the primary key in the Customer table and a foreign key in the Order table).

To define a one-to-many relationship between the two tables:

1. Click the **Relationships** button ⊞ on the Database toolbar. Access displays the Show Table dialog box on top of the Relationships window. See Figure 3-6.

Figure 3-6 ◄
Show Table
dialog box

add both tables

Relationships window

Each table participating in a relationship must be added to the Relationships window.

2. Click **Customer** (if necessary) and then click the **Add** button. The Customer table is added to the Relationships window.

3. Click **Order** and then click the **Add** button. The Order table is added to the Relationships window.

4. Click the **Close** button in the Show Table dialog box. Access closes the dialog box and reveals the entire Relationships window.

To form the relationship between the two tables, you drag the common field of CustomerNum from the primary table to the related table. Access then opens the Relationships dialog box in which you select the relationship options for the two tables.

5. Click **CustomerNum** in the Customer table list, and drag it to **CustomerNum** in the Order table list. When you release the mouse button, Access opens the Relationships dialog box. See Figure 3-7.

Figure 3-7 ◄
Relationships
dialog box

related table

primary table

common field

referential
integrity option

cascade options

type of relationship

The primary table, related table, and common field appear at the top of the dialog box. The type of relationship, one-to-many, appears at the bottom of the dialog box. When you click the Enforce Referential Integrity check box, the two cascade options become available. With the Cascade Update Related Fields option,

Access will change the appropriate foreign key values in the related table when you change a primary key value in the primary table. With the Cascade Delete Related Records option, when you delete a record in the primary table, Access will delete all records in the related table that have a matching foreign key value.

6. Click the **Enforce Referential Integrity** check box, click the **Cascade Update Related Fields** check box, and then click the **Cascade Delete Related Records** check box. You have now selected all the necessary relationship options.

7. Click the **Create** button to define the one-to-many relationship between the two tables and close the dialog box. The completed relationship appears in the Relationships window. See Figure 3-8.

Figure 3-8 ◀
Defined
relationship
in the
Relationships
window

"one" side of
the relationship

join line

The *join line* connects the CustomerNum fields, which are common to the two tables. The common field joins the two tables, which have a one-to-many relationship. The join line is thick at both ends; this signifies that you have chosen the option to enforce referential integrity. If you do not select this option, the join line is thin at both ends. The "one" side of the relationship has the digit 1 at its end, and the "many" side of the relationship has the infinity symbol ∞ at its end. The two tables are still separate tables, but you can use the data in them as if they were one table.

8. Click the **Save** button 🖫 on the Relationship toolbar to save the layout in the Relationships window.

9. Click the **Close** button ✕ on the Relationships window title bar. Access closes the Relationships window and returns you to the Database window.

Now that you have joined the Customer and Order tables, you can create a query to produce the information Barbara wants. As part of her tracking of payments received from restaurant customers, Barbara needs a query that displays the CustomerName, City, and State fields from the Customer table and the BillingDate, InvoiceAmt, and Paid fields from the Order table.

To create, run, and save the query using the Customer and Order tables:

1. From the Queries tab in the Database window, click the **New** button to open the New Query dialog box, click **Design View** in the dialog box, and then click the **OK** button. Access opens the Show Table dialog box on top of the Query window in Design view.

You need to add both tables to the Query window.

2. Click **Customer** in the Tables list box (if necessary), click the **Add** button, click **Order**, click the **Add** button, and then click the **Close** button. Access places the

Customer and Order field lists in the Query window and closes the Show Table dialog box. Note that the one-to-many relationship that exists between the two tables is shown in the Query window.

You need to place the CustomerName, City, and State fields from the Customer field list into the design grid, and then place the BillingDate, InvoiceAmt, and Paid fields from the Order field list into the design grid.

3. Double-click **CustomerName** in the Customer field list. Access places CustomerName in the design grid's first column Field text box.

4. Repeat Step 3 to add the **City** and **State** fields from the Customer table, and then add the **BillingDate**, **InvoiceAmt**, and **Paid** fields (in that order) from the Order table, so that these fields are placed in the second through sixth columns of the design grid.

The query specifications are complete, so you can now run the query.

5. Click the **Run** button ▮ on the Query Design toolbar. Access runs the query and displays the results in the datasheet.

6. Click the **Maximize** button ▢ on the Query window. See Figure 3-9.

Figure 3-9 ◀
Datasheet for the query based on the Customer and Order tables

fields from the Customer table

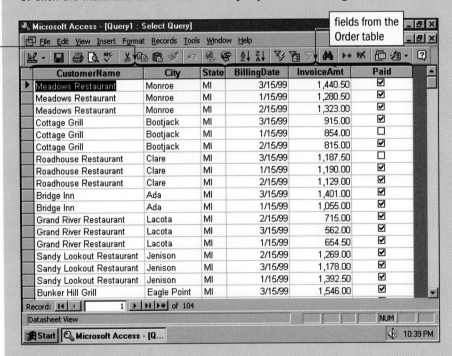

Only the six selected fields from the Customer and Order tables appear in the datasheet. The records are displayed in order according to the values in the primary key field, CustomerNum, even though this field is not included in the query datasheet.

Barbara plans on tracking the data retrieved by the query frequently, so she asks you to save the query as "Customer Orders."

7. Click the **Save** button 🖫 on the Query Datasheet toolbar. The Save As dialog box opens.

8. Type **Customer Orders** in the Query Name text box, and then press the **Enter** key. Access saves the query with the specified name and displays the name in the Query window title bar.

Barbara decides she wants the records displayed in alphabetical order by customer name. Because your query displays data in order by the field value of CustomerNum, the primary key for the Customer table, you need to sort the records by CustomerName to display the data in the order Barbara wants.

Sorting Data in a Query

Sorting is the process of rearranging records in a specified order or sequence. Often you need to sort data before displaying or printing it to meet a specific request. For example, Barbara might want to review order information arranged by the Paid field because she is interested in which orders are still unpaid. On the other hand, Leonard might want to view order information arranged by the InvoiceAmt totals for each customer because he tracks company sales.

When you sort data in a database, Access does not change the sequence of the records in the underlying tables. Only the records in the query datasheet are rearranged according to your specifications.

To sort records, you must select the **sort key**, which is the field used to determine the order of records in the datasheet. In this case, Barbara wants the data sorted by the customer name, so you need to specify the CustomerName field as the sort key. Sort keys can be text, number, date/time, currency, AutoNumber, or yes/no fields, but not memo, OLE object, or hyperlink fields. You sort records in either ascending (increasing) or descending (decreasing) order. Figure 3-10 shows the results of each type of sort for different data types.

Figure 3-10 ◀
Sorting results
for different
data types

Data Type	Ascending Sort Results	Descending Sort Results
Text	A to Z	Z to A
Number	lowest to highest numeric value	highest to lowest numeric value
Date/Time	oldest to most recent date	most recent to oldest date
Currency	lowest to highest numeric value	highest to lowest numeric value
AutoNumber	lowest to highest numeric value	highest to lowest numeric value
Yes/No	yes (check mark in check box) then no values	no then yes values

Access provides several methods for sorting data in a table or query datasheet and in a form. One method, clicking the toolbar sort buttons, lets you quickly sort the displayed records.

Using a Toolbar Button to Sort Data

The **Sort Ascending** and **Sort Descending** buttons on the toolbar allow you to sort records immediately, based on the selected field. First you select the column on which you want to base the sort, and then click the appropriate sort button on the toolbar to rearrange the records in either ascending or descending order. Unless you save the datasheet or form after you've sorted the records, the rearrangement of records is temporary.

Recall that in Tutorial 1 you used the Sort Ascending button to sort query results by the State field. You'll use this same button to sort the Customer Orders query results by the CustomerName field.

To sort the records using a toolbar sort button:

1. Click any visible CustomerName field value to establish this field as the current field.

2. Click the **Sort Ascending** button 🔼 on the Query Datasheet toolbar. Access rearranges the records in ascending order by customer name. See Figure 3-11.

Figure 3-11 ◄
Sorting records
on a single field
in a datasheet

Sort Ascending
button

Sort Descending
button

records sorted in
ascending order by
CustomerName

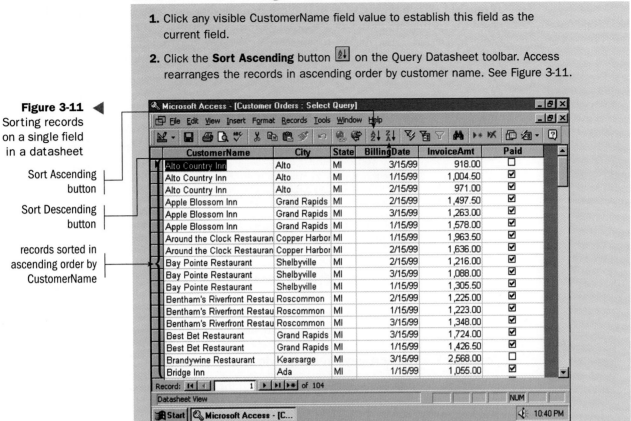

After viewing the query results, Barbara decides that she'd prefer the records to be arranged by the value in the Paid field so that she can determine more easily which invoices have been paid. She wants to view all the unpaid invoices before the paid invoices (descending order for the Paid field, which is a yes/no field); plus, she wants to display the records within each group in decreasing value of the InvoiceAmt field. To do this you need to sort using two fields.

Sorting Multiple Fields in Design View

Sort keys can be unique or nonunique. A sort key is **unique** if the value of the sort key field for each record is different. The CustomerNum field in the Customer table is an example of a unique sort key because each customer record has a different value in this field. A sort key is **nonunique** if more than one record can have the same value for the sort key field. The Paid field in the Order table is a nonunique sort key because more than one record has the same Paid value.

When the sort key is nonunique, records with the same sort key value are grouped together, but they are not in a specific order within the group. To arrange these grouped records in a specific order, you can specify a **secondary sort key**, which is a second sort key field. The first sort key field is called the **primary sort key**. Note that the primary sort key is not the same as a table's primary key field. A table has at most one primary key, which must be unique, whereas any field in a table can serve as a primary sort key.

Access lets you select up to 10 different sort keys. When you use the toolbar sort buttons, the sort key fields must be in adjacent columns in the datasheet. You highlight the columns, and Access sorts first by the first column and then by each other highlighted column in order from left to right.

Barbara wants the records sorted first by the Paid field and then by the InvoiceAmt field. Although the two fields are adjacent, they are in the wrong order. If you used a toolbar sort button, the InvoiceAmt field would be the primary sort key instead of the Paid field. When you have two or more nonadjacent sort keys or when the fields to be used for sorting are in the wrong order, you must specify the sort keys in the Query window in Design view. Access first uses the sort key that is leftmost in the design grid. Therefore, you must arrange the fields you want to sort from left to right in the design grid with the primary sort key being the leftmost sort key field.

REFERENCE
window

SORTING A QUERY DATASHEET

- In the query datasheet, select the field or adjacent fields on which you want to sort.
- Click the Sort Ascending button or the Sort Descending button on the Query Datasheet toolbar.
or
- In Design view, position the fields serving as sort keys from left (primary sort key) to right, and then select the sort order for each sort key.

To achieve the results Barbara wants, you need to switch to Design view, move the InvoiceAmt field to the right of the Paid field, and then specify the sort order for the two fields.

To select the two sort keys in Design view:

1. Click the **View** button for Design view ![icon] on the Query Datasheet toolbar. Access closes the window and opens the query in Design view.

   First, you'll move the InvoiceAmt field to the right of the Paid field.

2. If necessary, click the right arrow in the design grid's horizontal scroll bar to scroll to the right until both the InvoiceAmt and Paid fields are visible.

3. Position the pointer above the InvoiceAmt field name until the pointer changes to ↓ , and then click to select the field. See Figure 3-12.

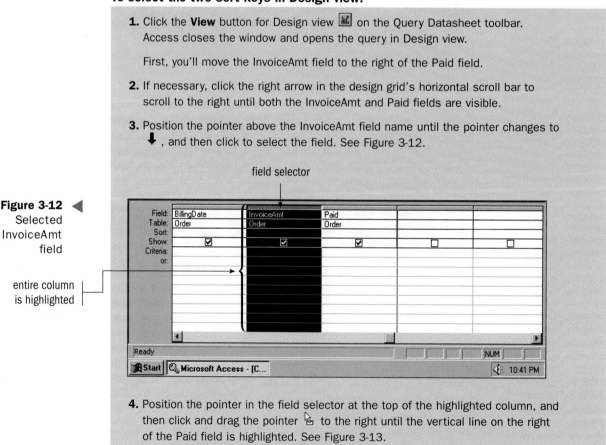

Figure 3-12 ◀
Selected
InvoiceAmt
field

entire column
is highlighted

field selector

4. Position the pointer in the field selector at the top of the highlighted column, and then click and drag the pointer ![icon] to the right until the vertical line on the right of the Paid field is highlighted. See Figure 3-13.

Access

Figure 3-13
Dragging the
field in the
design grid

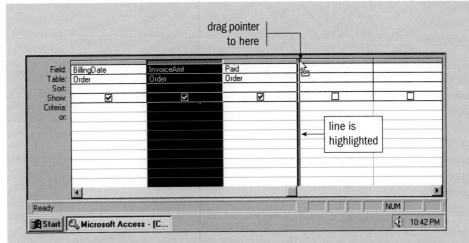

5. Release the mouse button. Access places the InvoiceAmt field to the right of the Paid field.

The fields are now in the correct order for the sort. Now you need to specify a descending sort order for each of the two fields.

6. Click the **Paid Sort** text box, click the **Sort** list arrow, and then click **Descending**. You've selected a descending sort order for the Paid field, which will be the primary sort key. The Paid field is a yes/no field, and a descending sort order for this type of field displays all the no (unpaid) values before the yes (paid) values.

7. Click the **InvoiceAmt Sort** text box, click the **Sort** list arrow, click **Descending**, and then click in the Criteria text box for the InvoiceAmt field. You've selected a descending sort order for the InvoiceAmt field, which will be the secondary sort key. See Figure 3-14.

Figure 3-14
Selecting two
sort keys in
Design view

primary sort key

secondary sort key

You have finished your query changes, so now you can run the query and then save the modified query with the same query name.

8. Click the **Run** button [!] on the Query Design toolbar. Access runs the query and displays the query datasheet. The records appear in descending order, based on the values of the Paid field. Within groups of records with the same Paid field value, the records appear in descending order by the values of the InvoiceAmt field. See Figure 3-15.

Figure 3-15
Datasheet
sorted on
two fields

primary sort key | secondary sort key

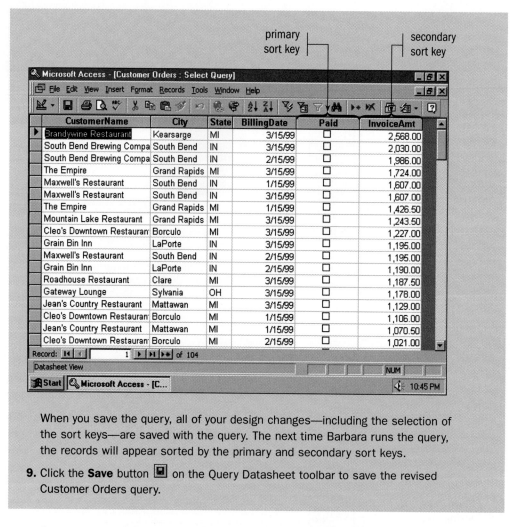

When you save the query, all of your design changes—including the selection of the sort keys—are saved with the query. The next time Barbara runs the query, the records will appear sorted by the primary and secondary sort keys.

9. Click the **Save** button 🖫 on the Query Datasheet toolbar to save the revised Customer Orders query.

Barbara wants to focus her attention for a few minutes on the orders in the datasheet that are unpaid. Because selecting only the unpaid orders is a temporary change Barbara wants in the datasheet, you do not need to switch to Design view and change the query. Instead, you can apply a filter.

Filtering Data

A **filter** is a set of restrictions you place on the records in an open datasheet or form to *temporarily* isolate a subset of the records. A filter lets you view different subsets of displayed records so you can focus on only the data you need. Unless you save a query or form with a filter applied, an applied filter is not available the next time you run the query or open the form. The simplest technique for filtering records is Filter By Selection. **Filter By Selection** lets you select all or part of a field value in a datasheet or form, and then display only those records that contain the selected value in the field.

REFERENCE window

USING FILTER BY SELECTION

- In the datasheet or form, select all or part of the field value that will be the basis for the filter.
- Click the Filter By Selection button on the toolbar.

For Barbara's request, you need to select an unchecked box in the Paid field, which represents an unpaid order, and then use Filter By Selection to display only those query records with this value.

To display the records using Filter By Selection:

1. Click any check box that is unchecked in the Paid column. When you click the check box, you select the field value, but you also change the check box from unchecked to checked. Because you've changed an unpaid order to a paid order, you need to click the same check box a second time.

2. Click the same check box a second time. The field value changes back to unchecked, which is now the selected field value.

3. Click the **Filter By Selection** button 🔽 on the Query Datasheet toolbar. Access displays the filtered results. Only the 25 query records that have an unchecked Paid field value appear in the datasheet; these records are the unpaid order records. Note that the status bar display and the selected Remove Filter button on the toolbar both indicate that records have been filtered. See Figure 3-16.

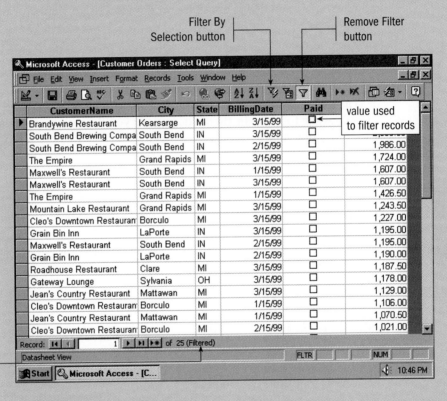

Figure 3-16 ◀
Using Filter
By Selection

Filter By Selection button | *Remove Filter button*

value used to filter records

indicates records have been filtered

Barbara asks you to print the current datasheet so that she can give the printout to a staff member who is tracking unpaid orders.

4. Click the **Print** button 🖨 on the Query Datasheet toolbar. Access prints the datasheet.

Now you can redisplay all the query records by clicking the Remove Filter button; this button works as a toggle to switch between the filtered and nonfiltered displays.

5. Click the **Remove Filter** button 🔽 on the Query Datasheet toolbar. Access redisplays all the records in the query datasheet.

6. Click the **Save** button 🖫 on the Query Datasheet toolbar, and then click the **Close** button ☒ on the menu bar to save and close the query and return to the Database window.

7. Click the **Restore** button 🗗 on the menu bar to return the Database window to its original size.

Quick Check

1 What is a select query?

2 Describe the field list and the design grid in the Query window in Design view.

3 How are a table datasheet and a query datasheet similar? How are they different?

4 The _____ is the "one" table in a one-to-many relationship, and the _____ is the "many" table in the relationship.

5 _____ is a set of rules that Access enforces to maintain consistency between related tables when you update data in a database.

6 For a date/time field, what is ascending sort order?

7 When must you define multiple sort keys in Design view instead of in the query datasheet?

8 A(n) _____ is a set of restrictions you place on the records in an open datasheet or form to temporarily isolate a subset of records.

The queries you've created will help Valle Coffee employees retrieve just the information they want to view. In the next session, you'll continue to create queries to meet their information needs.

SESSION

3.2

In this session you will specify an exact match condition in a query, change a datasheet's appearance, use a comparison operator to match a range of values, use the And and Or logical operators to define multiple selection criteria for queries, and perform calculations in queries.

Barbara wants to display customer and order information for all orders billed on 1/15/99 so she can see which orders have been paid. For this request, you need to create a query that displays selected fields from the Order and Customer tables and selected records that satisfy a condition.

Defining Record Selection Criteria for Queries

Just as you can display selected fields from a table in a query datasheet, you can display selected records. To tell Access which records you want to select, you must specify a condition as part of the query. A **condition** is a criterion, or rule, that determines which records are selected. To define a condition for a field, you place the condition in the field's Criteria text box in the design grid.

A condition usually consists of an operator, often a comparison operator, and a value. A **comparison operator** asks Access to compare the values of a database field to the condition value and to select all the records for which the relationship is true. For example, the condition >1000.00 for the InvoiceAmt field selects all records in the Order table having InvoiceAmt field values greater than 1000.00. The Access comparison operators are shown in Figure 3-17.

Figure 3-17 ◀
Access
comparison
operators

Operator	Meaning	Example
=	equal to (optional, default operator)	="Hall"
<	less than	<#1/1/94#
<=	less than or equal to	<=100
>	greater than	>"C400"
>=	greater than or equal to	>=18.75
<>	not equal to	<>"Hall"
Between ... And...	between two values (inclusive)	Between 50 And 325
In ()	in a list of values	In ("Hall", "Seeger")
Like	matches a pattern that includes wildcards	Like "706*"

Specifying an Exact Match

For Barbara's request, you need to create a query that will display only those records in the Order table with the value 1/15/99 in the BillingDate field. This type of condition is called an **exact match** because the value in the specified field must match the condition exactly in order for the record to be included in the query results. You'll use the Simple Query Wizard to create the query, and then you'll specify the exact match condition.

To create the query using the Simple Query Wizard:

1. If you took a break after the previous session, make sure that Access is running, the Restaurant database is open, and the Queries tab is displayed in the Database window, and then click the **New** button.

2. Click **Simple Query Wizard** and then click the **OK** button. Access opens the first Simple Query Wizard dialog box, in which you select the tables and fields for the query.

3. Click the **Tables/Queries** list arrow, and then click **Table: Order**. The fields in the Order table appear in the Available Fields list box. See Figure 3-18.

Figure 3-18 ◀
First Simple
Query Wizard
dialog box

selected table ──→

move needed
fields here

Except for the CustomerNum field, you will include all fields from the Order table in the query.

4. Click the >> button. Access removes all the fields from the Available Fields list box and places them in the same order in the Selected Fields list box.

5. Click **CustomerNum** in the Selected Fields list box, click the < button to move the CustomerNum field back to the Available Fields list box, and then click **BillingDate** in the Selected Fields list box.

Barbara also wants certain information from the Customer table included in the query results.

6. Click the **Tables/Queries** list arrow, and then click **Table: Customer**. The fields in the Customer table now appear in the Available Fields list box.

7. Click **CustomerName** in the Available Fields list box, and then click the > button to move CustomerName to the Selected Fields list box.

8. Repeat Step 7 for the **State**, **OwnerName**, and **Phone** fields.

9. Click the **Next** button to open the second Simple Query Wizard dialog box, in which you choose whether the query will display records from the selected tables or a summary of those records. Barbara wants to view the details for the records, not a summary.

10. Make sure the **Detail** option button is selected, and then click the **Next** button to open the last Simple Query Wizard dialog box, in which you choose a name for the query and complete the wizard. You need to enter a condition for the query, so you'll want to modify the query's design.

11. Type **January Orders**, click the **Modify the query design** option button, and then click the **Finish** button. Access saves the query as January Orders and opens the query in Design view. See Figure 3-19.

query name

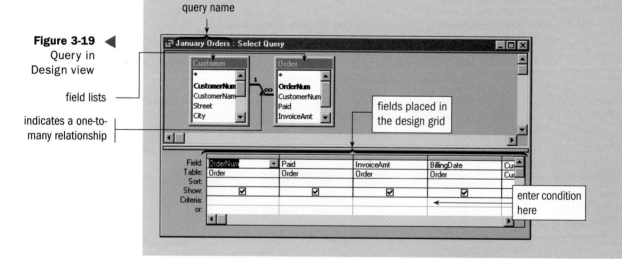

Figure 3-19 ◄
Query in
Design view

field lists

indicates a one-to-
many relationship

The field lists for the Customer and Order tables appear in the top portion of the window, and the join line indicating a one-to-many relationship connects the two tables. The selected fields appear in the design grid. Not all of the fields are visible in the grid; to see the other selected fields, you need to scroll to the right using the horizontal scroll bar.

To display the information Barbara wants, you need to enter the condition for the BillingDate field in its Criteria text box. Barbara wants to display only those records with a billing date of 1/15/99.

To enter the exact match condition, and then run the query:

1. Click the **BillingDate Criteria** text box, type **1/15/99**, and then press the **Enter** key. Access changes the condition to #1/15/99#.

   Access automatically placed number signs (#) before and after the condition. You must place date and time values inside number signs when using these values as selection criteria. If you omit the number signs, however, Access will include them automatically.

2. Click the **Run** button ⬚ on the Query Design toolbar. Access runs the query and displays the selected field values for only those records with a BillingDate field value of 1/15/99. A total of 36 records are selected and displayed in the datasheet. See Figure 3-20.

only records with a
BillingDate value
of 1/15/99
are selected

Figure 3-20
Datasheet
displaying
selected fields
and records

click here to
select all records

36 records selected

OrderNum	Paid	InvoiceAmt	BillingDate	CustomerName
201	☐	854.00	1/15/99	Cottage Grill
211	☑	703.50	1/15/99	Wagon Train Restaurant
202	☑	1,280.50	1/15/99	Meadows Restaurant
203	☑	1,190.00	1/15/99	Roadhouse Restaurant
204	☑	1,055.00	1/15/99	Bridge Inn
205	☑	654.50	1/15/99	Grand River Restaurant
206	☑	1,392.50	1/15/99	Sandy Lookout Restaura
207	☑	1,604.50	1/15/99	Bunker Hill Grill
208	☑	1,784.00	1/15/99	Florentine Restaurante
209	☐	1,106.00	1/15/99	Cleo's Downtown Restau
210	☑	1,223.00	1/15/99	Bentham's Riverfront Res
212	☑	1,220.50	1/15/99	Mountain Lake Restaurar
213	☑	1,426.50	1/15/99	Best Bet Restaurant

Record: 1 of 36

Barbara would like to see more fields and records on the screen at one time. She asks you to maximize the datasheet, change the datasheet's font size, and resize all the columns to their best fit.

Changing a Datasheet's Appearance

You can change the characteristics of a datasheet, including the font type and size of text in the datasheet, to improve its appearance or readability. You can also resize the datasheet columns to view more columns on the screen at the same time.

You'll maximize the datasheet, change the font size from the default 10 to 8, and then resize the datasheet columns.

To change the font size and resize columns in the datasheet:

1. Click the **Maximize** button ⬚ on the Query window title bar.

2. Click the **record selector** to the left of the field names at the top of the datasheet (see Figure 3-20). The entire datasheet is selected.

3. Click **Format** on the menu bar, and then click **Font** to open the Font dialog box.

4. Scroll the Size list box, click **8**, and then click the **OK** button. The font size for the entire datasheet changes to 8.

   Next you need to resize the columns to their best fit—that is, so each column is just wide enough to fit the longest value in the column.

5. Position the pointer in the OrderNum field selector. When the pointer changes to ↓, click to select the entire column.

6. Click the horizontal scroll right arrow until the Phone field is fully visible, and position the pointer in the Phone field selector until the pointer changes to ↓.

7. Press and hold the **Shift** key, and then click the mouse button. All the columns are selected. Now you can resize all of them at once.

8. Position the pointer at the right edge of the Phone field selector until the pointer changes to ↔. See Figure 3-21.

Figure 3-21
Preparing to resize all columns to their best fit

9. Double-click the mouse button. All columns are resized to their best fit, which makes each column just large enough to fit the longest *visible* field value in the column, including the field name at the top of the column. Scroll through the datasheet and resize individual columns as needed to completely display all field values.

10. If necessary, scroll to the left so that the OrderNum field is visible, and then click any field value box to deselect all columns. See Figure 3-22.

Figure 3-22
Datasheet after changing font size and column widths

TROUBLE? Your screen might show more or fewer columns depending on the monitor you are using.

11. Click the **Save** button ⊟ on the Query Datasheet toolbar, and then click the **Close** button ☒ on the menu bar. Access saves and closes the query, and you return to the Database window.

After viewing the query results, Barbara decides that she would like to see the same fields but only for those records whose InvoiceAmt exceeds $2,000. She wants to note this information and pass it along to her staff members so that they can contact those customers with higher outstanding invoices. To create the query needed to produce these results, you need to use a comparison operator to match a range of values—in this case, any InvoiceAmt value greater than $2,000.

Using a Comparison Operator to Match a Range of Values

Once you create and save a query, you can click the Open button to run it again, or you can click the Design button to change its design. Because the design of the query you need to create next is similar to the January Orders query, you will change its design, run the query to test it, and then save the query with a new name, keeping the January Orders query intact.

To change the January Orders query design to create a new query:

1. With the January Orders query selected in the Database window, click the **Design** button. Access opens the January Orders query in Design view.

2. Click the **InvoiceAmt Criteria** text box, type **>2000**, and then press the **Tab** key. See Figure 3-23.

Figure 3-23 ◀
Changing a
query's design
to create
a new query

new condition

condition to delete

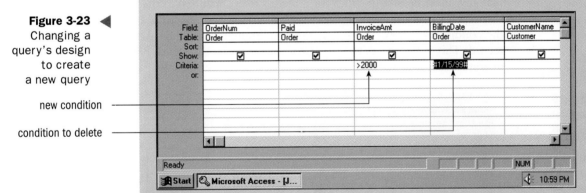

The new condition specifies that a record will be selected only if its InvoiceAmt field value exceeds 2000. Before you run the query, you need to delete the condition for the BillingDate field.

3. With the BillingDate field condition highlighted, press the **Delete** key. Access deletes the selected condition for the BillingDate field.

4. Click the **Run** button ❗ on the Query Design toolbar. Access runs the query and displays the selected fields for only those records with an InvoiceAmt field value greater than 2000. A total of four records are selected. See Figure 3-24.

Figure 3-24 ◀
Running the
modified query

only records with an
InvoiceAmt value
greater than 2,000
are selected

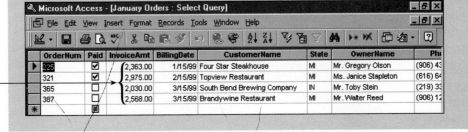

Of the records retrieved, Barbara notes that order numbers 365 and 387 have not yet been paid and the amount of each. She gives this information to her staff.

So that Barbara can display this information again, as necessary, you'll save the query as High Invoice Amounts.

5. Click **File** on the menu bar, and then click **Save As/Export** to open the Save As dialog box.

6. Type **High Invoice Amounts** in the New Name text box, and then press the **Enter** key. Access saves the query using the new query name and displays the new query name in the datasheet window title bar.

7. Click the **Close** button ☒ on the menu bar. The Database window becomes the active window.

Leonard asks Barbara for a list of the orders billed on 1/15/99 that are still unpaid. He wants to know which customers are slow in paying their invoices. To produce this data, you need to create a query containing two conditions.

Defining Multiple Selection Criteria for Queries

Multiple conditions require you to use **logical operators** to combine two or more conditions. When you want a record selected only if two or more conditions are met, you need to use the **And logical operator**. In this case, Leonard wants to see only those records with a BillingDate field value of 1/15/99 *and* a Paid field value of No. If you place conditions in separate fields in the *same* Criteria row of the design grid, all the conditions in that row must be met in order for a record to be included in the query results. However, if you place conditions in *different* Criteria rows, Access selects a record if at least one of the conditions is met. If none of the conditions is met, then Access does not select the record. This is known as the **Or logical operator**. The difference between these two logical operators is illustrated in Figure 3-25.

Figure 3-25 ◀
Logical operators And and Or for multiple selection criteria

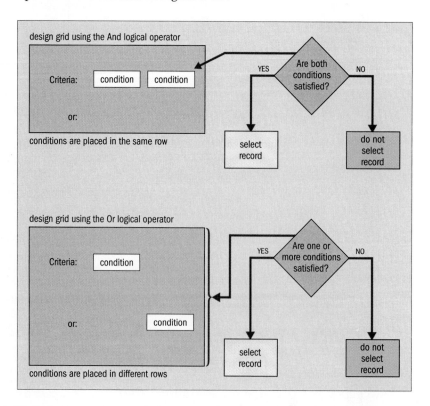

Access

The And Logical Operator

To create the query, you need to modify the existing January Orders query to show only the unpaid orders billed on 1/15/99. For the modified query, you must add a second condition in the same Criteria row. The condition #1/15/99# for the BillingDate field finds records billed on the specified date, and the condition "No" in the Paid field finds records whose invoices have not been paid. Because the conditions appear in the same Criteria row, Access selects records only if both conditions are met.

After modifying the query, you'll save it and rename it as "Unpaid January Orders," overwriting the January Orders query, which Barbara no longer needs.

To modify the January Orders query and use the And logical operator:

1. In the Queries tab of the Database window, click **January Orders** and then click the **Design** button to open the query in Design view.

2. Click the **Paid Criteria** text box, type **no**, and then press the **Tab** key. See Figure 3-26.

Figure 3-26 ◄
Query to
find unpaid
January orders

And logical operator:
conditions entered
in the same row

The condition for the BillingDate field is already entered, so you can run the query.

3. Click the **Run** button on the Query Design toolbar. Access runs the query and displays in the datasheet only those records that meet both conditions: a BillingDate field value of 1/15/99 and a Paid field value of No. A total of six records are selected. See Figure 3-27.

Figure 3-27 ◄
Results of
query using the
And logical
operator

Microsoft Access - [January Orders : Select Query]

File   Edit   View   Insert   Format   Records   Tools   Window   Help

OrderNum	Paid	InvoiceAmt	BillingDate	CustomerName	State	OwnerName	Ph
201	☐	854.00	1/15/99	Cottage Grill	MI	Ms. Doris Reaume	(616) 64
209	☐	1,106.00	1/15/99	Cleo's Downtown Restaurant	MI	Ms. Joan Hoffman	(616) 88
214	☐	1,070.50	1/15/99	Jean's Country Restaurant	MI	Ms. Jean Brooks	(517) 62
221	☐	1,607.00	1/15/99	Maxwell's Restaurant	IN	Ms. Barbara Feldon	(219) 33
235	☐	1,004.50	1/15/99	Embers Restaurant	IN	Mr. Clifford Merritt	(219) 81
239	☐	1,426.50	1/15/99	The Empire	MI	Ms. Curtis Haiar	(616) 78

Now you can save the changes to the query and rename it.

4. Click the **Save** button on the Query Datasheet toolbar, and then click the **Close** button on the menu bar.

5. Right-click **January Orders** in the Queries list box, and then click **Rename** on the shortcut menu.

6. Click to position the insertion point to the left of the word "January," type **Unpaid**, press the **spacebar**, and then press the **Enter** key. The query name is now Unpaid January Orders.

Leonard also wants to determine which restaurant customers are most valuable to Valle Coffee. Specifically, he wants to see a list of those customers who have been placing orders for many years or who place orders for a substantial amount of money. He needs this information so that he can call the customers personally and thank them for their business. To create this query, you need to use the Or logical operator.

The Or Logical Operator

For Leonard's request, you need a query that selects records when either one of two conditions is satisfied or when both conditions are satisfied. That is, a record is selected if the FirstContact field value is less than 1/1/92 (to find those customers who have been doing business with Valle Coffee the longest) *or* if the InvoiceAmt field value is greater than 2000 (to find those customers who spend more money). You will enter the condition for the FirstContact field in one Criteria row and the condition for the InvoiceAmt field in another Criteria row.

To display the information Leonard wants to view, you'll create a new query containing the CustomerName, OwnerName, Phone, and FirstContact fields from the Customer table and the InvoiceAmt field from the Order table. Then you'll specify the conditions using the Or logical operator.

To create the query and use the Or logical operator:

1. From the Queries tab of the Database window, click the **New** button to open the New Query dialog box, click **Design View**, and then click the **OK** button. Access opens the Show Table dialog box on top of the Query window in Design view.

2. Click **Customer** in the Tables list box (if necessary), click the **Add** button, click **Order**, click the **Add** button, and then click the **Close** button. Access places the Customer and Order field lists in the Query window and closes the Show Table dialog box.

3. Double-click **CustomerName** in the Customer field list. Access places CustomerName in the design grid's first column Field text box.

4. Repeat Step 3 to add the **OwnerName**, **Phone**, and **FirstContact** fields from the Customer table, and then add the **InvoiceAmt** field from the Order table.

   Now you need to specify the first condition, <1/1/92, in the FirstContact field.

5. Click the **FirstContact Criteria** text box, type **<1/1/92** and then press the **Tab** key.

   Because you want records selected if either of the conditions for the FirstContact or InvoiceAmt fields is satisfied, you must enter the condition for the InvoiceAmt field in the "or" row of the design grid.

6. Press the ↓ key, and then type **>2000**. See Figure 3-28.

Figure 3-28 ◀
Query window
with the Or
logical operator

Or logical operator:
conditions entered
in different rows

The query specifications are complete, so you can now run the query.

7. Click the **Run** button on the Query Design toolbar. Access runs the query and displays only those records that meet either condition: a FirstContact field value less than 1/1/92 or an InvoiceAmt field value greater than 2000. A total of 35 records are selected.

   Leonard wants the list displayed in alphabetical order by CustomerName.

8. Click any visible CustomerName field value to establish this field as the current field, and then click the **Sort Ascending** button on the Query Datasheet toolbar.

9. Resize all datasheet columns to their best fit. Be sure to scroll through the entire datasheet to make sure that all values are completely displayed. See Figure 3-29.

records with
InvoiceAmt values
greater than 2,000

Figure 3-29
Results of
query using the
Or logical
operator

records with
FirstContact values
earlier than 1/1/92

Now you'll save the query as Top Customers, print the query results, and then close the query.

10. Click the **Save** button on the Query Datasheet toolbar, type **Top Customers** in the Query Name text box, and then press the **Enter** key. Access saves the query with the specified name in the Restaurant database.

11. Click the **Print** button on the Query Datasheet toolbar to print the query results, and then click the **Close** button on the menu bar to close the query and return to the Database window.

Next, Leonard asks Barbara if the Restaurant database can be used to perform calculations. He is considering adding a 2% late charge to the unpaid invoices billed in January, and he wants to know exactly what these charges would be.

Performing Calculations

In addition to using queries to retrieve, sort, and filter data in a database, you can use a query to perform calculations. To perform a calculation, you define an **expression** containing a combination of database fields, constants, and operators. For numeric expressions, the data types of the database fields must be number, currency, or date/time; the constants are numbers such as .02 (for the 2% late charge); and the operators can be arithmetic operators (+ − * /) or other specialized operators. In complex expressions you can use parentheses ( ) to indicate which calculation should be performed first. In expressions without parentheses, Access calculates in the following order of precedence: multiplication and division before addition and subtraction. Access calculates operators that have equal precedence in order from left to right.

To perform a calculation in a query, you add a calculated field to the query. A **calculated field** is a field that displays the results of an expression. A calculated field appears in a query datasheet but does not exist in a database. When you run a query that contains a calculated field, Access evaluates the expression defined by the calculated field and displays the resulting value in the datasheet.

Creating a Calculated Field

To produce the information Leonard wants, you need to open the Unpaid January Orders query and create a calculated field that will multiply each InvoiceAmt field value by .02 to account for the 2% late charge Leonard is considering.

To enter an expression for a calculated field, you can type it directly in a Field text box in the design grid. Alternatively, you can open the Zoom box or Expression Builder and use either one to enter the expression. The **Zoom box** is a large text box for entering text, expressions, or other values. **Expression Builder** is an Access tool that contains an expression box for entering the expression, buttons for common operators, and one or more lists of expression elements, such as table and field names. Unlike a Field text box, which is too small to show an entire expression at one time, the Zoom box and Expression Builder are large enough to display lengthy expressions. In most cases Expression Builder provides the easiest way to enter expressions.

REFERENCE window	USING EXPRESSION BUILDER
	■ Display the query in Design view.
	■ In the design grid, position the insertion point in the Field text box of the field for which you want to create an expression.
	■ Click the Build button on the Query Design toolbar.
	■ Use the expression elements and common operators to build the expression.
	■ Click the OK button.

You'll begin by opening the Unpaid January Orders query in Design view and modifying it to show only the information Leonard wants to view.

To modify the Unpaid January Orders query:

1. In the Queries tab, click **Unpaid January Orders**, and then click the **Design** button.

   Leonard wants to see only the OrderNum, CustomerName, and InvoiceAmt fields. So, you'll first delete the unnecessary fields, and then uncheck the Show boxes for the Paid and BillingDate fields. You need to keep these two fields in the query because they specify the conditions for the query; however, they do not have to be included in the query results.

2. Scroll the design grid to the right until the last three fields—State, OwnerName, and Phone—are visible.

3. Position the pointer on the State field until the pointer changes to ↓, click and hold down the mouse button, drag the mouse to the right to highlight the State, OwnerName, and Phone fields, and then release the mouse button.

4. Press the **Delete** key to delete the three selected fields.

5. Scroll the design grid back to the left, click the **Show** check box for the Paid field to remove the check mark, and then click the **Show** check box for the BillingDate field to remove the check mark.

   Next, you'll move the InvoiceAmt field to the right of the CustomerName field so that the InvoiceAmt values will appear next to the calculated field values in the query results.

6. Make sure both the InvoiceAmt field and the empty field to the right of the CustomerName field are visible in the design grid.

7. Select the InvoiceAmt field, and then use the pointer ⊾ to drag the field to the right of the CustomerName field.

8. If necessary, scroll the design grid so that the empty field to the right of InvoiceAmt is visible, and then click anywhere in the design grid to deselect the InvoiceAmt field. See Figure 3-30.

Figure 3-30 ◀
Modified query
before adding
the calculated
field

Show boxes
unchecked

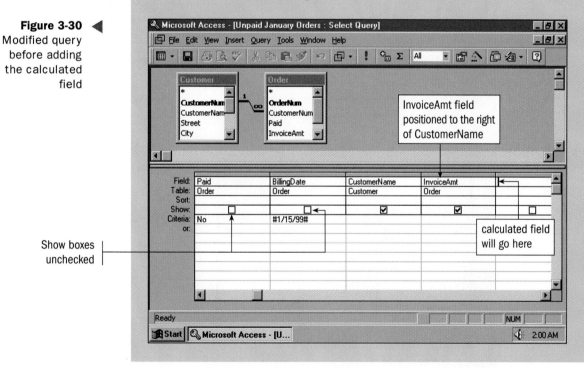

Now you're ready to use Expression Builder to enter the calculated field in the Unpaid January Orders query.

To add the calculated field to the Unpaid January Orders query:

1. Position the insertion point in the Field text box to the right of the InvoiceAmt field, and then click the **Build** button ▧ on the Query Design toolbar. The Expression Builder dialog box opens. See Figure 3-31.

Figure 3-31 ◀
Initial
Expression
Builder dialog
box

expression box

common operators

expression elements

You use the common operators and expression elements to help you build an expression. Note that the Unpaid January Orders query is already selected in the list box on the bottom left; the fields included in the query are listed in the center box.

The expression for the calculated field will multiply the InvoiceAmt field values by the numeric constant .02 (which represents a 2% late charge). To include a field in the expression, you select the field and then click the Paste button. To include a numeric constant, you simply type the constant in the expression.

2. Click **InvoiceAmt** and then click the **Paste** button. Access places [InvoiceAmt] in the expression box.

To include the multiplication operator in the expression, you click the asterisk (*) button.

3. Click the * button in the row of common operators, and then type **.02**. You have completed the entry of the expression. See Figure 3-32.

Figure 3-32 ◀
Completed
expression for
the calculated
field

expression

4. Click the **OK** button. Access closes the Expression Builder dialog box and adds the expression to the design grid.

Next, you need to specify a name for the calculated field as it will appear in the query results.

5. Press the **Home** key to position the insertion point to the left of the expression.

You'll enter the name LateCharge, which is descriptive of the field's contents; then you'll run the query.

6. Type **LateCharge:** Make sure you include the colon following the field name. The colon is used to separate the field name from its expression.

   Now you can run the query.

7. Click the **Run** button ⚑ on the Query Design toolbar. Access runs the query and displays the query datasheet, which contains the three specified fields and the calculated field. See Figure 3-33.

Figure 3-33 ◀
Datasheet
displaying the
calculated field

specified name for
calculated field

calculated field
values

You'll save the query as Unpaid With Late Charge, and then close the query.

8. Click **File** on the menu bar, click **Save As/Export**, type **Unpaid With Late Charge**, press the **Enter** key, and then click the **Close** button ☒ on the menu bar. The Database window becomes the active window.

Barbara prepares a report of Valle Coffee's restaurant business for Leonard on a regular basis. The information in the report includes a summary of the restaurant orders. Barbara lists the total invoice amount for all orders, the average invoice amount, and the total number of orders. She asks you to create a query to determine these statistics from data in the Order table.

Using Aggregate Functions

You can calculate statistical information, such as totals and averages, on the records selected in a query. To do this, you use the Access aggregate functions. **Aggregate functions** perform arithmetic operations on selected records in a database. Figure 3-34 lists the most frequently used aggregate functions. Aggregate functions operate on the records that meet a query's selection criteria. You specify an aggregate function for a specific field, and the appropriate operation applies to that field's values for the selected records.

Figure 3-34 ◀
Frequently used
aggregate
functions

Aggregate Function	Determines	Data Types Supported
Avg	Average of the field values for the selected records	AutoNumber, Currency, Date/Time, Number
Count	Number of records selected	AutoNumber, Currency, Date/Time, Memo, Number, OLE Object, Text, Yes/No
Max	Highest field value for the selected records	AutoNumber, Currency, Date/Time, Number, Text
Min	Lowest field value for the selected records	AutoNumber, Currency, Date/Time, Number, Text
Sum	Total of the field values for the selected records	AutoNumber, Currency, Date/Time, Number

To display the total, average, and count of all the invoice amounts in the Order table, you will use the Sum, Avg, and Count aggregate functions for the InvoiceAmt field.

To calculate the total, average, and count of all invoice amounts:

1. Click the **New** button to open the New Query dialog box, click **Design View** (if necessary), and then click the **OK** button. Access opens the Show Table dialog box on top of the Query window in Design view.

2. Click **Order**, click the **Add** button, and then click the **Close** button. Access adds the Order field list to the top of the Query window and closes the dialog box.

   To perform the three calculations on the InvoiceAmt field, you need to add the field three times to the design grid.

3. Double-click **InvoiceAmt** in the Order field list three times to add three copies of the field to the design grid.

   You need to select an aggregate function for each InvoiceAmt field. When you click the Totals button on the Query Design toolbar, Access adds a row labeled "Total" to the design grid. The Total row provides a list of the aggregate functions that can be selected.

4. Click the **Totals** button Σ on the Query Design toolbar. Access inserts a row labeled "Total" between the Table and Sort rows in the design grid. See Figure 3-35.

Figure 3-35 ◀
Total row
inserted in the
design grid

Total row ⟶

Totals
button

In the Total row, you specify the aggregate function you want to use for a field.

5. Click the right side of the first column's **Total** text box, and then click **Sum**. This field will calculate the total of all the InvoiceAmt field values.

   Access automatically assigns a datasheet column name of "SumOfInvoice Amount" for this field. You can change the datasheet column name to a more descriptive or readable name by entering the name you want in the Field text box. However, you must also keep InvoiceAmt in the Field text box because it identifies the field whose values will be summed. The Field text box will contain the datasheet column name you specify followed by the field name (InvoiceAmt) with a colon separating the two names.

6. Position the insertion point to the left of InvoiceAmt in the first column's Field text box, and then type **Total of Invoices:**. Be sure you include the colon at the end.

7. Click the right side of the second column's **Total** text box, and then click **Avg**. This field will calculate the average of all the InvoiceAmt field values.

8. Position the insertion point to the left of InvoiceAmt in the second column's Field text box, and then type **Average of Invoices:**.

9. Click the right side of the third column's **Total** text box, and then click **Count**. This field will calculate the total number of invoices (orders).

10. Position the insertion point to the left of InvoiceAmt in the third column's Field text box, and then type **Number of Invoices:**.

The query design is complete, so you can run the query.

11. Click the **Run** button [!] on the Query Design toolbar. Access runs the query and displays one record containing the three aggregate function values. The one row of summary statistics represents calculations based on the 104 records selected in the query.

You need to resize the three columns to their best fit to see the column names.

12. Resize each column by double-clicking the ╫ on the right edge of each column's field selector; then position the insertion point at the start of the field value in the first column. See Figure 3-36.

Figure 3-36
Results of the query using aggregate functions

Total of Invoices	Average of Invoices	Number of Invoices
$136,715.00	$1,314.57	104

You'll save the query as Invoice Statistics.

13. Click the **Save** button [🖫] on the Query Datasheet toolbar, type **Invoice Statistics**, and then press the **Enter** key.

Barbara's report to Leonard also includes the same invoice statistics (total, average, and count) for each month. Because Valle Coffee sends invoices to their restaurant customers once a month, each invoice in a month has the same billing date. Barbara asks you to display the invoice statistics for each different billing date in the Order table.

Using Record Group Calculations

In addition to calculating statistical information on all or selected records in selected tables, you can calculate statistics for groups of records. For example, you can determine the number of customers in each state or the total invoice amounts by billing date.

To create a query for Barbara's latest request, you can modify the current query by adding the BillingDate field and assigning the Group By operator to it. The **Group By operator** divides the selected records into groups based on the values in the specified field. Those records with the same value for the field are grouped together, and the datasheet displays one record for each group. Aggregate functions, which appear in the other columns of the design grid, provide statistical information for each group.

You need to modify the current query to add the Group By operator for the BillingDate field. This will display the statistical information grouped by billing date for the 104 selected records in the query.

To add the BillingDate field with the Group By operator, and then run the query:

1. Click the **View** button for Design view [☑] on the Query Datasheet toolbar to switch to Design view.

2. Scroll the Order field list, if necessary, and then double-click **BillingDate** to add the field to the design grid. Group By, which is the default option in the Total row, appears for the BillingDate field.

You've completed the query changes, so you can run the query.

3. Click the **Run** button ⚡ on the Query Design toolbar. Access runs the query and displays three records, one for each BillingDate group. Each record contains the three aggregate function values and the BillingDate field value for the group. Again, the summary statistics represent calculations based on the 104 records selected in the query. See Figure 3-37.

Figure 3-37 ◀
Aggregate functions grouped by BillingDate

aggregate function results

record groups

You'll save the query as Invoice Statistics by Billing Date, and then close the query.

4. Click **File** on the menu bar, and then click **Save As/Export**.

5. Position the insertion point to the right of the last character in the New Name text box, press the **spacebar**, type **by Billing Date**, and then press the **Enter** key.

6. Click the **Close** button ⊠ on the menu bar. The Database window becomes the active window.

7. Click the **Close** button ⊠ on the Access window title bar to close the Restaurant database and to exit Access.

Quick Check

1. A(n) _____ is a criterion, or rule, that determines which records are selected for a query datasheet.

2. In the design grid, where do you place the conditions for two different fields when you use the And logical operator? The Or logical operator?

3. To perform a calculation in a query, you define a(n) _____ containing a combination of database fields, constants, and operators.

4. How does a calculated field differ from a table field?

5. What is an aggregate function?

6. The _____ operator divides selected records into groups based on the values in a field.

The queries you've created and saved will help Leonard, Barbara, Kim, and other employees monitor and analyze the business activity of Valle Coffee's restaurant customers. The queries can be run at any time, modified as needed, or used as the basis for designing new queries to meet additional information requirements.

Tutorial Assignments

Barbara needs information from the Valle Products database, and she asks you to query the database by completing the following:

1. Make sure your Student Disk is in the disk drive, start Access, and then open the Valle Products database located in the TAssign folder on your Student Disk.

2. Create a select query based on the Product table. Display the ProductCode, WeightCode, and Price fields in the query results; sort in descending order based on the Price field values; and select only those records whose CoffeeCode value equals COLA. (*Hint*: Do not display the CoffeeCode field values in the query results.) Save the query as COLA Coffee, run the query, print the query datasheet, and then close the query.

3. Define a one-to-many relationship between the primary Coffee table and the related Product table, and then define a one-to-many relationship between the primary Weight table and the related Product table. (*Hint*: Add all three tables to the Relationships window, and then define the two relationships.) Select the referential integrity option and both cascade options for both relationships.

4. Create a select query based on the Coffee, Product, and Weight tables. Display the CoffeeType, CoffeeName, ProductCode, Price, and Weight/Size fields in that order. Sort in ascending order based on the CoffeeName field values. Select only those records whose CoffeeType equals "Special Import." Save the query as Special Imports, and then run the query. Resize all columns in the datasheet to fit the data. Print the datasheet and then close the query.

5. Create a query based on the Product table that shows all products that do not have a WeightCode field value of B, and whose Price field value is less than 30; display all fields except Decaf from the Product table. Save the query as Pricing, and then run the query.

6. Open the Pricing query in Design view. Create a calculated field named NewPrice that displays the results of increasing the Price values by 4%. Display the results in descending order by NewPrice. Save the query as New Prices, run the query, print the query datasheet, and then close the query.

7. Open the Special Imports query in Design view. Modify the query to display only those records with a CoffeeType field value of Special Import or with a Price field value greater than 50. Run the query, and then resize all columns in the datasheet to fit the data. Save the query as Special Imports Plus Higher Priced, print the query datasheet, and then close the query.

8. Create a new query based on the Product table. Use the Min and Max aggregate functions to find the lowest and highest values in the Price field. Name the two aggregate fields Lowest Price and Highest Price, respectively. Save the query as Lowest And Highest Prices, run the query, and then print the query datasheet.

9. Open the Lowest And Highest Prices query in Design view. Use the Show Table button on the Query Design toolbar to display the Show Table dialog box; then add the Weight table to the query. Modify the query so that the records are grouped by the Weight/Size field. Save the query as Lowest And Highest Prices By Weight/Size, run the query, print the query datasheet, and then close the query. Close the Valle Products database.

Case Problems

1. Ashbrook Mall Information Desk Sam Bullard wants to view specific information about jobs available at the Ashbrook Mall. He asks you to query the MallJobs database by completing the following:

1. Make sure your Student Disk is in the disk drive, start Access, and then open the MallJobs database located in the Cases folder on your Student Disk.

2. Define a one-to-many relationship between the primary Store table and the related Job table. Select the referential integrity option and both cascade options for the relationship.

3. Create a select query based on the Store and Job tables. Display the StoreName, Location, Position, and Hours/Week fields, in that order. Sort in ascending order based on the StoreName field values. Run the query, save the query as Store Jobs, and then print the datasheet.

4. Use Filter By Selection to temporarily display only those records with a Location field value of D1 in the Store Jobs query datasheet. Print the datasheet and then remove the filter.

5. Open the Store Jobs query in Design view. Modify the query to display only those records with a Position value of Clerk. Run the query, save the query as Clerk Jobs, and then print the datasheet.

6. Open the Clerk Jobs query in Design view. Modify the query to display only those records with a Position value of Clerk and with an Hours/Week value of 20-30. Run the query, save it with the same name, print the datasheet, and then close the query. Close the MallJobs database.

2. Professional Litigation User Services Raj Jawahir is completing an analysis of the payment history of PLUS clients. To help him find the information he needs, you'll query the Payments database by completing the following:

1. Make sure your Student Disk is in the disk drive, start Access, and then open the Payments database located in the Cases folder on your Student Disk.

2. Define a one-to-many relationship between the primary Firm table and the related Payment table. Select the referential integrity option and both cascade options for the relationship.

3. Create a select query based on the Firm and Payment tables. Display the Firm#, FirmName, AmtPaid, and DatePaid fields, in that order. Sort in descending order based on the AmtPaid field values. Select only those records whose AmtPaid is greater than 2,400.00. Save the query as Large Payments, and then run the query. Print the datasheet and then close the query.

4. For all payments on 6/2/99, display the Payment#, AmtPaid, DatePaid, and FirmName fields. Save the query as June 2 Payments, and then run the query. Switch to Design view, modify the query so that the DatePaid values do not appear in the query results, and then save the modified query. Run the query, print the query results, and then close the query.

5. For all firms that have Nancy Martinez as a PLUS account representative, display the FirmName, FirmContact, AmtPaid, and DatePaid fields. Save the query as Martinez Accounts, run the query, print the query results, and then close the query.

6. For all payments made on 6/11/99 or 6/12/99, display the DatePaid, AmtPaid, FirmName, and Firm# fields. Display the results in ascending order by DatePaid and then in descending order by AmtPaid. Save the query as Selected Dates, run the query, print the query datasheet, and then close the query.

Access

7. Use the Payment table to display the highest, lowest, total, average, and count of the AmtPaid field for all payments. Then do the following:
   a. Specify column names of HighestPayment, LowestPayment, TotalPayments, AveragePayment, and #Payments. Save the query as Payment Statistics, and then run the query. Resize all datasheet columns to their best fit, and then print the query results.
   b. Change the query to display the same statistics by DatePaid. Save the query as Payment Statistics By Date, run the query, and then print the query results.
   c. Change the Payment Statistics By Date query to display the same statistics by DatePaid then by Deposit#. Save the query as Payment Statistics By Date By Deposit, print the query results using landscape orientation, and then close the query. Close the Payments database.

3. Best Friends Noah and Sheila Warnick want to find specific information about the Walk-A-Thons they conduct for Best Friends. You'll help them find the information in the Walks database by completing the following:

1. Make sure your Student Disk is in the disk drive, start Access, and then open the Walks database located in the Cases folder on your Student Disk.

2. Define a one-to-many relationship between the primary Walker table and the related Pledge table. Select the referential integrity option and both cascade options for the relationship.

3. For all walkers with a PledgeAmt field value of greater than 20, display the WalkerID, LastName, PledgeNo, and PledgeAmt fields. Sort the query in descending order by PledgeAmt. Save the query as Large Pledges, run the query, print the query datasheet, and then close the query.

4. For all walkers who pledged less than $10 or who pledged $5 per mile, display the Pledger, PledgeAmt, PerMile, LastName, and FirstName fields. Save the query as Pledged Or Per Mile, run the query, and then print the query datasheet. Change the query to select all walkers who pledged less than $10 and who pledged $5 per mile. Save the query as Pledged And Per Mile, and then run the query. Describe the results. Close the query.

5. For all pledges, display the Pledger, Distance, PerMile, and PledgeAmt fields. Save the query as Difference. Create a calculated field named CalcPledgeAmt that displays the results of multiplying the Distance and PerMile fields; then save the query. Create a second calculated field named Difference that displays the results of subtracting the CalcPledgeAmt field from the PledgeAmt field. Format the calculated fields as fixed with two decimal places. (*Hint:* Choose the Properties option on the shortcut menu for the selected fields.) Display the results in ascending order by PledgeAmt. Save the modified query, and then run the query. Resize all datasheet columns to their best fit, print the query results, and then close the query.

6. Use the Pledge table to display the total, average, and count of the PledgeAmt field for all pledges. Then do the following:
   a. Specify column names of TotalPledge, AveragePledge, and #Pledges.

   b. Change properties so that the values in the TotalPledge and AveragePledge columns display two decimal places and the fixed format. (*Hint:* Choose the Properties option on the shortcut menu for the selected field.)
   c. Save the query as Pledge Statistics, run the query, resize all datasheet columns to their best fit, and then print the query datasheet.

   d. Change the query to display the sum, average, and count of the PledgeAmt field for all pledges by LastName. (*Hint:* Use the Show Table button on the Query Design toolbar to add the Walker table to the query.) Save the query as Pledge Statistics By Walker, run the query, print the query datasheet, and then close the query. Close the Walks database.

4. Lopez Lexus Dealerships Maria and Hector Lopez want to analyze data about the cars and different locations for their Lexus dealerships. Help them query the Lexus database by completing the following:

1. Make sure your Student Disk is in the disk drive, start Access, and then open the Lexus database located in the Cases folder on your Student Disk.

2. Define a one-to-many relationship between the primary Locations table and the related Cars table. Select the referential integrity option and both cascade options for the relationship.

3. For all vehicles, display the Model, Year, LocationCode, and SellingPrice fields. Save the query as Car Info, and then run the query. Resize all datasheet columns to their best fit. In Datasheet view, sort the query results in ascending order by the SellingPrice field. Print the query datasheet, and then save and close the query.

4. For all vehicles manufactured in 1998, display the Model, Year, Cost, SellingPrice, and LocationName fields. Sort the query in descending order by Cost. Save the query as 1998 Cars, and then run the query. Modify the query to remove the display of the Year field values from the query results. Save the modified query, run the query, print the query datasheet, and then close the query.

5. For all vehicles located in Houston or with a transmission of A4, display the Model, Year, Cost, SellingPrice, Transmission, LocationCode, and LocationName fields. Save the query as Location Or Trans, run the query, and then print the query datasheet using landscape orientation. Change the query to select all vehicles located in Houston and with a transmission of A4. Save the query as Location And Trans, run the query, print the query datasheet in landscape orientation, and then close the query.

6. For all vehicles, display the Model, Year, Cost, and SellingPrice fields. Save the query as Profit. Then create a calculated field named Profit that displays the difference between the vehicle's selling price and cost. Display the results in descending order by Profit. Save the query, run the query, print the query datasheet, and then close the query.

7. Use the Cars table to determine the total cost, average cost, total selling price, and average selling price of all vehicles. Use the Index tab in online Help to look up the word "caption"; then choose the topic "Change a field name in a query." Read the displayed information, and then choose and read the subtopic "Display new field names by changing the Caption property." Close the Help window. Set the Caption property of the four fields to Total Cost, Average Cost, Total Selling Price, and Average Selling Price, respectively. Save the query as Car Statistics, run the query, resize all datasheet columns to their best fit, and then print the query datasheet. Revise the query to show the car statistics by LocationName. (*Hint:* Use the Show Table button on the Query Design toolbar to display the Show Table dialog box.) Set the Caption property of the LocationName field to Location. Save the revised query as Car Statistics By Location, run the query, print the query datasheet, and then close the query.

8. Use the Office Assistant to ask the following question: "How do I create a Top Values query?" Choose the topic "Display only the highest or lowest values in the query's results." Read the displayed information, and then close the Help window and the Office Assistant. Open the Profit query in Design view, and then modify the query to display only the top five values for the Profit field. Save the query as Top Profit, run the query, print the query datasheet, and then close the query. Close the Lexus database.

Creating Forms and Reports

Creating an Order Data Form, a Customer Orders Form, and a Customers and Orders Report

Access

OBJECTIVES

In this tutorial you will:

- Create a form using the Form Wizard

- Change a form's AutoFormat

- Navigate a form and find data using a form

- Preview and print selected form records

- Maintain table data using a form

- Create a form with a main form and a subform

- Create a report using the Report Wizard

- Insert a picture on a report

- Preview and print a report

- Compact a database

CASE

Valle Coffee

Barbara Hennessey wants to continue to enhance the Restaurant database to make it easier for her office staff members and other Valle Coffee employees to find and maintain data. In particular, she wants the database to include a form for the Order table, similar to the Customer Data form, which is based on the Customer table. She also wants a form that shows data from both the Customer and Order tables at the same time, so that all the order information for each customer appears with the corresponding customer data, giving a complete picture of the restaurant customers and their orders.

In addition, Kim Carpenter would like a report showing customer and order data so that her marketing staff members have printed output to refer to when completing market analyses and planning strategies for selling to restaurant customers. She wants the information to be formatted attractively, perhaps including the Valle Coffee cup logo on the report for visual interest.

SESSION

4.1

In this session you will create a form using the Form Wizard, change a form's AutoFormat, navigate a form, find data using a form, print selected form records, and maintain table data using a form.

Creating a Form Using the Form Wizard

As you learned in Tutorial 1, a form is an object you use to maintain, view, and print records in a database. In Access, you can design your own forms or use Form Wizards to create them for you automatically.

Barbara asks you to create a new form her staff can use to view and maintain data in the Order table. In Tutorial 1, you used the AutoForm Wizard, which creates a form automatically using all the fields in the selected table or query, to create the Customer Data form. To create the form for the Order table, you'll use the Form Wizard. The **Form Wizard** allows you to choose some or all of the fields in the selected table or query, choose fields from other tables and queries, and display the chosen fields in any order on the form. You can also choose a style for the form.

To open the Restaurant database and activate the Form Wizard:

1. Place your Student Disk in the appropriate disk drive.

2. Start Access and open the Restaurant database located in the Tutorial folder on your Student Disk. The Restaurant database is displayed in the Access window.

3. Click the **Forms** tab in the Database window to select the tab. The Forms list includes the Customer Data form you created in Tutorial 1.

4. Click the **New** button in the Database window. The New Form dialog box opens.

5. Click **Form Wizard**, click the list arrow for choosing a table or query, click **Order** to select this table as the source for the form, and then click the **OK** button. The first Form Wizard dialog box opens. See Figure 4-1.

Figure 4-1 ◀
First Form Wizard dialog box

selected table ────

fields in the selected table ┤

Barbara wants the form to display all the fields in the Order table, but in a different order. She would like the Paid field to be placed at the bottom of the form so that it stands out more, making it easier to determine if an order has been paid.

To finish creating the form using the Form Wizard:

1. Click **OrderNum** in the Available Fields list box (if necessary), and then click the ▸ button to move the field to the Selected Fields list box.

2. Repeat Step 1 to select the **CustomerNum**, **InvoiceAmt**, **BillingDate**, and **Paid** fields, in that order.

3. Click the **Next** button to display the second Form Wizard dialog box, in which you select a layout for the form. See Figure 4-2.

Figure 4-2 ◀
Choosing a
layout for
the form

sample of the
selected layout

selected layout

The layout choices are columnar, tabular, datasheet, and justified. A sample of the selected layout appears on the left side of the dialog box.

4. Click each of the option buttons and review the corresponding sample layout.

The tabular and datasheet layouts display the fields from multiple records at one time, whereas the columnar and justified layouts display the fields from one record at a time. Barbara thinks the columnar layout is the appropriate arrangement for displaying and updating data in the table, so you'll choose this layout.

5. Click the **Columnar** option button (if necessary), and then click the **Next** button. Access displays the third Form Wizard dialog box, in which you choose a style for the form. See Figure 4-3.

Figure 4-3 ◀
Choosing a
style for
the form

Form Wizard
styles

sample of the
selected style

A sample of the selected style appears in the box on the left. If you choose a style, which is called an *AutoFormat*, and decide you'd prefer a different one after the form is created, you can change it.

6. Click each of the styles and review the corresponding sample.

Barbara likes the Evergreen style and asks you to use it for the form.

7. Click **Evergreen** and then click the **Next** button. Access displays the final Form Wizard dialog box and shows the table name as the default for the form name and for the title that will appear in the form title bar. See Figure 4-4.

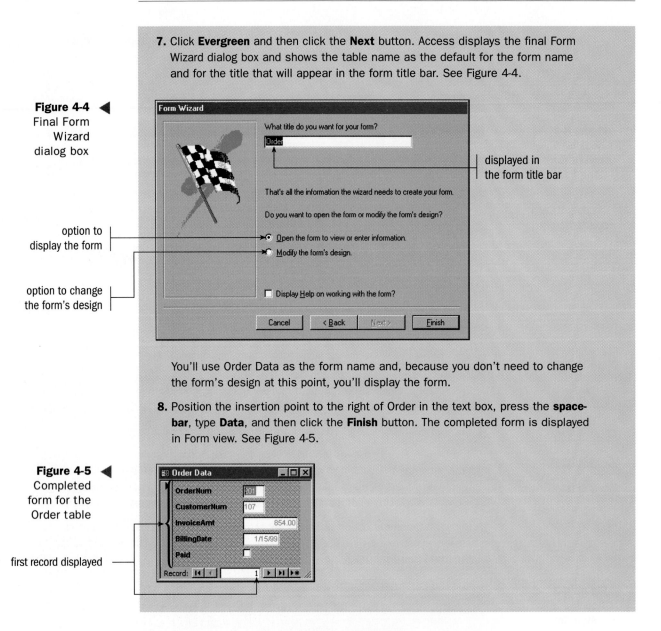

Figure 4-4 ◄
Final Form
Wizard
dialog box

option to
display the form

option to change
the form's design

displayed in
the form title bar

You'll use Order Data as the form name and, because you don't need to change the form's design at this point, you'll display the form.

8. Position the insertion point to the right of Order in the text box, press the **space-bar**, type **Data**, and then click the **Finish** button. The completed form is displayed in Form view. See Figure 4-5.

Figure 4-5 ◄
Completed
form for the
Order table

first record displayed

After viewing the form, Barbara decides that she doesn't like the form's style—the green background makes the field names difficult to read and the green type for the field values is too light. She asks you to change the form's style.

Changing a Form's AutoFormat

You can change a form's appearance by choosing a different AutoFormat for the form. As you learned when you created the Order Data form, an **AutoFormat** is a predefined style for a form (or report). The AutoFormats available for a form are the ones you saw when you selected the form's style using the Form Wizard. To change an AutoFormat, you must switch to Design view.

REFERENCE
window

CHANGING A FORM'S AUTOFORMAT

- Display the form in Design view.
- Click the AutoFormat button on the Form Design toolbar to open the AutoFormat dialog box.
- In the Form AutoFormats list box, click the AutoFormat you want for the form, and then click the OK button.

To change the AutoFormat for the Order Data form:

1. Click the **View** button for Design view on the Form View toolbar. The form is displayed in Design view. See Figure 4-6.

Figure 4-6
Form displayed
in Design view

Form window

TROUBLE? If your screen displays any other windows than those shown in Figure 4-6, click the Close button ☒ on the particular window's title bar to close it.

You use Design view to modify an existing form or to create a form from scratch. In this case, you need to change the AutoFormat for the Order Data form.

2. Click the **AutoFormat** button 🖫 on the Form Design toolbar. The AutoFormat dialog box opens.

3. Click the **Options** button to display the AutoFormat options. See Figure 4-7.

Figure 4-7
AutoFormat
dialog box

AutoFormats
for forms

AutoFormat options

A sample of the selected AutoFormat appears to the right of the Form AutoFormats list box. The options at the bottom of the dialog box allow you to apply the selected AutoFormat or just its font, color, or border.

Barbara decides that she prefers the Standard AutoFormat, because its field names and field values are easy to read.

4. Click **Standard** in the Form AutoFormats list box, and then click the **OK** button. The AutoFormat dialog box closes, the AutoFormat is applied to the form, and the Form window in Design view becomes the active window.

5. Click the **View** button for Form view 🖳 on the Form Design toolbar. The form is displayed in Form view with the new AutoFormat. See Figure 4-8.

Figure 4-8 ◀
Form displayed
with the new
AutoFormat

You have finished modifying the format of the form and can now save it.

6. Click the **Save** button 🖫 on the Form View toolbar to save the modified form.

Barbara wants to view some data in the Order table using the form. To view data, you need to navigate through the form.

Navigating a Form

To maintain and view data using a form, you must know how to move from field to field and from record to record. The mouse movement, selection, and placement techniques to navigate a form are the same techniques you've used to navigate a table datasheet and the Customer Data form you created in Tutorial 1. Also, the navigation mode and editing mode keystroke techniques are the same as those you used previously for datasheets (see Figure 2-29).

To navigate through the form:

1. Press the **Tab** key to move to the CustomerNum field value, and then press the **End** key to move to the Paid field. Because the Paid field is a yes/no field, its value is not highlighted; instead, a dashed box appears around the field name to indicate it is the current field.

2. Press the **Home** key to move back to the OrderNum field value. The first record in the Order table still appears in the form.

3. Press **Ctrl + End** to move to the Paid field in record 104, which is the last record in the table. The record number for the current record appears between the navigation buttons at the bottom of the form.

4. Click the **Previous Record** navigation button ◀ to move to the Paid field in record 103.

5. Press the ↑ key twice to move to the InvoiceAmt field value in record 103.

6. Position the insertion point between the numbers "2" and "6" in the InvoiceAmt field value to switch to editing mode, press the **Home** key to move the insertion point to the beginning of the field value, and then press the **End** key to move the insertion point to the end of the field value.

7. Click the **First Record** navigation button ◀◀ to move to the InvoiceAmt field value in the first record. The entire field value is highlighted because you have switched from editing mode to navigation mode.

8. Click the **Next Record** navigation button ▶ to move to the InvoiceAmt field value in record 2, which is the next record.

Barbara asks you to display the records for Jean's Country Restaurant, whose customer number is 407, because she wants to review the orders for this customer.

Finding Data Using a Form

The **Find** command allows you to search the data in a form and to display only those records you want to view. You choose a field to serve as the basis for the search by making that field the current field; then you enter the value you want Access to match in the Find in field dialog box. You can use the Find command for a form or datasheet, and you can activate the command from the Edit menu or by clicking the toolbar Find button.

REFERENCE window

FINDING DATA

- On a form or datasheet, click anywhere in the field value you want to search.
- Click the Find button on the toolbar to open the Find in field dialog box.
- In the Find What text box, type the field value you want to find.
- Complete the remaining options, as necessary, to specify the type of search you want Access to perform.
- Click the Find First button to have Access begin the search at the beginning of the table, or click the Find Next button to begin the search at the current record.
- Click the Find Next button to continue the search for the next match.
- Click the Close button to stop the search operation.

You need to find all records in the Order table for Jean's Country Restaurant, whose customer number is 407.

To find the records using the Order Data form:

1. Position the insertion point in the CustomerNum field value box. This is the field for which you will find matching values.

2. Click the **Find** button [icon] on the Form View toolbar to open the Find in field dialog box. Note that the title bar of the dialog box specifies the name of the field that Access will search, in this case, the CustomerNum field.

3. If the Find in field dialog box covers any part of the form, move the dialog box by dragging its title bar. See Figure 4-9.

Figure 4-9 ◀
Find in field
dialog box

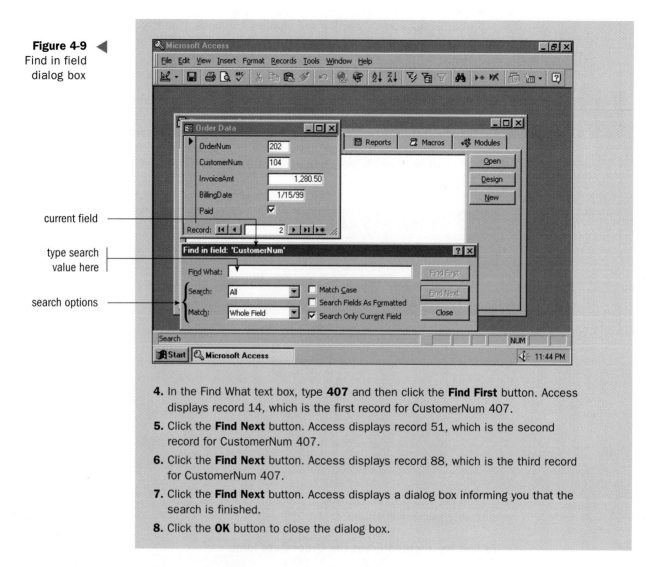

current field

type search
value here

search options

4. In the Find What text box, type **407** and then click the **Find First** button. Access displays record 14, which is the first record for CustomerNum 407.

5. Click the **Find Next** button. Access displays record 51, which is the second record for CustomerNum 407.

6. Click the **Find Next** button. Access displays record 88, which is the third record for CustomerNum 407.

7. Click the **Find Next** button. Access displays a dialog box informing you that the search is finished.

8. Click the **OK** button to close the dialog box.

The search value you enter can be an exact value, such as the customer number 407 you just entered, or it can include wildcard characters. A **wildcard character** is a placeholder you use when you know only part of a value or when you want to start or end with a specific character or match a certain pattern. Figure 4-10 shows the wildcard characters you can use when finding data.

Figure 4-10 ◀
Wildcard
characters

Wildcard Character	Purpose	Example
*	Match any number of characters. It can be used as the first and/or last character in the character string.	th* finds *the, that, this, therefore,* and so on
?	Match any single alphabetic character.	a?t finds *act, aft, ant,* and *art*
[ ]	Match any single character within the brackets.	a[fr]t finds *aft* and *art* but not *act* and *ant*
!	Match any character not within brackets.	a[!fr]t finds *act* and *ant* but not *aft* and *art*
-	Match any one of a range of characters. The range must be in ascending order (a to z, not z to a).	a[d-p]t finds aft and ant but not act and art
#	Match any single numeric character.	#72 finds *072, 172, 272, 372,* and so on

To check if their orders have been paid, Barbara wants to view the order records for two customers: Cheshire Restaurant (CustomerNum 515) and Around the Clock Restaurant (CustomerNum 597). You'll use the * wildcard character to search for these customers' orders.

To find the records using the * wildcard character:

1. Double-click **407** in the Find What text box to select the entire value, and then type **5***.

   Access will match any field value in the CustomerNum field that starts with the digit 5.

2. Click the **Find First** button. Access displays record 16, which is the first record for CustomerNum 515. Note that the Paid field value is checked, indicating that this order has been paid.

3. Click the **Find Next** button. Access displays record 17, which is the first record for CustomerNum 597.

4. Click the **Find Next** button. Access displays record 39, which is the second record for CustomerNum 597.

5. Click the **Find Next** button. Access displays record 68, which is the second record for CustomerNum 515.

6. Click the **Find Next** button. Access displays record 82, which is the third record for CustomerNum 515.

7. Click the **Find Next** button. Access displays a dialog box informing you that the search is finished.

8. Click the **OK** button to close the dialog box.

9. Click the **Close** button to close the Find in field dialog box.

All five orders have been paid, but Barbara wants to make sure Valle Coffee has a record of payment for order number 375. She asks you to print the data displayed on the form for record 82, which is for order number 375, so she can ask a staff member to look for the payment record for this order.

Previewing and Printing Selected Form Records

Access prints as many form records as can fit on a printed page. If only part of a form record fits on the bottom of a page, the remainder of the record prints on the next page. Access allows you to print all pages or a range of pages. In addition, you can print the currently selected form record.

Before printing record 82, you'll preview the form record to see how it will look when printed.

To preview the form and print the data for record 82:

1. Make sure record 82 is the current record in the Order Data form.

2. Click the **Print Preview** button 🔍 on the Form View toolbar. The Print Preview window opens, showing the form records for the Order table in miniature.

3. Click the **Maximize** button 🔲 on the form title bar.

4. Click the **Zoom** button 🔍 on the Print Preview toolbar, and then use the vertical scroll bar to view the contents of the window. See Figure 4-11.

Figure 4-11
Print Preview
window
displaying
form records

Zoom button

form records

form's Restore
button

Each record from the Order table appears in a separate form. Access places as many forms as will fit on each page.

5. Click the **Restore** button 🗗 on the Print Preview menu bar, and then click the **Close** button on the Print Preview toolbar to return to the table in Form view.

6. Click **File** on the menu bar, and then click **Print**. The Print dialog box opens.

7. Click the **Selected Record(s)** option button to print only the current form record (record 82).

8. Click the **OK** button to close the dialog box and print the selected record.

Barbara has identified several updates she wants you to make to the Order table using the Order Data form, as shown in Figure 4-12.

Figure 4-12
Updates to the
Order table

Order Number	Update Action
319	Change InvoiceAmt to 1,175.00 Change Paid to Yes
392	Delete record
400	Add new record for CustomerNum 135, InvoiceAmt of 1,350.00, BillingDate of 3/15/99, and Paid status of No

Maintaining Table Data Using a Form

Maintaining data using a form is often easier than using a datasheet, because you can concentrate on all the changes required to a single record at a time. You already know how to navigate a form and find specific records. Now you'll make the changes Barbara requested to the Order table using the Order Data form.

First, you'll update the record for OrderNum 319.

To change the record using the Order Data form:

1. Make sure the Order Data form is displayed in Form view.

The current record number appears between the sets of navigation buttons at the bottom of the form. If you know the number of the record you want to change, you can type the number and press the Enter key to go directly to the record. When she reviewed the order data to identify possible corrections, Barbara noted that 48 is the record number for order number 319.

2. Select the number 82 that appears between the navigation buttons, type **48**, and then press the **Enter** key. Record 48 is now the current record.

You need to change the InvoiceAmt field value to 1,175.00 and the Paid field value to Yes for this record.

3. Position the insertion point between the numbers 9 and 5 in the InvoiceAmt field value, press the **Backspace** key, and then type **7**. Note that the pencil symbol appears in the top left of the form, indicating that the form is in editing mode.

4. Press the **Tab** key twice to move to the Paid field value, and then press the **spacebar** to insert a check mark in the check box. See Figure 4-13.

Figure 4-13 ◀
Order record
after changing
field values

indicates
editing mode

field values changed

You have completed the changes for order number 319. Barbara's next update is to delete the record for order number 392. The customer who placed this order canceled it before the order was filled and processed.

To delete the record using the Order Data form:

1. Click anywhere in the OrderNum field value to make it the current field.

2. Click the **Find** button 🔍 on the Form View toolbar. The Find in field dialog box opens.

3. Type **392** in the Find What text box, click the **Find First** button, and then click the **Close** button. The record for order number 392 is now the current record.

To delete the record, you first need to select the entire record by clicking anywhere in the large rectangular area surrounding the record selector.

4. Click the **record selector** in the top left of the form to select the entire record. See Figure 4-14.

Figure 4-14
Entire record
selected

click to select
the entire record

5. Click the **Delete Record** button on the Form View toolbar. A dialog box opens, asking you to confirm the record deletion.

6. Click the **Yes** button. The dialog box closes and the record for order number 392 is deleted from the table.

Barbara's final maintenance change is to add a record for a new order placed by Topview Restaurant.

To add the new record using the Order Data form:

1. Click the **New Record** button on the Form View toolbar. Record 104, the next record available for a new record, becomes the current record. All field value boxes are empty, and the insertion point is positioned at the beginning of the field value for OrderNum.

2. Refer to Figure 4-15 and enter the value shown for each field, pressing the Tab key to move from field to field.

Figure 4-15
Completed
form for the
new record

TROUBLE? Compare your screen with Figure 4-15. If any field value is wrong, correct it now using the methods described earlier for editing field values.

3. After entering the value for BillingDate, press the **Tab** key twice (if necessary). Record 105, the next record available for a new record, becomes the current record, and the record for order number 400 is saved in the Order table.

You've completed Barbara's changes to the Order table, so you can close the Order Data form.

4. Click the **Close** button on the form title bar. The form closes and you return to the Database window. Notice that the Order Data form is listed in the Forms list box.

Quick Check

1 Describe the difference between creating a form using the AutoForm Wizard and creating a form using the Form Wizard.

2 What is an AutoFormat, and how do you change one for an existing form?

3　Which table record is displayed in a form when you press Ctrl + End?

4　You can use the Find command to search for data in a form or _____.

5　Which wildcard character matches any single alphabetic character?

6　How many form records does Access print by default on a page?

7　How do you select an entire form record?

The Order Data form will enable Barbara and her staff to enter and maintain data easily in the Order table. In the next session, you'll create another form for working with data in both the Order and Customer tables at the same time. You'll also create a report showing data from both tables.

SESSION

4.2

In this session you will create a form with a main form and a subform, create a report using the Report Wizard, insert a picture on a report, preview and print a report, and compact a database.

Barbara would like you to create a form so that she can view the data for each customer and all the orders for the customer at the same time. The type of form you need to create will include a main form and a subform.

Creating a Form with a Main Form and a Subform

To create a form based on two tables, you must first define a relationship between the two tables. In Tutorial 3, you defined a one-to-many relationship between the Customer (primary) and Order (related) tables, so you are ready to create the form based on both tables.

When you create a form containing data from two tables that have a one-to-many relationship, you actually create a main form for data from the primary table and a subform for data from the related table. Access uses the defined relationship between the tables to automatically join the tables through the common field that exists in both tables.

Barbara and her staff will use the form when contacting customers about the status of their order payments. Consequently, the main form will contain the customer number and name, owner name, and phone number; the subform will contain the order number, paid status, invoice amount, and billing date.

You'll use the Form Wizard to create the form.

To activate the Form Wizard to create the form:

1. If you took a break after the previous session, make sure that Access is running, the Restaurant database is open, and the Forms tab is displayed in the Database window, and then click the **New** button. The New Form dialog box opens.

   When creating a form based on two tables, you first choose the primary table and select the fields you want to include in the main form; then you choose the related table and select fields from it for the subform.

2. Click **Form Wizard**, click the list arrow for choosing a table or query, click **Customer** to select this table as the source for the main form, and then click the **OK** button. The first Form Wizard dialog box opens, in which you select fields in the order you want them to appear on the main form.

   Barbara wants the form to include only the CustomerNum, CustomerName, OwnerName, and Phone fields from the Customer table.

3. Click **CustomerNum** in the Available Fields list box (if necessary), and then click the ![>] button to move the field to the Selected Fields list box.

4. Repeat Step 3 for the **CustomerName**, **OwnerName**, and **Phone** fields.

The CustomerNum field will appear in the main form, so you do not have to include it in the subform. Otherwise, Barbara wants the subform to include all the fields from the Order table.

5. Click the **Tables/Queries** list arrow, and then click **Table: Order**. The fields from the Order table appear in the Available Fields list box. The quickest way to add the fields you want to include is to move all the fields to the Selected Fields list box, and then remove only the field you don't want to include (CustomerNum).

6. Click the ![>>] button to move all the fields from the Order table to the Selected Fields list box.

7. Click **Order.CustomerNum** in the Selected Fields list box, and then click the ![<] button to move the field back to the Available Fields list box. Note that the table name (Order) is included in the field name to distinguish it from the same field (CustomerNum) in the Customer table.

8. Click the **Next** button. The next Form Wizard dialog box opens. See Figure 4-16.

Figure 4-16 ◀
Choosing a
main/subform
format

primary table ——

related table ——

option for a form
with a subform

In this dialog box, the list box on the left shows the order in which you will view the selected data: first by data from the Customer table (primary table), then by data from the Order table (related table). The form will be displayed as shown in the right side of the dialog box, with the fields from the Customer table at the top in the main form, and the fields from the Order table at the bottom in the subform. The selected option button specifies a main form with a subform.

The default options shown in Figure 4-16 are correct for creating a form with Customer data in the main form and Order data in the subform.

To finish creating the form:

1. Click the **Next** button. The next Form Wizard dialog box opens, in which you choose the subform layout.

The tabular layout displays subform fields as a table, whereas the datasheet layout displays subform fields as a table datasheet. The layout choice is a matter of personal preference. You'll use the datasheet layout.

Access

2. Click the **Datasheet** option button (if necessary), and then click the **Next** button. The next Form Wizard dialog box opens, in which you choose the form's AutoFormat.

Barbara wants all forms to have the same style, so you will choose the Standard AutoFormat, which is the same AutoFormat you used to create the Order Data form earlier.

3. Click **Standard** (if necessary) and then click the **Next** button. The next Form Wizard dialog box opens, in which you choose names for the main form and the subform.

You will use Customer Orders as the main form name and Order Subform as the subform name.

4. Position the insertion point to the right of the last letter in the Form text box, press the **spacebar**, and then type **Orders**. The main form name is now Customer Orders. Note that the default subform name, Order Subform, is the name you want, so you don't need to change it.

You have answered all the Form Wizard questions.

5. Click the **Finish** button. The completed form is displayed in Form view.

Notice that some columns in the subform are not wide enough to display the field names entirely. You need to resize the columns to their best fit.

6. Double-click the pointer ✛ at the right edge of each column in the subform. The columns are resized to their best fit and all field names are fully displayed. See Figure 4-17.

Figure 4-17 ◀
Completed
form

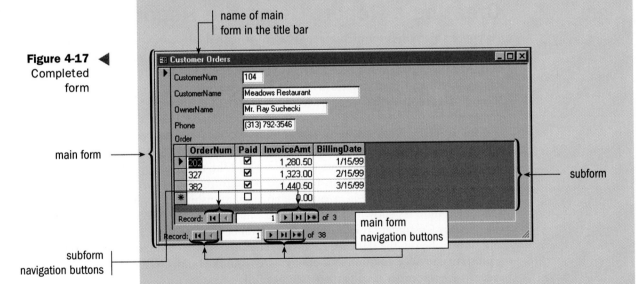

In the main form, Access displays the fields from the first record in the Customer table in columnar format. The records in the main form appear in primary key sequence by customer number. Customer 104 has three related records in the Order table; these records are shown at the bottom in a datasheet format. The form shows that Meadows Restaurant has placed three orders with Valle Coffee, and each order has been paid.

Two sets of navigation buttons appear near the bottom of the form. You use the top set of navigation buttons to select records from the related table in the subform and the bottom set to select records from the primary table in the main form.

You'll use the navigation buttons to view different records.

To navigate to different main form and subform records:

1. Click the **Last Record** navigation button ▶❘ in the main form. Record 38 in the Customer table for Embers Restaurant becomes the current record in the main form. The subform shows that this customer placed three orders with Valle Coffee, all of which are unpaid.

2. Click the **Last Record** navigation button ▶❘ in the subform. Record 3 in the Order table becomes the current record in the subform.

3. Click the **Previous Record** navigation button ◀ in the main form. Record 37 in the Customer table for The Empire becomes the current record in the main form. This customer has placed two orders, both of which are unpaid.

   You have finished your work with the form, so you can close it.

4. Click the **Close** button ✖ on the form title bar. The form closes, and you return to the Database window. Notice that both the main form, Customer Orders, and the subform, Order Subform, appear in the Forms list box.

Kim would like a report showing data from both the Customer and Order tables so that all the pertinent information about restaurant customers and their orders is available in one place.

Creating a Report Using the Report Wizard

As you learned in Tutorial 1, a report is a formatted hardcopy of the contents of one or more tables in a database. In Access, you can create your own reports or use the Report Wizard to create them for you. Like the Form Wizard, the **Report Wizard** asks you a series of questions and then creates a report based on your answers. Whether you use the Report Wizard or design your own report, you can change the report's design after you create it.

Kim wants you to create a report that includes selected customer data from the Customer table and all the orders from the Order table for each customer. Kim sketched a design of the report she wants (Figure 4-18). Like the Customer Orders form you just created, which includes a main form and a subform, the report will be based on both tables, which are joined in a one-to-many relationship through the common field of CustomerNum. As shown in the sketch in Figure 4-18, the selected customer data from the primary Customer table includes the customer number, name, city, state, owner name, and phone. Below the data for each customer, the report will include the order number, paid status, invoice amount, and billing date from the related Order table. The set of field values for each order is called a **detail record**.

Figure 4-18 ◄
Report sketch
for the
Customers and
Orders report

fields from Customer
table: primary table

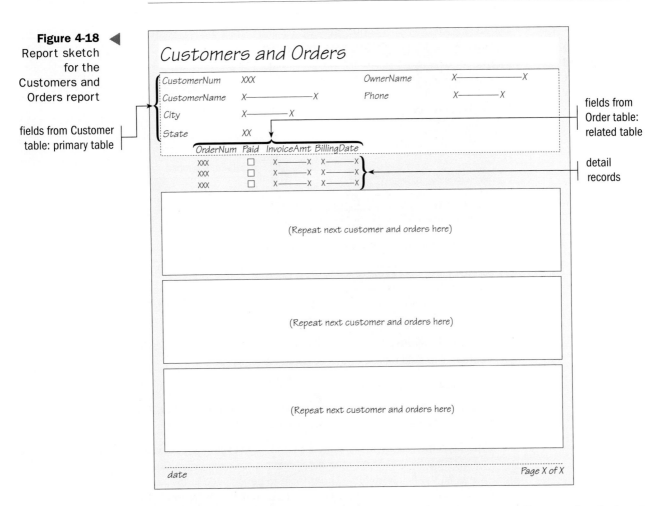

You'll use the Report Wizard to create the report according to the design in Kim's sketch.

To activate the Report Wizard and select the fields to include in the report:

1. Click the **Reports** tab in the Database window to display the Reports list box. You have not created and saved any reports, so the list box is empty.

2. Click the **New** button in the Database window. The New Report dialog box opens.

Although the data for the report exists in two tables (Customer and Order), you can choose only one table or query to be the data source for the report in the New Report dialog box. However, in the Report Wizard dialog boxes you can include data from other tables. You will select the primary Customer table in the New Report dialog box.

3. Click **Report Wizard**, click the list arrow for choosing a table or query, and then click **Customer**. See Figure 4-19.

Figure 4-19 ◀
Completed
New Report
dialog box

method for
creating the report

primary source of
data for the report

4. Click the **OK** button. The first Report Wizard dialog box opens.

In the first Report Wizard dialog box, you select fields in the order you want them to appear on the report. Kim wants the CustomerNum, CustomerName, City, State, OwnerName, and Phone fields from the Customer table to appear on the report.

5. Click **CustomerNum** in the Available Fields list box, and then click the [>] button. The field moves to the Selected Fields list box.

6. Repeat Step 5 for **CustomerName**, **City**, **State**, **OwnerName**, and **Phone**.

7. Click the **Tables/Queries** list arrow, and then click **Table: Order**. The fields from the Order table appear in the Available Fields list box.

The CustomerNum field will appear on the report with the customer data, so you do not have to include it in the detail records for each order. Otherwise, Kim wants all the fields from the Order table to be included in the report. The easiest way to include the necessary fields is to add all the Order table fields to the Selected Fields list box and then to remove the only field you don't want to include—CustomerNum.

8. Click the [>>] button to move all the fields from the Available Fields list box to the Selected Fields list box.

9. Click **Order.CustomerNum** in the Selected Fields list box, click the [<] button to move the selected field back to the Available Fields list box, and then click the **Next** button. The second Report Wizard dialog box opens. See Figure 4-20.

Figure 4-20 ◀
Choosing a
grouped or
ungrouped
report

grouped by table

click to display
tips and examples

You can choose to arrange the selected data grouped by table, which is the default, or ungrouped. For a grouped report, the data from a record in the primary table appears as a group, followed by the joined records from the related table. For the report you are creating, data from a record in the Customer table appears in a group, followed by the records for the customer from the Order table. An example of an ungrouped report would be a report of records from the Customer and Order tables in order by OrderNum. Each order and its associated customer data would appear together; the data would not be grouped by table.

You can display tips and examples for the choices in the Report Wizard dialog box by clicking the ⟫ button ("Show me more information").

To display tips about the options in the Report Wizard dialog box:

1. Click the ⟫ button. The Report Wizard Tips dialog box opens. Read the displayed information in the dialog box.

   You can display examples of different grouping methods by clicking the ⟫ button ("Show me examples").

2. Click the ⟫ button. The Report Wizard Examples dialog box opens. See Figure 4-21.

Figure 4-21 ◀
Report Wizard
Examples
dialog box

click to
display examples

click to return to
Report Wizard Tips
dialog box

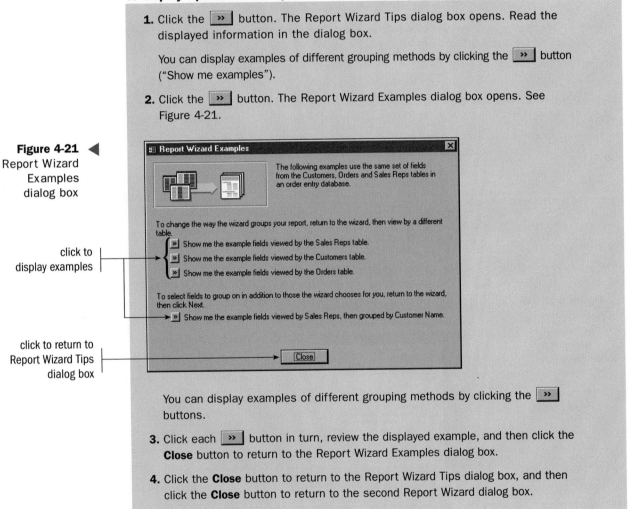

You can display examples of different grouping methods by clicking the ⟫ buttons.

3. Click each ⟫ button in turn, review the displayed example, and then click the **Close** button to return to the Report Wizard Examples dialog box.

4. Click the **Close** button to return to the Report Wizard Tips dialog box, and then click the **Close** button to return to the second Report Wizard dialog box.

The default options shown on your screen are correct for the report Kim wants, so you can continue responding to the Report Wizard questions.

To finish creating the report using the Report Wizard:

1. Click the **Next** button. The next Report Wizard dialog box opens, in which you choose additional grouping levels.

Two grouping levels are shown: one for each customer's data, the other for a customer's orders. Grouping levels are useful for reports with multiple levels, such as those containing month, quarter, and annual totals; or containing city and country groups. Kim's report contains no further grouping levels, so you can accept the default options.

2. Click the **Next** button. The next Report Wizard dialog box opens, in which you choose the sort order for the detail records. See Figure 4-22.

Figure 4-22 ◀
Choosing the sort order for detail records

click to display field list

The records from the Order table for a customer represent the detail records for Kim's report. She wants these records to appear in increasing, or ascending, order by the value in the OrderNum field.

3. Click the **1** list arrow, click **OrderNum**, and then click the **Next** button. The next Report Wizard dialog box opens, in which you choose a layout and page orientation for the report. See Figure 4-23.

Figure 4-23 ◀
Choosing the report layout and page orientation

layout sample

orientation options

layout options

A sample of each layout appears in the box on the left.

4. Click each layout option and examine each sample that appears. You'll use the Outline 2 layout option because it resembles the layout shown in Kim's sketch of the report.

5. Click the **Outline 2** option button, and then click the **Next** button. The next Report Wizard dialog box opens, in which you choose a style for the report.

CREATING FORMS AND REPORTS **TUTORIAL 4** **A** 4.21

A sample of the selected style, or AutoFormat, appears in the box on the left. You can always choose a different AutoFormat after you create the report, just as you could when creating a form. Kim likes the appearance of the Corporate AutoFormat, so you'll choose this one for your report.

6. Click **Corporate** and then click the **Next** button. The last Report Wizard dialog box opens, in which you choose a report name, which also serves as the printed title on the report.

According to Kim's sketch, the report title you need to specify is "Customers and Orders."

7. Type **Customers and Orders** and then click the **Finish** button. The Report Wizard creates the report based on your answers and saves it to your Student Disk. Then Access opens the Customers and Orders report in Print Preview.

To better view the report, you need to maximize the report window.

8. Click the **Maximize** button on the Customers and Orders title bar.

To view the entire page, you need to change the Zoom setting.

9. Click the **Zoom** list arrow on the Print Preview toolbar, and then click **Fit**. The first page of the report is displayed in Print Preview. See Figure 4-24.

Figure 4-24
Report displayed in Print Preview

Zoom list arrow

When a report is displayed in Print Preview, you can use the pointer to toggle between a full-page display and a close-up display of the report. Kim asks you to check the report to see if any adjustments need to be made. To do so, you need to view a close-up display of the report.

To view a close-up display of the report and make any necessary corrections:

1. Click the pointer ⊕ at the top center of the report. The display changes to show the report close up. See Figure 4-25.

Figure 4-25 ◀
Close-up view
of the report

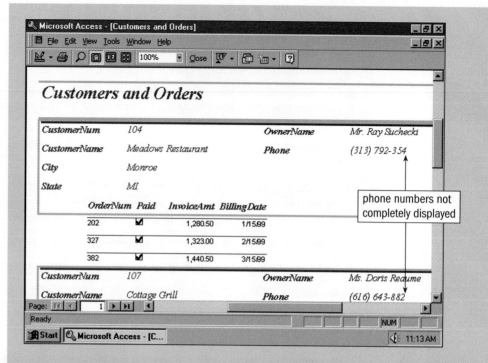

TROUBLE? Scroll your screen as necessary so that it matches the screen in Figure 4-25.

Notice that the last digit in each phone number is not visible in the report. To fix this, you need to first display the report in Design view.

2. Click the **View** button for Design view on the Print Preview toolbar. Access displays the report in Design view. See Figure 4-26.

Figure 4-26 ◀
Report
displayed in
Design view

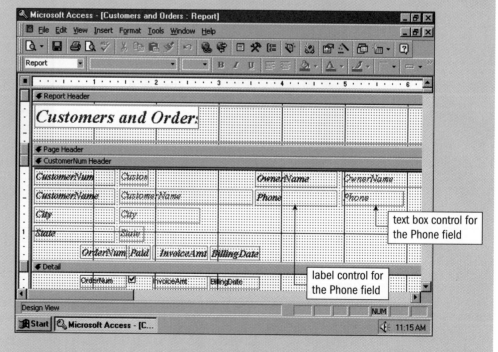

TROUBLE? If the Toolbox is displayed on your screen, close it by clicking its Close button ☒.

You use the Report window in Design view to modify existing reports and to create custom reports.

Each item on a report in Design view is called a *control*. For example, the Phone field consists of two controls: the label "Phone," which appears on the report to identify the field value, and the Phone text box in which the actual field value appears. You need to widen the text box control for the Phone field so that the entire field value is visible in the report.

3. Click the text box control for the Phone field to select it. Notice that small black boxes appear on the border around the control. These boxes, which are called *handles*, indicate that the control is selected and can be manipulated.

4. Position the pointer on the center right handle of the Phone text box control until the pointer changes to ↔. See Figure 4-27.

Figure 4-27 ◀
Resizing the Phone text box control

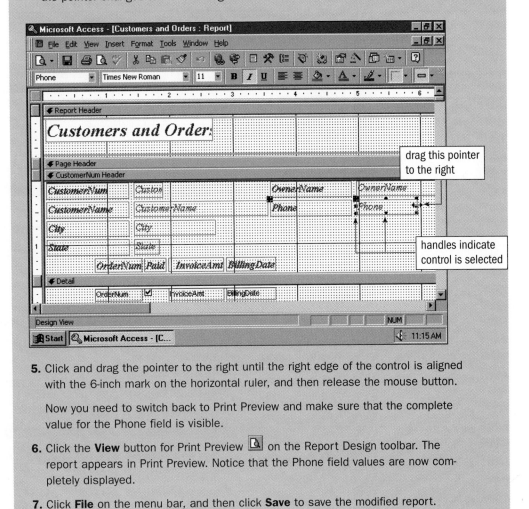

5. Click and drag the pointer to the right until the right edge of the control is aligned with the 6-inch mark on the horizontal ruler, and then release the mouse button.

Now you need to switch back to Print Preview and make sure that the complete value for the Phone field is visible.

6. Click the **View** button for Print Preview [Q] on the Report Design toolbar. The report appears in Print Preview. Notice that the Phone field values are now completely displayed.

7. Click **File** on the menu bar, and then click **Save** to save the modified report.

Kim decides that she wants the report to include the Valle Coffee cup logo to the right of the report title, for visual interest. You can add the logo to the report by inserting a picture of the coffee cup.

Inserting a Picture on a Report

In Access, you can insert a picture or other graphic image on a report or form to enhance the appearance of the report or form. Sources of graphic images include Microsoft Paint, other drawing programs, and scanners. The file containing the picture you need to insert is named ValleCup, and is located in the Tutorial folder on your Student Disk.

To insert the picture on the report:

1. Click the **Close** button on the Print Preview toolbar to display the report in Design view. See Figure 4-28.

click to select Report
Header section

Figure 4-28 ◄
Inserting a
picture in
Design view

Report
Header section

insert picture here

Kim wants the picture to appear on the first page of the report only; therefore, you need to insert the picture in the Report Header section (see Figure 4-28). Any text or graphics placed in this section appear once at the beginning of the report.

2. Click the **Report Header** bar to select this section of the report. The bar is high-lighted to indicate the section is selected.

3. Click **Insert** on the menu bar, and then click **Picture**. The Insert Picture dialog box opens. See Figure 4-29.

Figure 4-29 ◄
Insert Picture
dialog box

selected picture file

4. Make sure Tutorial appears in the Look in text box, click **ValleCup** to select the picture of the Valle Coffee cup, and then click the **OK** button. The picture is inserted at the far left of the Report Header section, covering some of the report title text. See Figure 4-30.

Figure 4-30 ◀
Picture
inserted
in report

inserted picture ⎯⎯

Notice that handles appear on the border around the picture, indicating that the picture is selected and can be manipulated.

Kim wants the picture to appear to the right of the report title, so you need to move the picture using the mouse.

5. Position the pointer on the picture until the pointer changes to 🖑, and then click and drag the mouse to move the picture to the right so that its left edge aligns with the 3-inch mark on the horizontal ruler and its top edge is just below the top border line above the report title (see Figure 4-30).

6. Release the mouse button. The picture appears in the new position. See Figure 4-31.

Figure 4-31 ◀
Repositioned
picture in
the report

TROUBLE? If your picture is in a different location from the one shown in Figure 4-31, use the pointer 🖑 to reposition the picture until it is in approximately the same position shown in the figure. Be sure that the top edge of the picture is below the top border line of the report.

7. Click the **View** button for Print Preview 🔍 on the Report Design toolbar to view the report in Print Preview. The report now includes the inserted picture. If necessary, click the **Zoom** button 🔍 on the Print Preview toolbar to display the entire report page. See Figure 4-32.

Figure 4-32 ◀
Print Preview
of report
with picture

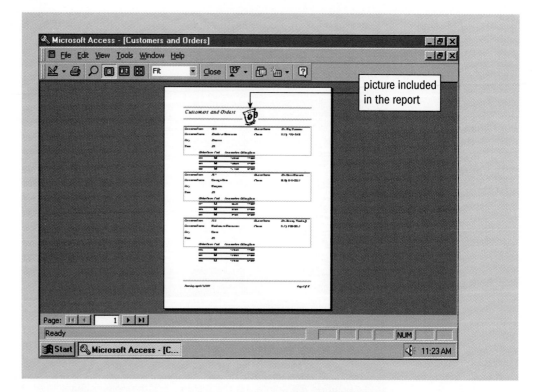

The report is now complete. You'll print a hardcopy of just the first page of the report so that Kim can review the report layout and the inserted picture.

To print page 1 of the report:

1. Click **File** on the menu bar, and then click **Print**. The Print dialog box opens.

2. In the Print Range section, click the **Pages** option button. The insertion point now appears in the From text box so that you can specify the range of pages to print.

3. Type **1** in the From text box, press the **Tab** key to move to the To text box, and then type **1**. These settings specify that only page 1 of the report will be printed.

4. Click the **OK** button. The Print dialog box closes and the first page of the report is printed. See Figure 4-33.

Figure 4-33 ◀
First page
of the
Customers and
Orders report

report title

fields from
Customer table

fields from
Order table

page footer

inserted picture

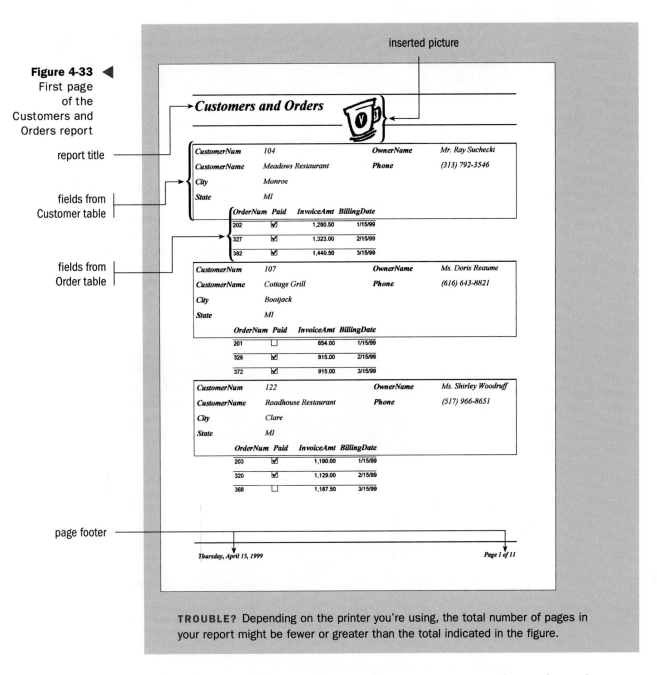

TROUBLE? Depending on the printer you're using, the total number of pages in your report might be fewer or greater than the total indicated in the figure.

Kim approves of the report layout and contents, so you can close and save the report.

To close and save the report:

1. Click the **Close** button ✕ on the menu bar.

TROUBLE? If you click the Close button on the Print Preview toolbar by mistake, Access redisplays the report in Design view. Click the Close button ✕ on the menu bar.

Access displays a dialog box asking if you want to save the changes to the design of your report.

2. Click the **Yes** button to save and close the report and return to the Database window.

You no longer need to have the Database window maximized, so you can restore it now.

3. Click the **Restore** button on the Database window.

Before you exit Access, you'll compact the Restaurant database to free up disk space.

Compacting a Database

When you delete records in an Access table, the space occupied by the deleted records on disk does not become available for other records. The same is true if you delete an object, such as a table, query, or form. To make the space available, you must compact the database. **Compacting** a database rearranges the data and objects in a database and creates a smaller copy of the database. Unlike making a copy of a database file, which you do to protect your database against loss or damage, you compact the database to make it smaller, thereby making more space available on your disk. Before compacting a database, you must close it.

REFERENCE window

COMPACTING A DATABASE

- Make sure the database you want to compact is closed.
- In the Access window, click Tools on the menu bar, point to Database Utilities, and then click Compact Database to open the Database to Compact From dialog box.
- In the Look in box, select the drive and directory containing the database you want to compact; in the File name box, select the database you want to compact.
- Click the Compact button. Access opens the Compact Database Into dialog box.
- In the Save in box, select the drive and directory for the location of the compacted database; in the File name text box, type the name you want to assign to the compacted database.
- Click the Save button.

You'll compact the Restaurant database, delete the original (uncompacted) database file, and then rename the compacted file.

To compact the Restaurant database:

1. Click the **Close** button ☒ on the Database window title bar.

2. Click **Tools** on the menu bar, point to **Database Utilities**, and then click **Compact Database**. Access opens the Database to Compact From dialog box, in which you select the database you want to compact.

3. Make sure Tutorial appears in the Look in list box, click **Restaurant** in the list box, and then click the **Compact** button. Access opens the Compact Database Into dialog box, in which you enter the filename for the compacted copy of the database and select its drive and folder location.

Usually you would make a backup copy of the database as a safeguard before compacting. Here, you'll save the compacted database with a different name, delete the original database file, and then rename the compacted database to the original database name.

4. Type **Compacted Restaurant** in the File name text box, make sure Tutorial appears in the Save in list box, and then click the **Save** button. Access compacts the Restaurant database, creating the copied file named Compacted Restaurant, and returns you to the Access window.

Now you need to exit Access, delete the original Restaurant database, and then rename the compacted database as Restaurant. To delete and rename the necessary files, you'll open the Exploring window from the desktop.

To open the Exploring window and delete and rename the database files:

1. Click the **Close** button ☒ on the Access window title bar. Access closes and you return to the Windows 95 desktop.

2. Using the right mouse button, click the **Start** button on the taskbar, and then click **Explore**. The Exploring window opens.

3. Scrolling as necessary, click the plus symbol to the left of the drive that contains your Student Disk in the All Folders list box, and then click **Tutorial**. The list of files in the Tutorial folder on your Student Disk appears in the Contents of 'Tutorial' list box. See Figure 4-34.

Figure 4-34 ◄
Original and
compacted
database files
in Exploring
window

original database file —

Verify that both database files—the original Restaurant database and the Compacted Restaurant database—are included in the window. Note the difference in size of the two files.

TROUBLE? The size of your files might be different from those in the figure.

Now you need to delete the original (uncompacted) database file and then rename the compacted file.

4. Click **Restaurant** in the list box, click **File** on the menu bar, and then click **Delete**. The Confirm File Delete dialog box opens and asks you to confirm the deletion.

5. Click the **Yes** button to delete the file.

6. Click **Compacted Restaurant** in the list box, click **File** on the menu bar, and then click **Rename**. The filename appears highlighted inside a box to indicate it is selected for editing.

7. Position the insertion point to the left of the word "Compacted," and then use the **Delete** key to delete the word "Compacted" and the space following it.

8. Press the **Enter** key. The filename of the compacted file is now Restaurant.

9. Click the **Close** button ☒ on the Exploring title bar to close the Exploring window and return to the desktop.

Quick Check

1. How are a related table and a primary table associated with a form that contains a main form and a subform?

2. Describe how you use the navigation buttons to move through a form containing a main form and a subform.

3. When you use the Report Wizard, the report name is also used as the _____ .

4. To insert a picture on a report, the report must be displayed in _____ .

5. Any text or graphics placed in the _____ section of a report appear only on the first page of the report.

6. What is the purpose of compacting a database?

Barbara is satisfied that both forms—the Order Data form and the Customer Orders form—will make it easier to enter, view, and update data in the Restaurant database. The Customers and Orders report presents important information about Valle Coffee's restaurant customers in an attractive, professional format, which will help Kim and her staff in their sales and marketing efforts.

Tutorial Assignments

Barbara wants to enhance the Valle Products database with forms and reports, and she asks you to complete the following:

1. Make sure your Student Disk is in the disk drive, start Access, and then open the Valle Products database located in the TAssign folder on your Student Disk.

2. Use the Form Wizard to create a form based on the Product table. Select all fields for the form, the Columnar layout, the Stone style, and the title name of Product Data.

3. Using the form you created in the previous step, print the fifth form record, change the AutoFormat to Standard, save the changed form, and then print the fifth form record again.

4. Use the Product Data form to update the Product table as follows:
   a. Navigate to the record with the ProductCode 2310. Change the field values for WeightCode to A, Price to 8.99, and Decaf to Null for this record.
   b. Use the Find command to move to the record with the ProductCode 4306, and then delete the record.
   c. Add a new record with the following field values:
      ProductCode: 2306
      CoffeeCode: AMAR
      WeightCode: A
      Price: 8.99
      Decaf: Null
      Print only this form record, and then save and close the form.

5. Use the Form Wizard to create a form containing a main form and a subform. Select the CoffeeName and CoffeeType fields from the Coffee table for the main form, and select all fields except CoffeeCode from the Product table for the subform. Use the Tabular layout and the Standard style. Specify the title Coffee Products for the main form and the title Product Subform for the subform. Print the fourth main form record and its subform records.

6. Use the Report Wizard to create a report based on the primary Coffee table and the related Product table. Select all fields from the Coffee table except Decaf, and select all fields from the Product table except CoffeeCode. In the third Report Wizard dialog box, specify the CoffeeType field as an additional grouping level. Sort the detail records by ProductCode. Choose the Align Left 1 layout and the Casual style for the report. Specify the title Valle Coffee Products for the report.

7. Insert the ValleCup picture, which is located in the TAssign folder on your Student Disk, in the Report Header section of the Valle Coffee Products report. Position the picture so that its left edge aligns with the 4-inch mark on the horizontal ruler and its top edge is just below the top border line of the report.

8. Print only the first page of the report, and then close and save the modified report.

9. Compact the Valle Products database; name the copy of the database Compacted Valle Products. After the compacting process is complete, delete the original Valle Products database, and then rename the Compacted Valle Products file as Valle Products.

Case Problems

1. Ashbrook Mall Information Desk Sam Bullard wants the MallJobs database to include forms and reports that will help him track and distribute information about jobs available at the Ashbrook Mall. You'll create the necessary forms and reports by completing the following:

1. Make sure your Student Disk is in the disk drive, start Access, and then open the MallJobs database located in the Cases folder on your Student Disk.

2. Use the Form Wizard to create a form based on the Store table. Select all fields for the form, the Columnar layout, and the Clouds style. Specify the title Store Data for the form.

3. Change the AutoFormat for the Store Data form to Flax.

4. Use the Find command to move to the record with the Store value of TC, and then change the Contact field value for this record to Sarah Pedicini.

5. Use the Store Data form to add a new record with the following field values:
   Store: PW
   StoreName: Pet World
   Location: B2
   Contact: Killian McElroy
   Extension: 2750
   Print only this form record, and then save and close the form.

6. Use the Form Wizard to create a form containing a main form and a subform. Select all the fields from the Store table for the main form, and select all fields except Store from the Job table for the subform. Use the Tabular layout and the Flax style. Specify the title Jobs By Store for the main form and the title Job Subform for the subform.

7. Display the Jobs By Store form in Design view. To improve the appearance of the form, you need to reduce the width of the subform so that it does not block out the Flax background. Maximize the Form window, if necessary. Click the subform to select it; handles will appear around the subform to indicate it is selected. Position the pointer on the right middle handle until the pointer changes to ↔, click and drag the mouse to the left until the right edge

of the subform aligns with the 4-inch mark on the horizontal ruler, and then release the mouse button. Restore the Form window and then display the form in Form view.

8. Print the eighth main form record and its subform records, and then save and close the Jobs By Store form.

9. Use the Report Wizard to create a report based on the primary Store table and the related Job table. Select all fields from the Store table, and select all fields from the Job table except Store. Sort the detail records by Job. Choose the Block layout and Landscape orientation for the report. Choose the Bold style. Specify the title Available Jobs for the report, and then print and close the report.

10. Compact the MallJobs database; name the copy of the database Compacted MallJobs. After the compacting process is complete, delete the original MallJobs database, and then rename the Compacted MallJobs file as MallJobs.

2. Professional Litigation User Services Raj Jawahir continues his work with the Payments database to track and analyze the payment history of PLUS clients. To help him, you'll enhance the Payments database by completing the following:

1. Make sure your Student Disk is in the disk drive, start Access, and then open the Payments database located in the Cases folder on your Student Disk.

2. Use the Form Wizard to create a form containing a main form and a subform. Select the Firm# and FirmName fields from the Firm table for the main form, and select all fields except Firm# from the Payment table for the subform. Use the Datasheet layout and the Dusk style. Specify the title Firm Payments for the main form and the title Payment Subform for the subform. Resize all columns in the subform to their best fit. Print the first main form record and its displayed subform records.

3. For the form you just created, change the AutoFormat to Colorful 2, save the changed form, and then print the first main form record and its displayed subform records.

4. Navigate to the third record in the subform for the first main record, and then change the AmtPaid field value to 1,500.00.

5. Use the Find command to move to the record with the Firm# 1136, and delete the record. Answer Yes to any warning messages about deleting the record.

 6. Use the appropriate wildcard character to find all records with the abbreviation "DA" (for District Attorney) in the firm name. (*Hint:* You must enter the wildcard character before and after the text you are searching for.) How many records did you find?

 7. Use the Report Wizard to create a report based on the primary Firm table and the related Payment table. Select all fields from the Firm table except Extension, and select all fields from the Payment table except Firm#. In the third Report Wizard dialog box, specify the PLUSAcctRep field as an additional grouping level. Sort the detail records by AmtPaid in *descending* order. Choose the Outline 1 layout and the Formal style for the report. Specify the title Payments By Firms for the report.

8. Insert the Plus picture, which is located in the Cases folder on your Student Disk, in the Report Header section of the Payments By Firms report. Leave the picture in its original position at the left edge of the report header.

 9. Use the Office Assistant to ask the following question: "How do I move an object behind another?" Choose the topic "Move a control in front of or behind other controls." Read the information and then close the Help window. Make sure the Plus picture is still selected, and then move it behind the Payments By Firms title.

10. Use the Office Assistant to ask the following question: "How do I change the background color of an object?" Choose the topic "Change the background color of a control or section." Read the information and then close the Help window and the Office Assistant. Select the Payments By Firms title object, and then change its background color to Transparent. Select each of the two horizontal lines in the Report Header section that cut through the middle of the Plus picture, and then use the Delete key to delete each line.

11. Display the report in Print Preview. Print just the first page of the report, and then close and save the report.

12. Compact the Payments database; name the copy of the database Compacted Payments. After the compacting process is complete, delete the original Payments database, and then rename the Compacted Payments file as Payments.

3. Best Friends Noah and Sheila Warnick want to create forms and reports for the Walks database. You'll help them create these database objects by completing the following:

1. Make sure your Student Disk is in the disk drive, start Access, and then open the Walks database located in the Cases folder on your Student Disk.

2. Use the Form Wizard to create a form based on the Walker table. Select all fields for the form, the Columnar layout, and the Colorful 1 style. Specify the title Walker Data for the form.

3. Use the Walker Data form to update the Walker table as follows:
   a. For the record with the WalkerID 223, change the LastName to Hoban and the Distance to 0.
   b. Add a new record with the following values:
      WalkerID: 225
      LastName: DelFavero
      FirstName: Cindi
      Phone: 711-1275
      Distance: 2.0
      Print just this form record.
   c. Delete the record with the WalkerID field value of 123.

4. Change the AutoFormat of the Walker Data form to Pattern, save the changed form, and then use the form to print the last record in the Walker table. Close the form.

5. Use the Form Wizard to create a form containing a main form and a subform. Select all the fields from the Walker table for the main form, and select the PledgeAmt, PaidAmt, and DatePaid fields from the Pledge table for the subform. Use the Tabular layout and the Standard style. Specify the title Walkers And Pledges for the main form and the title Pledge Subform for the subform. Use the navigation buttons to find the first main form record that contains values in the subform. Print this main form record and its subform records.

6. Use the Report Wizard to create a report based on the primary Walker table and the related Pledge table. Select all fields from the Walker table, and select all fields from the Pledge table except WalkerID. Sort the detail records by PledgeNo. Choose the Align Left 2 layout and Landscape orientation for the report. Choose the Soft Gray style. Specify the title Walk-A-Thon Walkers And Pledges for the report.

7. View both pages of the report in Print Preview. (*Hint:* Use a toolbar button.) Notice that the pledge data for the third record appears at the top of the second page. You need to decrease the size of the bottom margin so that the pledge data will appear with its corresponding walker data. Use the Office Assistant to ask the question, "How do I change the margins in a report?" Choose the topic "Set margins, page orientation, and other page setup options" and then read the displayed Help information. Use the Page Setup command to change the bottom margin of the report to .5".

8. Print the entire report.

9. Compact the Walks database; name the copy of the database "Compacted Walks." After the compacting process is complete, delete the original Walks database, and then rename the Compacted Walks file as Walks.

4. Lopez Lexus Dealerships Maria and Hector Lopez want to create forms and reports that will help them track and analyze data about the cars and different locations for their Lexus dealerships. Help them enhance the Lexus database by completing the following:

1. Make sure your Student Disk is in the disk drive, start Access, and then open the Lexus database located in the Cases folder on your Student Disk.

2. Use the Form Wizard to create a form containing a main form and a subform. Select all the fields from the Locations table for the main form, and select the VehicleID, Model, Class, Year, Cost, and SellingPrice fields from the Cars table for the subform. Use the Datasheet layout and the International style. Specify the title Locations And Cars for the main form and the title Cars Subform for the subform. Resize all columns in the subform to their best fit. Print the first main form record and its displayed subform records.

3. For the form you just created, change the AutoFormat to Standard, save the changed form, and then print the first main form record and its displayed subform records.

4. Navigate to the second record in the subform for the fifth main record, and then change the SellingPrice field value to $42,175.00.

5. Use the Find command to move to the record with the LocationCode P1, and delete the record. Answer Yes to any warning messages about deleting the record.

6. Use the appropriate wildcard character to find all records with a LocationCode value that begins with the letter "A." How many records did you find?

7. Use the Report Wizard to create a report based on the primary Locations table and the related Cars table. Select all fields from the Locations table, and select all fields from the Cars table except Manufacturer and LocationCode. Specify two sort fields for the detail records: first, the VehicleID field in ascending order, then the Cost field in descending order. Choose the Align Left 1 layout and Landscape orientation for the report. Choose the Compact style. Specify the title Dealership Locations And Cars for the report, and then print just the first page of the report.

8. Compact the Lexus database; name the copy of the database Compacted Lexus. After the compacting process is complete, delete the original Lexus database, and then rename the Compacted Lexus file as Lexus.

Answers to Quick Check Questions

SESSION 1.1

1 field

2 common field

3 primary key; foreign key

4 records; fields

5 current record symbol

6 Use the horizontal and vertical scroll bars to view fields or records not currently visible in the datasheet; use the navigation buttons to move vertically through the records.

SESSION 1.2

1 query

2 primary key

3 AutoForm Wizard

4 The form displays each field name on a separate line to the left of its field value, which appears in a box; the widths of the boxes represent the size of the fields.

5 Click the Office Assistant button on any toolbar, type a question in the text box, click the Search button, and then choose a topic from the list displayed.

6 Print Preview

SESSION 2.1

1 Identify all the fields needed to produce the required information; group related fields into tables; determine each table's primary key; include a common field in related tables; avoid data redundancy; and determine the properties of each field.

2 The data type determines what field values you can enter for the field and what other properties the field will have.

3 text fields and number fields

4 Order numbers will not be used for calculations.

5 null

6 the record being edited; the next row available for a new record

SESSION 2.2

1 The field and all its values are removed from the table.

2 In Design view, right-click the row selector for the row above which you want to insert the field, click Insert Rows on the shortcut menu, and then define the new field.

3 yes/no

4 Format property

5 Access allows you to have only one database open at a time.

6 In navigation mode, the entire field value is selected and anything you type replaces the field value; in editing mode, you can insert or delete characters in a field value based on the location of the insertion point.

SESSION 3.1

1 a general query in which you specify the fields and records you want Access to select

2 The field list contains the table name at the top of the list box and the table's fields listed in the order in which they appear in the table; the design grid displays columns that contain specifications about a field you will use in the query.

3 A table datasheet and a query datasheet look the same, appearing in Datasheet view, and can be used to update data in a database. A table datasheet shows the permanent data in a table, whereas a query datasheet is temporary and its contents are based on the criteria you establish in the design grid.

4 primary table; related table

5 referential integrity

6 oldest to most recent date

7 when you have two or more nonadjacent sort keys or when the fields to be used for sorting are in the wrong order

8 filter

SESSION 3.2

1 condition

2 in the same Criteria row; in different Criteria rows

3 expression

4 A calculated field appears in a query datasheet but does not exist in a database, as does a table field.

5 a function that performs an arithmetic operation on selected records in a database

6 Group By

SESSION 4.1

1 The AutoForm Wizard creates a form automatically using all the fields in the selected table or query; the Form Wizard allows you to choose some or all of the fields in the selected table or query, choose fields from other tables and queries, and display fields in any order on the form.

2 An AutoFormat is a predefined style for a form (or report). To change a form's AutoFormat, display the form in Design view, click the AutoFormat button on the Form Design toolbar, click the new AutoFormat in the Form AutoFormats list box, and then click OK.

3 the last record in the table

4 datasheet

5 the question mark (?)

6 as many form records as can fit on a printed page

7 Click the record selector in the top left of the form.

SESSION 4.2

1 The main form displays the data from the primary table and the subform displays the data from the related table.

2 You use the top set of navigation buttons to select and move through records from the related table in the subform and the bottom set to select and move through records from the primary table in the main form.

3 report title

4 Design view

5 Report Header

6 to make the database smaller and make more space available on your disk

Microsoft Access 97

LEVEL II

TUTORIALS

Read This **Before You Begin**

STUDENT DISKS

To complete Access 97 Tutorials 5–7, you need three Student Disks. Your instructor will either provide you with Student Disks or ask you to make your own.

If you are supposed to make your own Student Disks, you will need three blank, formatted, high-density disks. You will need to copy a set of folders from a file server or standalone computer onto your disks. Your instructor will tell you which computer, drive letter, and folders contain the files you need. The following table shows you which folders go on each of your disks, so that you will have enough disk space to complete all the tutorials, Tutorial Assignments, and Case Problems:

Student Disk	Write this on the disk label	Put these folders on the disk
1	Student Disk 1: Access 97 Tutorials 5–7 Tutorials and Tutorial Assignments	Tutorial and TAssign from Disk 1 folder
2	Student Disk 2: Access 97 Case Problems 1 and 2	Cases from Disk 2 folder
3	Student Disk 3: Access 97 Case Problems 3 and 4	Cases from Disk 3 folder

When you begin each tutorial, be sure you are using the correct Student Disk. See the inside front or inside back cover of this book for more information on Student Disk files, or ask your instructor or technical support person for assistance.

USING YOUR OWN COMPUTER

If you are going to work through this book using your own computer, you need:

■ **Computer System** Microsoft Windows 95 or Microsoft Windows NT Workstation 4.0 (or a later version) and Microsoft Access 97 must be installed on your computer. This book assumes a typical installation of Microsoft Access 97.

■ **Student Disks** Ask your instructor or technical support person for details on how to get the Student Disks. You will not be able to complete the tutorials or end-of-tutorial assignments in this book using your own computer until you have Student Disks. The Student Files may also be obtained electronically over the Internet. See the inside front or inside back cover of this book for more details.

TO THE INSTRUCTOR

To complete Access 97 Tutorials 5–7, your students must use a set of files on three Student Disks. These files are included in the Instructor's Resource Kit, and they may also be obtained electronically over the Internet. See the inside front or inside back cover of this book for more details. Follow the instructions in the Readme file to copy the files to your server or standalone computer. You can view the Readme file using WordPad. Once the files are copied, you can make Student Disks for the students yourself, or you can tell students where to find the files so they can make their own Student Disks.

COURSE TECHNOLOGY STUDENT FILES

You are granted a license to copy the Student Files to any computer or computer network used by students who have purchased this book.

Creating More Advanced Queries and Custom Forms

Making the Restaurant Database Easier to Use

OBJECTIVES

In this tutorial you will:

- Create a Lookup Wizard field in a table

- Define multiple selection criteria in a query

- Use the In, Like, and Not operators in a query

- Use both the And and Or logical operators in the same query

- Create a parameter query

- Design and create a custom form

- Select, move, and delete controls

- Add form headers and footers

- Add a graphic image to a form

- Use Control Wizards to create a multi-page form

- Use a filter to select and sort records in a form

CASE

Valle Coffee

Ten years ago Leonard Valle became president of Algoman Imports, a small distributor of inexpensive coffee beans to supermarkets in western Michigan. Since that time, Leonard has transformed the company into a popular distributor of gourmet coffees to restaurants and offices. He took over company ownership, changed the company name to Valle Coffee, and expanded its market area to include Indiana and Ohio.

Leonard has incorporated the use of computers in all aspects of the business, including financial management, inventory, production, and sales. The company has developed the Restaurant database of customer information and uses **Microsoft Access 97** (or simply **Access**) to manage it.

The Restaurant database contains tables, queries, forms, and reports that Barbara Hennessey, office manager, and Kim Carpenter, director of marketing, use to keep track of customer orders and billing and marketing information.

Leonard, Kim, and Barbara are pleased with the information they are able to get from the Restaurant database. They are interested in taking better advantage of the power of Access to make the database easier to use and to create more sophisticated queries and custom forms. For example, Kim wants to obtain lists of customers in certain area codes and Barbara needs a list of unpaid invoices for customers in Indiana or Ohio. Barbara also wants to make a change to the design of the Order table to make it easier to enter the CustomerNum value for an Order record. In this tutorial, you'll make the necessary modifications and customizations to the Restaurant database.

In this session you will change the CustomerNum field in the Order table to a Lookup Wizard field. You will also create a pattern match query, a list-of-values query, and a query selecting non-matching values. Finally, you will construct complex selection criteria using And with Or, and you'll create a parameter query.

Creating a Lookup Wizard Field

The Order table in the Restaurant database contains information about orders placed by Valle Coffee's customers. Barbara wants to make it easier for her staff members to enter data in the table. In particular, it would be easier for them if they did not have to remember the correct customer number of the customer who placed the order. So, Barbara wants to change the CustomerNum field in the Order table to a Lookup Wizard field. A **Lookup Wizard field** allows the user to select a value from a list of possible values. For the CustomerNum field, the user will be able to select from the list of customer names in the Customer table rather than having to remember the correct customer number. The CustomerNum field in the Order table will store the customer number, but the customer name will appear in Datasheet view. This makes it easier for the user and guarantees that the customer number entered is valid.

Barbara asks you to change the CustomerNum field in the Order table to a Lookup Wizard field. You begin by opening the Order table in Design view.

To open the Order table in Design view:

1. Make sure you have created your copy of the Access Student Disk, and then place your Student Disk in the appropriate disk drive.

   TROUBLE? If you don't have a Student Disk, you need to get one before you can proceed. Your instructor will either give you one or ask you to make your own. (See your instructor for information.) In either case, be sure you have made a copy of your Student Disk before you begin; in this way, the original Student Disk files will be available on the copied disk in case you need to start over because of an error or problem.

2. Start Access and open the Restaurant database located in the Tutorial folder on your Student Disk. The Restaurant database is displayed in the Access window.

3. Click the **Tables** tab (if necessary), click **Order**, and then click the **Design** button to display the Order table in Design view. See Figure 5-1.

Figure 5-1 ◀
Order table in
Design view

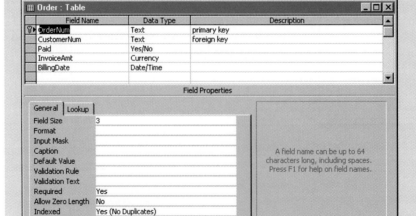

Now you can change the data type of the CustomerNum field to Lookup Wizard.

To change the CustomerNum field to a Lookup Wizard field:

1. Click the **Data Type** text box for the CustomerNum field, click the **Data Type** list arrow, and then click **Lookup Wizard**. Access displays the first Lookup Wizard dialog box. See Figure 5-2.

Figure 5-2 ◀
First Lookup Wizard dialog box

make sure this option is selected

This dialog box allows you to specify a list of values that are allowed for the CustomerNum value in a record in the Order table. You can specify a table or query from which the value is selected or you can enter a new list of values. You want the CustomerNum value to come from the Customer table.

2. Make sure the option for looking up the values in a table or query is selected, and then click the **Next** button to display the next Lookup Wizard dialog box.

3. Make sure **Customer** is selected, and then click the **Next** button. See Figure 5-3.

Figure 5-3 ◀
Selecting the Customer table fields

select these two fields

click to select highlighted field

This dialog box allows you to select the necessary fields from the Customer table. You need to select the CustomerNum field because it is the common field that links the Customer and Order tables. You also must select the CustomerName field because Barbara wants the user to be able to select from a list of customer names when entering a new order record.

4. Click the [>] button to select the CustomerNum field from the Customer table to be included in the lookup column. Click the [>] button to select the CustomerName field, and then click the **Next** button. See Figure 5-4.

Figure 5-4 ◄
Adjusting the
width of the
lookup column

In this dialog box you can adjust the width of the CustomerName column. This column will appear when a user enters a CustomerNum for the order in the Order table. The user can select a CustomerName and Access will enter the correct CustomerNum. The selected "Hide key column" option means that the list of CustomerNum values will not appear in the datasheet.

5. Place the pointer on the right edge of the CustomerName field column heading. When the pointer changes to ↔, double-click to resize the column to fit the data, and then click the **Next** button.

In this dialog box you can specify the caption that will appear for the field in Datasheet view. The default value is the field name, CustomerNum. Because the field will show customer names in Datasheet view, you will change the caption to CustomerName.

6. Type **CustomerName** in the text box, and then click the **Finish** button.

To create the Lookup Wizard field, Access must save the table design and create the necessary relationship so that Access can enter the correct CustomerNum value when the user selects a customer name. Access displays a dialog box asking you to confirm saving the table.

7. Click the **Yes** button. Access creates the Lookup Wizard field and returns to the Order table in Design view. See Figure 5-5.

Figure 5-5 ◄
Lookup Wizard
field defined

new caption ————

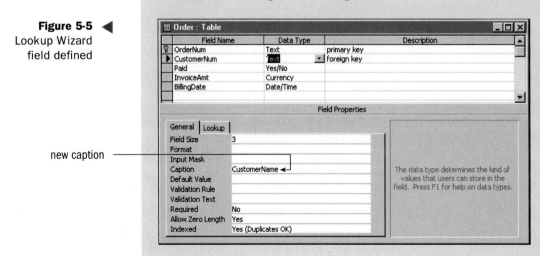

> The Data Type value for the CustomerNum field still says Text, because this field contains text data. However, Access will now use the CustomerNum field value to look up and display customer names from the Customer table.
>
> **8.** Click the **Save** button 🖫 on the Table Design toolbar to save the changes to the table design.

Barbara asks you to enter a new record in the Order table (Figure 5-6). To do so you need to switch to Datasheet view.

Figure 5-6 ◀
The new Order
table record

OrderNum	CustomerName	Paid	InvoiceAmt	BillingDate
401	Roadhouse Restaurant	No	1,100.00	3/15/99

To enter the new order record:

1. Click the **View** button for Datasheet view 🖩 on the Table Design toolbar to display the Order table in Datasheet view. Notice that the customer names instead of the customer numbers now appear in the second column, as specified by the Lookup Wizard field.

You need to widen the CustomerName column to display the complete field values.

2. Place the pointer on the right edge of the CustomerName column heading. When the pointer changes to ➕, double-click to resize the column to fit the data.

3. Click the **New Record** button ▶* on the Table Datasheet toolbar. Access displays a new blank record (number 105).

4. In the OrderNum field, type **401** and then press the **Tab** key to move to the CustomerNum field, which has the caption CustomerName. Access displays a list arrow at the right of the CustomerNum field text box.

5. Click the list arrow. Access displays the list of CustomerName field values from the Customer table. See Figure 5-7.

Figure 5-7 ◀
List of
CustomerName
field values

Lookup Wizard
list box

OrderNum	CustomerName	Paid	InvoiceAmt	Bill
384	Sandy Lookout Restaurant	☑	1,178.00	
385	Florentine Restaurante	☑	1,840.00	
386	Four Star Steakhouse	☑	1,407.00	
387	Brandywine Restaurant	☐	2,568.00	
388	Bay Pointe Restaurant	☑	1,088.00	
389	Best Bet Restaurant	☑	1,724.00	
390		☑	903.00	
391	Meadows Restaurant	☐	868.00	
393	Cottage Grill	☐	1,227.00	
394	Roadhouse Restaurant	☐	1,195.00	
395	Bridge Inn	☑	1,348.00	
398	Grand River Restaurant	☑	1,426.50	
399	Sandy Lookout Restaurant	☑	1,246.00	
400	Bunker Hill Grill	☐	1,350.00	
401	Florentine Restaurante	☐	0.00	

Record: 105 of 105

6. Click **Roadhouse Restaurant** to select this field value. Access closes the list box and displays Roadhouse Restaurant in the CustomerNum field text box. Access also stores the value 122, the CustomerNum for Roadhouse Restaurant, in the CustomerNum field for this order.

7. Refer to Figure 5-6 and enter the remaining field values for the new order record.

8. Click the **Close** button ☒ on the Table window title bar to close the Order table.

9. Click the **Yes** button when Access asks if you want to save changes.

You are now ready to create the queries that Barbara and Kim have requested. You are already familiar with queries that use an exact match or a range of values (using the > comparison operator) to select records. Access provides many other operators for creating select queries. These operators allow you to create more complicated queries that are difficult or impossible to create with exact match or range of values selection criteria.

Barbara and Kim have created a list of questions they want to answer using the Restaurant database:

- What customers are located in the 313 area code?

- What is the customer information for customers 123, 135, and 202?

- What is the customer information for all customers *except* customers 123, 135, and 202?

- What are the customer numbers, customer names, order numbers, and invoice amounts for unpaid invoices for customers in Indiana or Ohio?

- What are the customer names, amounts overdue, and potential late charges for customers with overdue January invoices in a particular state? For this query, the user specifies the state.

You will create the necessary queries to answer these questions. To do so you'll use the Query window in Design view.

Using a Pattern Match in a Query

Kim wants to view the records for all customers in the 313 area code. She will be travelling in that area next week and wants to contact those customers. To answer Kim's question, you can create a query that uses a pattern match. A **pattern match** selects records that have a value for the selected field matching the pattern of the simple condition value, in this case, to select customers with 313 area codes. You do this using the Like comparison operator.

The **Like comparison operator** selects records by matching field values to a specific pattern that includes one or more wildcard characters—asterisk (*), question mark (?), and number symbol (#). The asterisk represents any string of characters, the question mark represents any single character, and the number symbol represents any single digit. Using a pattern match is similar to using an exact match, except that a pattern match includes wildcard characters.

To create the query, you must first place the Customer table field list in the Query window in Design view.

To create the pattern match query in Design view:

1. Click the **Queries** tab in the Database window, and then click the **New** button. The New Query dialog box opens.

2. Click **Design View** in the list box (if necessary), and then click the **OK** button. Access opens the Show Table dialog box on top of the Query window.

3. Click **Customer** in the Tables list box, click the **Add** button, and then click the **Close** button. Access places the Customer table field list in the Query window.

Access

4. Double-click the title bar of the Customer field list to highlight all the fields, click and drag one of the highlighted fields to the design grid, and then release the mouse button. Access places each field in a separate column in the design grid, in the same order that the fields appear in the table. See Figure 5-8.

Figure 5-8 ◀
Adding the
fields for the
query

all Customer table
fields in the design
grid

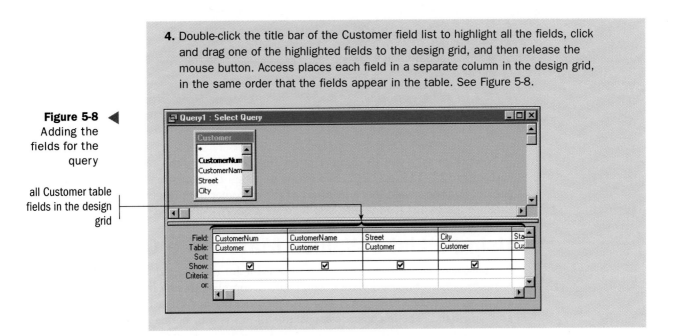

You will now enter the pattern match condition Like "(313)*" for the Phone field. Access will select records that have a Phone field value containing (313) in positions one through five. The asterisk (*) wildcard character specifies that any characters can appear in the remaining positions of the field value.

To select records that match the specified pattern:

1. Scroll the design grid until the Phone field is visible.

2. Click the **Phone Criteria** text box, and then type **Like "(313)*"**. See Figure 5-9. (Note that if you omit the operator Like, Access will automatically add it when you run the query.)

Figure 5-9 ◀
Record
selection based
on matching a
specific pattern

pattern match
selection criterion

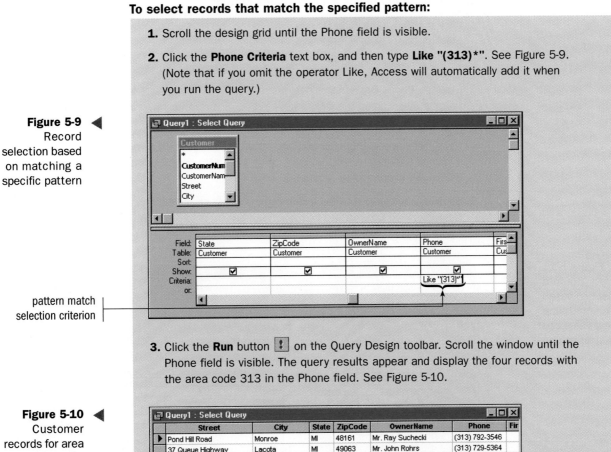

3. Click the **Run** button 🔱 on the Query Design toolbar. Scroll the window until the Phone field is visible. The query results appear and display the four records with the area code 313 in the Phone field. See Figure 5-10.

Figure 5-10 ◀
Customer
records for area
code 313

Street	City	State	ZipCode	OwnerName	Phone	Fir
Pond Hill Road	Monroe	MI	48161	Mr. Ray Suchecki	(313) 792-3546	
37 Queue Highway	Lacota	MI	49063	Mr. John Rohrs	(313) 729-5364	
2890 Canyonside Way	Romulus	MI	48174	Ms. Nancy Mills	(313) 888-7778	
3509 Garfield Avenue	Romulus	MI	48174	Mr. Shannon Petree	(313) 461-8899	

Now you can save the query.

4. Click the **Save** button 🖫 on the Query Datasheet toolbar. The Save As dialog box opens.

5. Type **313 Area Code** in the Query Name text box, and then press the **Enter** key. Access saves the query in the Restaurant database on your Student Disk.

Next, Kim asks you to create a query that will display the customer information for customers 123, 135, and 202. She wants to assign these customers to a particular salesperson, and she would like a printout of the customer data to give to the salesperson. To produce the results Kim wants, you'll create a query using a list-of-values match.

Using a List-of-Values Match in a Query

A **list-of-values match** selects records whose value for the selected field matches one of two or more simple condition values. You could accomplish this by including several Or conditions in the design grid, but Access also provides the In comparison operator that works as a shorthand. The **In comparison operator** allows you to define a condition with two or more values. If a record's field value matches at least one value from the list of values, Access selects that record for inclusion in the query results.

To display the information Kim requested, you want records selected if the CustomerNum field value is equal to 123, 135, or 202. These are the values you will use with the In comparison operator.

To create the query using a list-of-values match:

1. Click the **View** button for Design view 🔍 on the Query Datasheet toolbar to display the Query window in Design view.

   First you need to delete the condition for the previous query you created.

2. Click the **Phone Criteria** text box, press the **F2** key to highlight the entire condition, and then press the **Delete** key to remove the condition.

   Now you can enter the criteria for the new query using the In comparison operator. When you use this operator, the list of values you want to match must be enclosed within parentheses. Each value must also be surrounded by quotation marks and separated by a comma.

3. Scroll the design grid to the left to display the CustomerNum column, click the **CustomerNum Criteria** text box, and then type **In ("123","135","202")**. See Figure 5-11.

Figure 5-11 ◄
Record
selection based
on matching
field values to
a list of values

list-of-values selection
criterion

4. Click the **Run** button [!] on the Query Design toolbar. Access runs the query and displays the results, which show the three records with 123, 135, or 202 in the CustomerNum field.

Now you can print the query results for Kim. Also, because Kim won't need to display this information again, you don't have to save this query.

5. Click the **Print** button [printer icon] on the Query Datasheet toolbar. Access prints the query results.

Kim wants to assign the remaining customers to other salespersons in her group. She needs a list of all the customers except customers 123, 135, and 202 to help her plan the assignments. You can create this query by modifying the previous one to include a non-matching value.

Using a Non-Matching Value in a Query

A **non-matching value** selects records whose value for the selected field does not match the simple condition value. You create the selection criterion using the Not logical operator. The **Not logical operator** negates a criterion. For example, if you enter Not = "MI" in the Criteria text box for the State field in the Customer table, the query results will show the records for which the State field value is not MI; that is, all customers not located in Michigan.

To create Kim's query, you will combine the Not operator with the In operator to select customer records whose CustomerNum field value is not in the list ("123","135","202").

To create the query using a non-matching value:

1. Click the **View** button for Design view [icon] on the Query Datasheet toolbar to switch back to Design view.

2. If necessary, position the insertion point immediately to the left of the word "In" in the Criteria text box for the CustomerNum field.

3. Type **Not** and then press the **spacebar**. Access will select a record only if the CustomerNum field value is not in the list ("123","135","202"). See Figure 5-12.

Figure 5-12 ◄
Record selection based on not matching a list of values

negation operator with list-of-values selection criterion

4. Click the **Run** button [!] on the Query Design toolbar. Access runs the query and displays only those records with a CustomerNum field value that is not 123, 135, or 202. A total of 35 records are included in the query results. See Figure 5-13.

Figure 5-13
Results of query using non-matching values

customers 123, 135, and 202 not selected

	CustomerNum	CustomerName	Street	City	State	Zi
▶	04	Meadows Restaurant	Pond Hill Road	Monroe	MI	48
	107	Cottage Grill	82 Mix	Bootjack	MI	49
	122	Roadhouse Restaurant	8408 E. Fletcher Road	Clare	MI	48
	128	Grand River Restaurant	37 Queue Highway	Lacota	MI	49
	129	Sandy Lookout Restaurant	95 North Bay Boulevard	Jenison	MI	49
	131	Bunker Hill Grill	15365 Old Bedford Trail	Eagle Point	MI	49
	133	Florentine Restaurante	2874 Western Avenue	Drenthe	MI	49
	136	Cleo's Downtown Restaurant	4090 Division Street NW	Borculo	MI	49
	163	Bentham's Riverfront Restaurant	1366 36th Street	Roscommon	MI	48
	165	Sullivan's Restaurant & Lounge	1935 Snow Street SE	Saugatuck	MI	49
	201	Wagon Train Restaurant	5480 Alpine Lane	Selkirk	MI	48
	203	Mountain Lake Restaurant	701 Bagley Street	Grand Rapids	MI	49
	322	Alto Country Inn	114 Lexington Parkway	Alto	MI	49
	325	Best Bet Restaurant	56 Four Mile Road	Grand Rapids	MI	49
	407	Jean's Country Restaurant	44 Tower Lane	Mattawan	MI	49

313 Area Code : Select Query

Record: 1 of 35

5. Click the **Print** button [printer icon] on the Query Datasheet toolbar to print the query results.

Now you can close the query without saving it, because Kim will not need to run this query again.

6. Click the **Close** button [X] on the Query window to close it, and then click the **No** button when Access asks if you want to save the query.

You are now ready to create the query to answer Barbara's question about unpaid invoices in Indiana or Ohio.

Using Both the And and Or Operators in the Same Query

Barbara wants to see the customer numbers, customer names, order numbers, and invoice amounts for unpaid invoices for customers in Indiana or Ohio. To create this query, you need to use both the And and Or logical operators to create two compound conditions. That is, you will create conditions that select records for customers located in Indiana *and* who have unpaid invoices *or* customers located in Ohio *and* who have unpaid invoices. Because you want the customer names shown with the invoice information in the query results, you will use fields from both the Customer and Order tables.

To add the fields to the query design:

1. From the Queries tab of the Database window, click the **New** button. Access opens the New Query dialog box.

2. Click **Design View** (if necessary), and then click the **OK** button. The Show Table dialog box opens on top of the Query window in Design view.

3. Double-click **Customer** to add the Customer table to the Query window.

4. Double-click **Order** to add the Order table to the Query window, and then click the **Close** button to close the Show Table dialog box.

5. Double-click **CustomerNum**, double-click **CustomerName**, and then double-click **State** in the Customer field list to add these fields to the design grid.

6. Double-click **OrderNum**, double-click **Paid**, and then double-click **InvoiceAmt** in the Order field list to add these fields to the design grid.

You've selected all the fields to include in the query. Now you're ready to add the selection criteria, which will include both the And and Or logical operators.

To specify the criteria using the And logical operator with the Or logical operator:

1. Click the **State Criteria** text box, and then type **="IN"**.

   Kim wants to view data for customers in Indiana or Ohio, so you need to enter the Or condition for the State field.

2. Press the ↓ key and then type **="OH"**.

   Now, for each of the existing conditions, you need to enter the And condition that selects only those records for customers who have not paid their invoices.

3. Scroll right to display the Paid field, click the **Paid Criteria** text box, and then type **=No**.

4. Press the ↓ key and then type **=No**.

   When you save this query, you'll specify a name that indicates the data is for unpaid invoices. Therefore, you don't have to display the Paid field values in the query results.

5. Click the **Show** check box for the Paid field to remove the check mark. The query definition is now complete. See Figure 5-14.

Figure 5-14 ◄
And and Or
conditions in
the design grid

one-to-many
relationship

first And condition

or row for Or
condition

second And
condition

6. Click the **Run** button on the Query Design toolbar. Access runs the query and displays the results. See Figure 5-15.

Figure 5-15 ◄
Results of
query using
And with Or

Indiana customers
selected

Ohio customer
selected

The query results show the records for customers in Indiana or Ohio that have unpaid invoices. Because you unchecked the Show box for the Paid field, it does not appear in the query results. Next, you'll save the query with a name indicating that the query selects unpaid invoices.

7. Click the **Save** button on the Query Datasheet toolbar, type **IN and OH Unpaid Invoices** in the Query Name text box, and then press the **Enter** key to save the query.

8. Click the **Close** button ☒ on the Query window.

Creating a Parameter Query

Barbara's final query asks for the customer name, amount overdue, and late charge for customers with overdue January invoices in a particular state. For this query, she wants to be able to specify the state, such as MI (Michigan), IN (Indiana), or OH (Ohio).

To create this query, you will modify the existing Unpaid With Late Charge query. You could create a simple condition using an exact match for the State field, which you would need to change in Design view every time you run the query. Instead, you will create a parameter query. A **parameter query** is a query that prompts you for information when the query runs. In this case, you want to create a query that prompts you for the state of the customers to select from the table. You enter the prompt in the Criteria text box for the State field.

When Access runs the query, it will display a dialog box and prompt you to enter the state. Access then creates the query results just as if you had changed the criteria in Design view.

REFERENCE window	CREATING A PARAMETER QUERY
	■ Create a select query that includes all the fields that will appear in the query results. Also choose the sort keys and set the criteria that do not change when you run the query.
	■ Decide on the fields that will have prompts when you run the query. In the Criteria text box for each of these fields, type the prompt you want to appear in a message box when you run the query, and enclose the prompt in brackets.

Now you can open the Unpaid With Late Charge query in Design view and change its design to create the parameter query.

To create the parameter query based on an existing query:

1. From the Queries tab of the Database window, click **Unpaid With Late Charge**, and then click the **Design** button to display the query in Design view.

   Now you need to add the State field to the query design and enter a prompt in the Criteria box for the State field.

2. Scroll the design grid to the right to display the first blank column.

3. Double-click **State** in the Customer field list to add this field in the next available column in the design grid.

   Next you must enter the criteria for the parameter query. In this case, Kim wants the query to prompt users to enter the state for the customer information they want to view. So, you need to enter the prompt in the Criteria text box for the State field. The text of the prompt must be enclosed within brackets.

Access

4. Scroll right to display the State field, click the **State Criteria** text box, and then type **[Enter the state:]**. See Figure 5-16.

Figure 5-16 ◀
Specifying the prompt for the parameter query

specifies unpaid invoices

prompt

5. Click the **Run** button ⬆ on the Query Design toolbar. Access runs the query and displays a dialog box prompting you for the name of the state. See Figure 5-17.

Figure 5-17 ◀
Enter Parameter Value dialog box

enter value here

The text you specified in the Criteria text box of the State field appears above a text box, in which you must type a State field value. You must enter the value exactly as it appears in the table.

6. To see the January unpaid invoices for customers in Indiana, type **IN**, and then click the **OK** button. Access displays the data for the customers in Indiana who have unpaid January invoices (in this case, only two customers). See Figure 5-18.

Figure 5-18 ◀
Results of the parameter query

OrderNum	BillingDate	CustomerName	InvoiceAmt	LateCharge	State
221	1/15/99	Maxwell's Restaurant	1,607.00	32.14	IN
235	1/15/99	Embers Restaurant	1,004.50	20.09	IN

Indiana customers selected

Barbara plans on running this query frequently to monitor the payment activity of the restaurant customers, so she asks you to save it with a new name (to keep the original query intact).

7. Click **File** on the menu bar, and then click **Save As/Export**. The Save As dialog box opens.

8. Position the insertion point immediately to the right of the "e" in Charge, press the **spacebar**, type **Parameter**, and then press the **Enter** key.

9. Click the **Close** button ☒ on the Query window.

Quick Check

1. What is a Lookup Wizard field?

2. What comparison operator is used to select records based on a specific pattern?

3. What is the purpose of the asterisk (*) in a pattern match query?

4. When do you use the In comparison operator?

5. How do you negate a selection criterion?

6. When do you use a parameter query?

The Lookup Wizard field you specified and the queries you created will make the Restaurant database easier to use. In the next session, you will create a custom form for the database, which will help Valle Coffee's employees enter and maintain data more easily.

SESSION 5.2

In this session, you will create a custom form for customer information. You will work in Design view to add form controls, create a form header with a title and a graphic image, and add color to the background of the form.

Creating a Custom Form

Barbara has been using the Customer Orders form to enter and view information about Valle Coffee's customers and their orders. She likes having all the information on a single form, but she would like to have the fields rearranged and a graphic image added to the form. To make the form easier to read, she wants to have the customer and order information on separate pages, like the tabs in a dialog box. She asks you to create a new form to display the information in this way. Because this form is significantly different from the Customer Orders form, you will create a new custom form.

To create a custom form, you can modify an existing form or design and create a form from scratch. In either case, you create a custom form working in the Form window in Design view. A custom form can be designed to match a paper form, to display some fields side by side and others top to bottom, to highlight certain sections with color, or to add special buttons and list boxes. A multi-page form displays the form on more than one page on a single screen. Each page is labeled with a tab like the tabs in the Database window. By clicking a tab, you can display the information on that page.

Designing a Custom Form

Whether the custom form you want to create is a simple or complex form, it is always best to plan the form's content and appearance first. Figure 5-19 shows Barbara's design for the custom form that she wants you to create.

Figure 5-19
Barbara's design for the multi-page custom form

title label

picture created by drawing application software

first page of form

second page of form

Notice that the top of the form displays a title and graphic image. Below these are the CustomerNum and CustomerName fields. Also, notice that Barbara's form contains two pages. The first page, labeled "Customer Information," displays the address and contact information for the customer. The second page, labeled "Orders," displays order information for the customer. Each field value from the Customer table will appear in a text box and will be preceded by a label. The label will be the value of the field's Caption property (if any) or the field name. The locations and lengths of each field value are indicated by a series of Xs in Barbara's form design. For example, the three Xs that follow the CustomerNum field label indicate that the field value will be three characters long. The Order table fields appear in a subform on the second page.

With the design for the custom form in place, you are ready to create it. You could use an AutoForm Wizard or the Form Wizard to create a basic form and then customize it in Design view. However, you would need to make many modifications to a basic form to create the form Barbara wants, so you will design the entire form directly in Design view.

The Form Window in Design View

You use the Form window in Design view to create and modify forms. To create Barbara's custom form, you'll create a blank form based on the Customer table and then add the Order table fields in a subform.

REFERENCE
window

CREATING A FORM IN DESIGN VIEW

- In the Database window, click the Forms tab to display the Forms list.
- Click the New button to display the New Form dialog box, and then click Design View.
- Select the table or query on which the form will be based, and then click the OK button.
- Place the necessary controls in the Form window in Design view. Modify the size, position, and other properties of the controls as necessary.
- Click the Save button on the Form Design toolbar, and then enter a name for the form.

To create a blank form in Design view:

1. If you took a break after the previous session, make sure that Access is running and the Restaurant database from the Tutorial folder on your Student Disk is open.

2. Click the **Forms** tab to display the Forms list in the Database window, and then click the **New** button. The New Form dialog box opens.

3. Click **Design View** (if necessary), click the list arrow for choosing a table or query, click **Customer**, and then click the **OK** button. Access displays the Form window in Design view.

Access

4. Click the **Maximize** button 🗖 on the Form window to maximize the window. See Figure 5-20.

Figure 5-20 ◄
Form window in Design view

View button

rulers

Detail section

grid

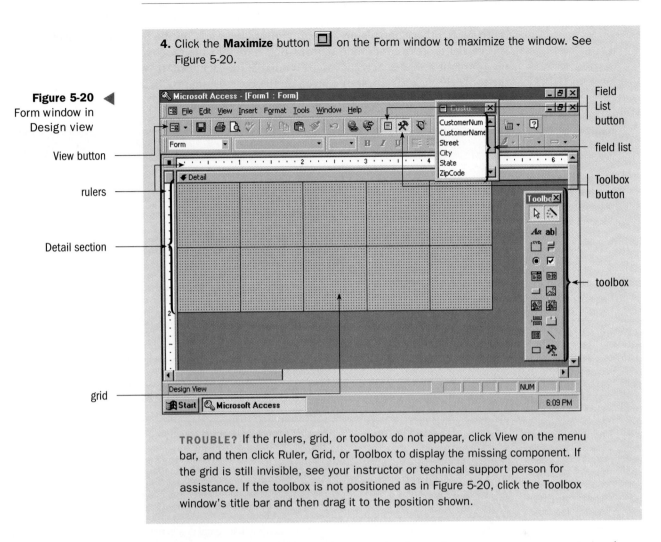

Field List button

field list

Toolbox button

toolbox

TROUBLE? If the rulers, grid, or toolbox do not appear, click View on the menu bar, and then click Ruler, Grid, or Toolbox to display the missing component. If the grid is still invisible, see your instructor or technical support person for assistance. If the toolbox is not positioned as in Figure 5-20, click the Toolbox window's title bar and then drag it to the position shown.

The Form window in Design view contains the tools necessary to create a custom form. You create the form by placing objects on the blank form in the window. Each object—such as a text box, list box, rectangle, or command button—that you place on a form is called a **control**. There are three kinds of controls that you can place on a form:

■ A **bound control** is linked, or bound, to a field in the underlying table or query. You use a bound control to display table field values.

■ An **unbound control** is not linked to a field in the underlying table or query. You use an unbound control to display text, such as a form title or instructions, or to display graphics and pictures from other software programs. An unbound control that displays text is called a **label**.

■ A **calculated control** displays a value calculated from data from one or more fields.

To create a bound control, you use the Field List button on the Form Design toolbar to display a list of fields available from the underlying table or query. Then you drag fields from the field list box to the Form window and place the bound controls where you want them to appear on the form.

To place other controls on a form, you use the tools on the toolbox. The **toolbox** is a specialized toolbar containing buttons that represent the tools you use to place controls on a form or a report. ScreenTips are available for each tool. If you want to show or hide the toolbox, click the Toolbox button on the Form Design toolbar. The tools available on the toolbox are described in Figure 5-21.

Figure 5-21 ◄
Summary of tools available in the toolbox for a form or report

Button	Tool Name	Purpose on a Form or a Report	Control Wizard Available
	Select Objects	Select, move, size, and edit controls	No
	Control Wizards	Activate Control Wizards for certain other toolbox tools	No
	Label	Display text, such as title or instructions; an unbound control	No
	Text Box	Display a label attached to a text box that contains a bound control or a calculated control	No
	Option Group	Display a group frame containing toggle buttons, option buttons, or check boxes	Yes
	Toggle Button	Display a toggle button control bound to a Yes/No field	Yes
	Option Button	Display an option button control bound to a Yes/No field	Yes
	Check Box	Display a check box control bound to a Yes/No field	Yes
	Combo Box	Display a control that combines the features of a list box and a text box; you can type in the text box or select an entry in the list box to add a value to an underlying field	Yes
	List Box	Display a control that contains a scrollable list of values	Yes
	Command Button	Display a control button you can use to link to an action, such as finding a record, printing a record, or applying a form filter	Yes
	Image	Display a graphic image	Yes
	Unbound Object Frame	Display a frame for enclosing an unbound OLE object, such as a Microsoft Excel spreadsheet	Yes
	Bound Object Frame	Display a frame for enclosing an bound OLE object stored in an Access database table	Yes
	Page Break	Begin a new screen on a form or a new page on a report	No
	Tab Control	Display a tab control with multiple pages	No
	Subform/ Subreport	Display data from more than one table	Yes
	Line	Display a line	No
	Rectangle	Display a rectangle	No
	More Controls	Display a list of all available controls	No

The Form window in Design view also contains a Detail section, which appears as a light gray rectangle, in which you place the fields, labels, and values for your form. You can change the size of the Detail section size by dragging its edges. The grid consists of the dots that appear in the Detail section to help you position controls precisely on a form.

The rulers at the top and at the left edge of the Detail section define the horizontal and vertical dimensions of the form and serve as a guide to the placement of controls on the form.

Your first task is to add bound controls to the Detail section for the CustomerNum and CustomerName fields from the Customer table.

Adding Fields to a Form

When you add a bound control to a form, Access adds a field-value text box and, to its left, a label. The text box displays the field values from the table or query, and the label identifies the values. To create a bound control, you display the field list by clicking the Field List button. Then you select one or more fields from the field list box and drag them to the form. You select a single field by clicking the field. You select two or more fields by holding down the Ctrl key and clicking each field; and you select all fields by double-clicking the field list title bar.

You will add bound controls to the Detail section for two of the fields in the field list. Because you will not need the toolbox for a while, you can close it.

To add bound controls for the CustomerNum and CustomerName fields:

1. Click the **Close** button ☒ on the toolbox to close it.

2. If necessary, click the **Field List** button ▣ on the Form Design toolbar to display the field list.

3. Click **CustomerNum** in the field list, press and hold the **Ctrl** key, and then click **CustomerName** in the field list. Both fields are selected.

4. Click the highlighted fields and then drag them to the form's Detail section. Release the mouse button when the pointer ▱ is positioned at the 1-inch mark on the horizontal ruler and just below the top of the Detail section. Access adds two bound controls—one for the CustomerNum field and one for the CustomerName field—in the Detail section of the form. See Figure 5-22.

Figure 5-22 ◀
Adding text boxes and attached labels as bound controls to the form

two attached labels ———

position the pointer here

field list

two text boxes are bound controls linked to the table field values

> **TROUBLE?** Your controls do not have to be in the exact same position as the controls in Figure 5-22. However, they should be in approximately the same position. If you did not position the bound controls properly in the Detail section, click the Undo button 🔄 on the Form Design toolbar to delete the text boxes and labels from the Detail section. Then repeat Steps 3 and 4 to add the bound controls.
>
> 4. Click the **Close** button ✕ on the field list to close it.

Working on a form in Design view might seem awkward at first. With practice you will become comfortable with creating a custom form. Remember that you can always click the Undo button immediately after you make an error or undesired form adjustment.

Comparing the form's Detail section with Barbara's design, notice that you need to arrange the text boxes so that they appear next to each other. To do so you must select and move the controls.

Selecting and Moving Controls

Two text boxes now appear in the form's Detail section, one below the other. Each text box is a bound control linked to a field in the underlying table and has a label box attached to its left. This means that if you move the text box, the label will move with it. Each text box and each label is an object on the form and appears with square boxes on the corners and edges. These boxes are called **handles**. Handles appear around an object when it is selected and they allow you to move or resize the control.

REFERENCE window	**SELECTING AND MOVING CONTROLS**
	▪ Click the control to select it. To select several controls at once, press and hold the Shift key while clicking each control. Handles appear around all selected controls.
	▪ To move a single selected control, click the control's move handle and drag it to its new position.
	▪ To move a group of selected controls, click any selected control (but do not click its move handle) and then drag the group of selected controls to its new position.

To move a single bound control, you must first select just that control. All the controls on your form are currently selected and will move together if you move any one of them. You first need to deselect all of the bound controls and then select the CustomerName control to move it to the right of the CustomerNum control. The CustomerName control consists of the CustomerName field-value text box and the corresponding label to its left.

Access

To select the CustomerName bound control:

1. Click the gray area outside the Detail section to deselect the selected controls.

2. Click the **CustomerName field-value text box** to select it. Move handles, which are the larger handles, appear on the upper-left corner of the field-value text box and its attached label box. Sizing handles appear but only on the field-value text box. See Figure 5-23.

Figure 5-23 ◀
Selecting a
single bound
control

label boxes

move handles

sizing handles

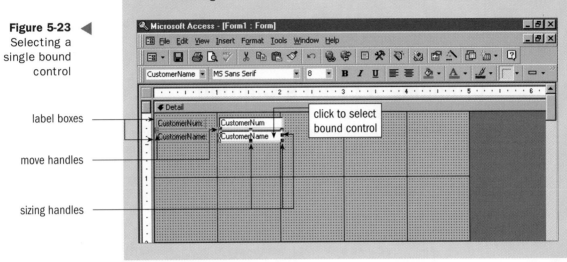

You can move a field-value text box and its attached label box together. To move them, place the pointer anywhere on the border of the field-value text box, but not on a move handle or a sizing handle. When the pointer changes to ✋, you can drag the field-value text box and its attached label box to the new location. As you move the boxes, their outline moves to show you the changing position.

You can also move either the field-value text box or its label box individually. If you want to move the field-value text box but not its label box, for example, place the pointer on the text box's move handle. When the pointer changes to ☝, drag the field-value text box to the new location. You use the label box's move handle in a similar way to move just the label box.

To arrange the text boxes to match Barbara's design, you must move the CustomerName control up and to the right.

To move the CustomerName control:

1. Place the pointer on the CustomerName control, but not on a move handle or a sizing handle. When the pointer changes to ✋, click and drag the control up and to the right. An outline of the control appears as you change its position to guide you in the move operation. Use the grid dots in the Detail section to help you position the control as shown in Figure 5-24.

Figure 5-24 ◀
Moving the
CustomerName
control

> **TROUBLE?** Your control does not have to be in the exact same position as the control in Figure 5-24. However, it should be in approximately the same position, and it should be aligned with the CustomerNum control. If you did not place the control correctly, click the Undo button on the Form Design toolbar, and then repeat Step 1.

According to Barbara's design, the labels for the two controls should be "Customer No.:" and "Customer Name:" (respectively). To modify the text of the labels, you need to change each label's caption.

Changing a Label's Caption

The text in a label is defined by the field name or by the field's Caption property. By default, a label displays the field name as it exists in the underlying table or query. If you want the label to display different text, you need to change the label's Caption property value.

REFERENCE window

CHANGING A LABEL'S CAPTION

- Click the label to select it.
- Click the right mouse button to display the shortcut menu, and then click Properties to display the property sheet.
- If necessary, click the Format tab to display the Format page of the property sheet.
- Edit the existing label in the Caption text box, or double-click the Caption text box to select the current value, and then type a new caption.
- Click the property sheet Close button to close it.

You need to change the Caption property of the two labels on your form to "Customer No.:" and "Customer Name:" (respectively).

To change the Caption property value for the two labels:

1. Click the **CustomerNum label box** to select it.

2. Click the right mouse button to display the shortcut menu, and then click **Properties**. The property sheet for the CustomerNum label opens.

3. If necessary, click the property sheet title bar and drag the property sheet down until the CustomerNum and CustomerName label boxes are visible.

4. If necessary, click the **Format** tab to display the Format page of the property sheet.

5. Position the insertion point between the "r" and the "N" in CustomerNum, and then press the **spacebar**.

6. Position the insertion point between the "m" in Num and the colon following it, press the **Backspace** key twice, and then type **o.** (including the period). The value should now be Customer No.:. See Figure 5-25.

Figure 5-25 ◀
Changing the
Caption
property for
the label

property sheet

Caption value

TROUBLE? Some of the property values on your screen might be different from those shown in Figure 5-25, such as the Left and Top margin values, if your controls are in slightly different positions from those in the figure.

7. Click the **CustomerName label box** to select it. The property sheet now displays the properties for the CustomerName label, and the CustomerNum label in the Detail section now displays Customer No.:.

8. Position the insertion point between the "r" and "N" in CustomerName, and then press the **spacebar**. The label should now be Customer Name:.

9. Click the **Close** button [X] on the property sheet to close it.

When you create a form, you should periodically check your progress by displaying the form in Form view. You might see adjustments you want to make on your form in Design view. Next, you'll save the current form design and then view the form in Form view.

To save the form and switch to Form view:

1. Click the **Save** button [🖫] on the Form Design toolbar. The Save As dialog box opens.

2. Type **Customer Information Multi-page**, and then press the **Enter** key. Access saves the form design.

3. Click the **View** button for Form view [▦] on the Form Design toolbar. Access closes the Form window in Design view and displays the form in Form view. See Figure 5-26.

Figure 5-26 ◀
Form window in
Form view

record displayed in
custom form

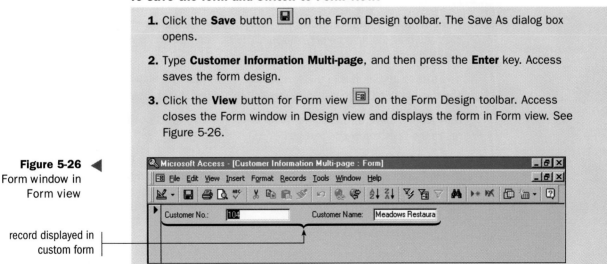

Access displays the CustomerNum and CustomerName field values for the first record in the Customer table (Meadows Restaurant). You can use the navigation buttons to view other records from the table in the form.

The form displayed in Form view reveals some adjustments you need to make to the form design. The CustomerNum field-value text box is too large for the field value, and the CustomerName field-value text box is too small for the field value. So you will resize both of the text boxes.

Resizing Controls

A selected object displays seven sizing handles, one on each side of the object and one at each corner except the upper-left corner. The upper-left corner displays the move handle. Positioning the pointer over a sizing handle changes the pointer to a two-headed arrow; the direction in which the arrows are pointing indicates the direction in which you can resize the selected object. When you drag a sizing handle, you resize the control. Thin lines appear, which guide you as you resize the control.

REFERENCE
window

RESIZING A CONTROL

- Click the control to select it and display the sizing handles.
- Place the pointer over the sizing handle you want, and then click and drag the edge of the object until it is the size you want.

You'll begin by resizing the CustomerNum text box, which is much larger than necessary to display the three-digit customer number. Then you'll resize the CustomerName text box to make it large enough to display the complete customer name.

To resize the two text boxes:

1. Click the **View** button for Design view 🔲 on the Form View toolbar to return to the Form window in Design view.

2. Click the **CustomerNum text box** to select it.

3. Place the pointer on the middle right handle. When the pointer changes to ↔, click and drag the right border horizontally to the left until the text box is approximately the size of the text box shown in Figure 5-27.

   TROUBLE? If you change the vertical size of the box by mistake, just click the Undo button 🔲 on the Form Design toolbar and then repeat Step 3.

   Now you will move the CustomerName control to its correct position, and then resize the CustomerName text box.

4. Click the **CustomerName text box** to select the bound control. Place the pointer on the CustomerName text box, but not on a move handle or a sizing handle. When the pointer changes to 🖐, click and drag the control to the left until its left edge is at the 2-inch mark on the horizontal ruler. Release the mouse button.

5. Place the pointer on the middle right handle of the control. When the pointer changes to ↔, click and drag the right border horizontally to the right until the right edge of the text box is at the 4¾-inch mark on the horizontal ruler. Release the mouse button. See Figure 5-27.

Figure 5-27 ◀
CustomerNum
and
CustomerName
text boxes
moved and
resized

CustomerNum text
box resized

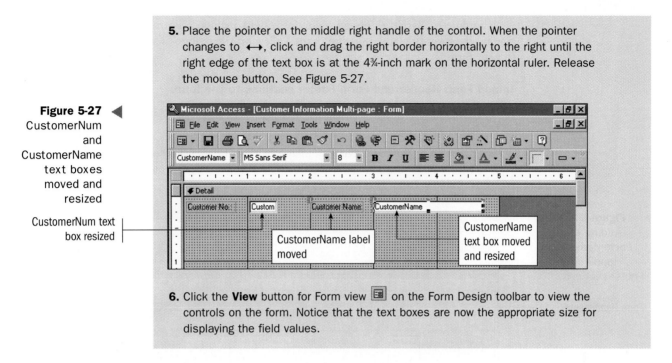

6. Click the **View** button for Form view 🔳 on the Form Design toolbar to view the controls on the form. Notice that the text boxes are now the appropriate size for displaying the field values.

Now you will add the title and picture to the top of the form.

Using Form Headers and Form Footers

The Form Header and Form Footer sections allow you to add titles, instructions, command buttons, and other information to the top and bottom of your form, respectively. Controls placed in the Form Header or Form Footer sections remain on the screen whenever the form is displayed; they do not change when the contents of the Detail section change. To add either a header or footer to your form, you must first add both the Form Header and Form Footer sections as a pair to the Form window in Design view. If your form needs one of these sections but not the other, you can remove a section by setting its height to zero, which is the method you would use to remove any section on a form.

REFERENCE
window

ADDING AND REMOVING FORM HEADER AND FORM FOOTER SECTIONS

■ Display the form in Design view.
■ Click View on the menu bar, and then click Form Header/Footer to add a Form Header section and a Form Footer section to the form.
■ To remove a Form Header or Form Footer section, click and drag the bottom edge of that section up until the section area disappears.

According to Barbara's design, your form must include a Form Header section that will contain the form title and a picture of the Valle Coffee cup logo. You need to add this section to your form.

To add Form Header and Form Footer sections to the form:

1. Click the **View** button for Design view 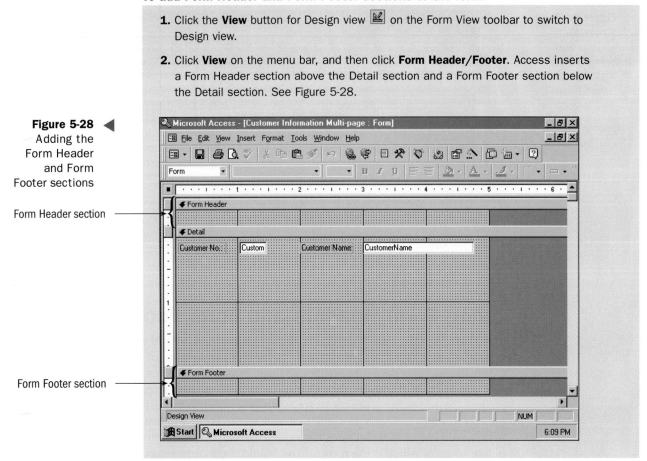 on the Form View toolbar to switch to Design view.

2. Click **View** on the menu bar, and then click **Form Header/Footer**. Access inserts a Form Header section above the Detail section and a Form Footer section below the Detail section. See Figure 5-28.

Figure 5-28 ◀
Adding the
Form Header
and Form
Footer sections

Form Header section ──

Form Footer section ──

You do not need a Form Footer section in this form, so you'll remove it by making its height zero.

To remove the Form Footer section:

1. Place the pointer at the bottom edge of the Form Footer section. When the pointer changes to ✛, click and drag the bottom edge of the section up until it disappears. Even though the words Form Footer remain, the area defining the section is set to zero, and the section will not appear in the form.

You can now add the title to the Form Header section with the Label tool on the toolbox.

Access

Adding a Label to a Form

The form design shows a title at the top of the form. You can add a title or other text to a form by using the Label tool on the toolbox.

REFERENCE
window

ADDING A LABEL TO A FORM

- If necessary, click the Toolbox button on the Form Design toolbar to display the toolbox.
- Click the Label tool on the toolbox.
- Place the pointer at the position for the upper-left corner of the label.
- Click the left mouse button. Access places a box in the form where the label will appear.
- Type the text for the label in the label box.
- Click anywhere outside of the label box to enter the text.

You'll begin by placing a label box for the title in the Form Header section.

To place a label on the form:

1. Click the **Toolbox** button 🛠 on the Form Design toolbar to display the toolbox.

2. Click the **Label** tool ⟨Aa⟩ on the toolbox.

3. Move the pointer to the Form Header section. The pointer changes to $^+\!A$.

4. Place the pointer in the upper-left corner of the Form Header section. This will be the upper-left corner of the label.

5. Click the left mouse button. Access inserts a small label box in the Form Header section and places the insertion point in the label box.

6. Type **Valle Coffee Customer Information** in the label box, and then click anywhere outside of the label box to deselect the label box and enter the text. See Figure 5-29.

Figure 5-29 ◄
Label placed
in the Form
Header
section

label added ────

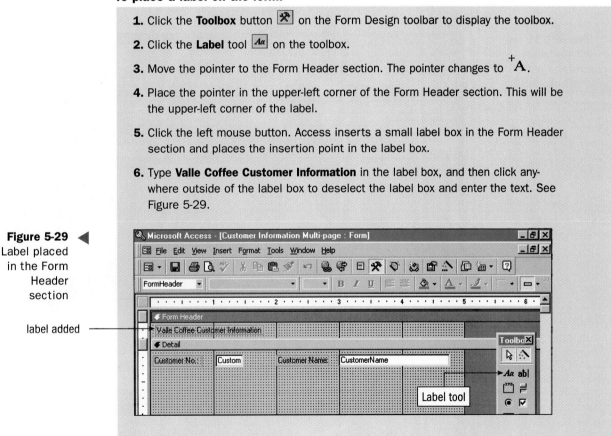

Barbara wants the title to be prominent on the form, so you will change the format of the text in the label to increase its font size and change the font weight to bold. You do this by using the buttons on the Formatting toolbar.

To change the font size and weight for the title:

1. Click the **title label control** to select it.

2. Click the **Font Size** list arrow on the Formatting toolbar, and then click **14**.

3. Click the **Bold** button �B on the Formatting toolbar. See Figure 5-30.

Figure 5-30 ◀
Setting the
properties for
the title label
control

label font size and
weight changed

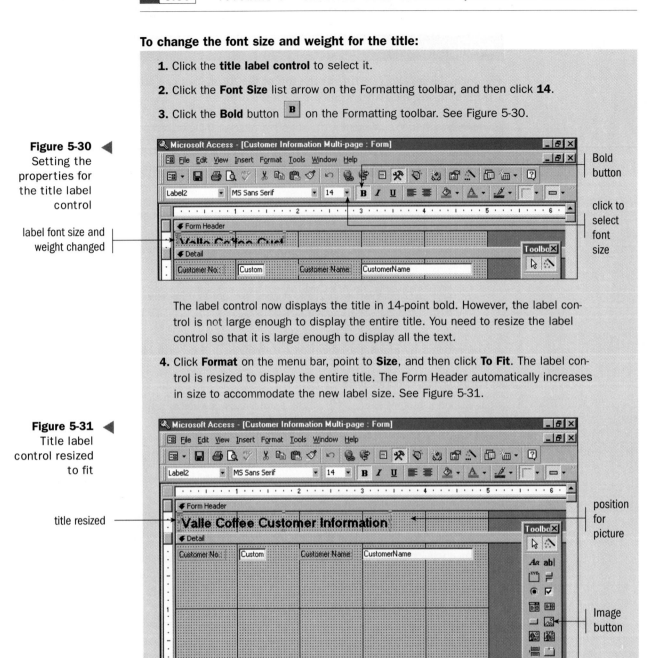

Bold
button

click to
select
font
size

The label control now displays the title in 14-point bold. However, the label control is not large enough to display the entire title. You need to resize the label control so that it is large enough to display all the text.

4. Click **Format** on the menu bar, point to **Size**, and then click **To Fit**. The label control is resized to display the entire title. The Form Header automatically increases in size to accommodate the new label size. See Figure 5-31.

Figure 5-31 ◀
Title label
control resized
to fit

title resized

position
for
picture

Image
button

Barbara also wants the Valle Coffee logo, which is a picture of a coffee cup, to appear at the top of the form. You will now add the picture to the Form Header section.

Adding a Picture to a Form

Access has the ability to use files and data created by other software programs. To enhance the appearance of a form or report, for example, you can include a picture or other graphic image on the form or report. To do so you use the Image tool on the toolbox.

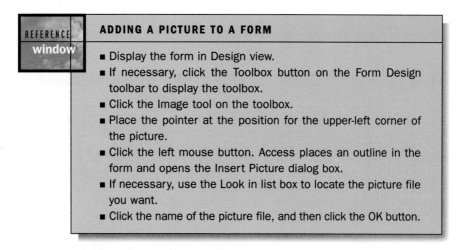

In this case, the Valle Coffee logo was created in a drawing program and saved in a file named ValleCup. Now you'll add this picture to the top right of the form.

To place the picture on the form:

1. Click the **Image** tool 🖼 on the toolbox.

2. Move the pointer to the Form Header section. The pointer changes to ⁺🖼.

3. Using the ruler as a guide, place the pointer slightly below the top of the Form Header section, approximately ¼-inch from the right edge of the title label control. (See Figure 5-31 for the correct position.) This will be the upper-left corner of the picture.

4. Click the left mouse button. Access places an outline in the Form Header section and opens the Insert Picture dialog box. See Figure 5-32.

Figure 5-32 ◄
Insert Picture
dialog box

place this picture
in form

5. Make sure Tutorial appears in the Look in list box, click **ValleCup** to select the picture file, and then click the **OK** button.

Access closes the Insert Picture dialog box and inserts the picture. The Form Header section automatically enlarges to accommodate the size of the image.

Now view the form with the new header.

6. Click the **View** button for Form view 🖹 on the Form Design toolbar to view the form. See Figure 5-33.

Figure 5-33 ◀
Viewing the
form with the
new header

Form Header section ⟶

Detail section ⟶

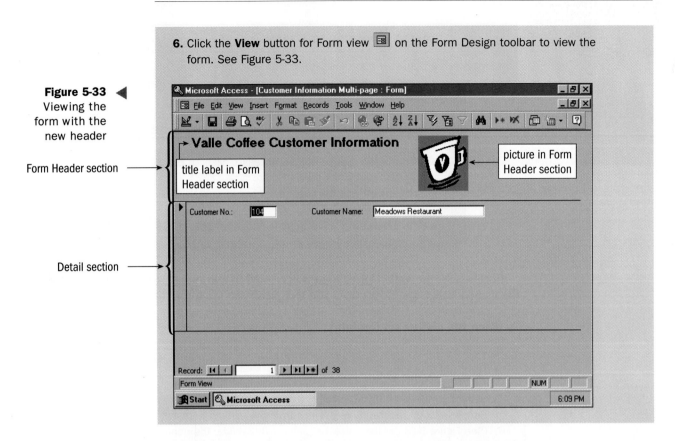

Barbara views the form and confirms that the title and picture are correctly placed, formatted, and sized. However, she would like the background color of the form to be dark gray to match the background color of the picture, so that the picture will blend in better with the form.

Changing the Background Color of a Form Object

You can change the background color of a form or of a specific section or object on the form by using tools available in Design view.

REFERENCE
window

CHANGING THE BACKGROUND COLOR OF AN OBJECT

- Click the control to select it.
- Click the Fill/Back Color list arrow on the Form Design toolbar to display the palette of available colors.
- Click the box of the color you want to apply to the control.

You need to change the background color of the Form Header section and the Detail section of the form to match the background color of the picture. This will cause the picture to blend in with the form.

To change the background color of the Detail and Form Header sections:

1. Click the **View** button for Design view 🔲 on the Form View toolbar to switch to Design view.

2. Click an empty area of the Detail section. This makes the Detail section the selected control.

3. Click the list arrow for the **Fill/Back Color** button 🔲 on the Form Design toolbar. Access displays the palette of available colors. See Figure 5-34.

Figure 5-34
Changing the background color of the form sections

Fill/Back Color button

Fill/Back Color palette

Fill/Back Color list arrow

click to select medium gray

4. Click the medium gray box in the color palette at the right end of the second row (see Figure 5-34). The background of the Detail section changes to the medium gray color.

Now you need to apply the same color to the Form Header section. To do so, you do not have to redisplay the color palette; once you select a color from the palette, it remains in effect so that you can apply the color to other objects by simply clicking the Fill/Back Color button.

5. Click an empty area of the Form Header section. This makes the Form Header section the selected control.

6. Click the **Fill/Back Color** button 🔲 (not the list arrow) on the Form Design toolbar. The Form Header section now appears with the medium gray background.

Now you can save the form and view your changes in Form View.

7. Click the **Save** button 🔲 on the Form Design toolbar to save the form.

8. Click the **View** button for Form view 🔲 on the Form Design toolbar to view the form. See Figure 5-35.

Figure 5-35
Form with new background color

medium gray background color applied

Quick Check

1. What is the difference between a bound control and an unbound control?

2. How do you move a control and its label together?

3. How do you change a label name?

4. How do you resize a control?

5. What is the Form Header section?

6. How do you insert a picture, created using another software program, in a form?

You are now ready to add the two pages to the form to display the customer address and contact information on one page and the order information on another.

SESSION 5.3

In this session, you will create a multi-page form and use Control Wizards to add a subform. You will also use the custom form to filter the data and save the filter as a query.

Creating a Multi-page Form Using Tab Controls

You can create a multi-page form in two ways: by inserting a page break control in the form or by using a tab control. If you insert a page break control in a form, the user can move between pages using the Page Up and Page Down keys on the keyboard. If you use a tab control, the control appears with tabs at the top, one tab for each page. The user can switch between pages by clicking the tabs.

Barbara wants to include a tab control with two pages on the Valle Coffee Customer Information form. The first page of the tab control will contain customer information, such as the customer name, address, and other fields from the Customer table. The second page of the tab control will contain a subform with order information for that customer.

First you will resize the Detail section of the form to make room for the tab control.

To resize the Detail section:

1. If you took a break after the previous session, make sure that Access is running, that the Restaurant database from the Tutorial folder on your Student Disk is open, and that the Customer Information Multi-page form is open and the window is maximized.

2. Click the **View** button for Design view 🔲 on the Form View toolbar to display the form in Design view.

3. Place the pointer on the right edge of the Detail section. When the pointer changes to ✛, click and drag the edge to the right until it is at the 5½-inch mark on the horizontal ruler. Release the mouse button.

Now you can place the tab control on the form.

To place the tab control on the form:

1. Click the **Tab Control** tool 🔲 on the toolbox.

2. Place the pointer at the left edge of the Detail section, approximately ½-inch below the top of the Detail section, and then click the left mouse button. (Refer to Figure 5-36 for the correct position for the tab control.) Access places a tab control in the Detail section.

   Now you will resize the tab control so that it is large enough to display the remaining fields for the form.

3. Scroll down the Form window until the tab control is completely visible, click the right middle handle of the tab control, and then drag it to the right until it is three grid dots from the right edge of the form. Release the mouse button. See Figure 5-36.

Figure 5-36 ◀
Tab control placed in the Detail section and resized

tab for second page of tab control

tab for first page of tab control

tab control in form

Tab Control tool

sizing handles

TROUBLE? The page tabs on your screen might show different page numbers in the labels, depending on how you completed the previous steps. This will not affect the form. Just continue with the tutorial.

The top of the tab control displays two tabs. Each tab indicates a separate page on the form. On the first page, you will place the controls for the fields from the Customer table. On the second page, you will place a subform displaying the fields from the Order table for that customer. The user can move between the two pages by clicking the tabs.

To add the fields to the tab control:

1. Click the **Field List** button 🔲 on the Form Design toolbar to display the field list.

2. Click the **Street** field in the field list, scroll to the end of the field list, press and hold the **Shift** key, and then click the **FirstContact** field. All the fields in the list, except CustomerNum and CustomerName, should be selected.

3. Drag the selected fields to the tab control and release the mouse button when the pointer is approximately at the 1-inch mark on the horizontal ruler.

4. Click the **Close** button ☒ on the field list to close it.

5. Click a blank area of the tab control to deselect the text boxes and their labels.

   Now you need to move and resize the text boxes to match Barbara's form design.

6. Click the **Street text box** to select it, and then place the pointer on its move handle in the upper-left corner. When the pointer changes to 🖑 , click and drag the Street text box to the left to the ¾-inch mark (approximately) on the horizontal ruler. Refer to Figure 5-37 to help you position the text box.

7. Place the pointer on the middle right handle of the Street text box. When the pointer changes to ↔, click and drag the right border to the right until the text box is approximately the size of the text box shown in Figure 5-37.

8. Move and resize the text boxes for the remaining fields. Use Figure 5-37 as a guide for positioning and sizing the text boxes.

Figure 5-37 ◀
Customer fields
placed in the
tab control

bound controls added
to the first page of
the tab control

TROUBLE? Your controls do not have to be in the exact same position as the controls in Figure 5-37. However, they should be in approximately the same position. If you did not place the controls correctly, move and resize them now.

Notice that the label boxes on the form are left-justified; that is, they are aligned on their left edges. Barbara thinks that the form will look better if these labels are right-justified, or aligned on their right edges. To align them, you will select all of the labels and use the shortcut menu.

REFERENCE
window

ALIGNING OBJECTS ON A FORM

- Select the objects you want to align.
- Right-click any one of the selected objects to display the shortcut menu.
- Point to Align, and then click the alignment you want.

To select and align all the label boxes on the right:

1. Click the **Street label box** to select it.

2. Press and hold the **Shift** key while you click each of the remaining label boxes below the Street label so that all four are selected, and then release the Shift key.

3. Right-click any one of the selected label boxes to display the shortcut menu.

4. Point to **Align**, and then click **Right**. Access aligns the label boxes on their right edges. See Figure 5-38.

Figure 5-38 ◀
Aligning the
label boxes

label boxes
right-aligned

TROUBLE? If the text boxes were realigned as well, click the Undo button on the Form Design toolbar, and then repeat Steps 1 through 4.

5. Select the three label boxes on the right (OwnerName, Phone, and FirstContact), and then repeat Steps 3 and 4 to right-align them.

6. Click the **View** button for Form view on the Form Design toolbar to view the form. See Figure 5-39.

Figure 5-39 ◀
First record in
Form view

page tabs

controls moved and
realigned

You are now ready to add the Order table fields as a subform on the second page of the form.

Adding a Subform Using Control Wizards

You use the Subform/Subreport tool on the toolbox to add a subform to a form. If you want help in defining the subform, you can first select one of the Access Control Wizards. A **Control Wizard** asks you a series of questions and then creates a control on a form or report based on your answers. Access offers Control Wizards for the Combo Box, List Box, Option Group, Command Button, and Subform/Subreport tools, among others.

You will use the Subform/Subreport Wizard to add the subform for the Order table records. This subform will appear on the second page of the form.

To add the subform to the form:

1. Click the **View** button for Design view 🖾 on the Form View toolbar to switch to Design view.

2. Make sure the **Control Wizards** tool 🖾 on the toolbox is selected.

3. Click the tab for the second page (the tab on the right) to select that page.

4. Click the **Subform/Subreport** tool 🎛 on the toolbox.

5. Place the pointer near the upper-left corner of the tab control, and then click the left mouse button. Access places a subform control in the tab control and displays the first Subform/Subreport Wizard dialog box.

   This dialog box allows you to create a new subform based on a table or query, or use an existing subform. You will use the Order table as the basis for a new subform.

6. Make sure the **Table/Query** option button is selected, and then click the **Next** button. Access displays the next Subform/Subreport Wizard dialog box. See Figure 5-40.

Figure 5-40 ◄
Selecting the table and fields for the subform

click to display list of tables and queries

This dialog box allows you to select the table or query on which the subform is based and to select the fields from that table or query.

7. Click the **Tables and Queries** list arrow to display the list of tables and queries in the Restaurant database, and then click **Table: Order**. The Available Fields list box shows the fields in the Order table.

8. Click the ⬥⬥ button to move all available fields to the Selected Fields list box, and then click the **Next** button. See Figure 5-41.

Figure 5-41 ◀
Selecting the linking field

make sure this option is selected |

make sure this link is selected |

This dialog box allows you to select the link between the Customer table and the Order table.

9. Make sure the **Choose from a list** option button is selected and that the first link is highlighted, and then click the **Next** button. The next Subform/Subreport Wizard dialog box allows you to specify a name for the subform.

10. Type **Customer Information Subform** and then click the **Finish** button. Access inserts a subform object in the tab control where the Order records will appear.

11. Click the **View** button for Form view 📧 on the Form Design toolbar to view the form. See Figure 5-42.

Figure 5-42 ◀
Viewing the form with the tab control

click to display second page |

first page of tab control |

The tab control shows the customer information on the current page. You can view the order information for the customer by clicking the second page.

12. Click the page tab on the right to display the order information. See Figure 5-43.

Figure 5-43 ◄
Viewing the
subform on the
tab control

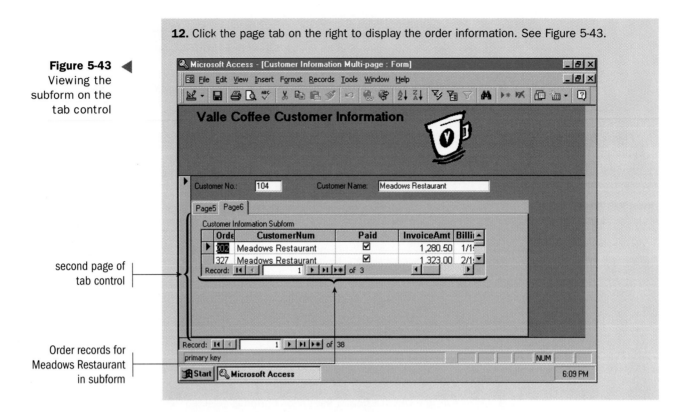

second page of
tab control

Order records for
Meadows Restaurant
in subform

After viewing the form, Barbara identifies several modifications she'd like you to make. The subform is not properly sized and the field values in the subform are not displayed completely. She wants you to resize the subform and the field values so that the entire field values are visible. She also wants you to delete the CustomerNum field from the subform, because the labels at the top of the form already provide both the customer number and the customer name. Finally, she asks you to delete the Customer Information Subform label and edit the labels for the tabs in the tab control so that they indicate the contents of each page.

You can resize the subform, edit the labels, and delete the CustomerNum field from the subform in Design view. Then you can resize the Order columns in Form view. You will begin by resizing the subform, deleting its labels, and editing the labels for the tabs.

To resize the subform, delete its label, and edit the labels for the tabs:

1. Click the **View** button for Design view ☑ on the Form View toolbar.

2. Scroll down until the bottom of the subform is visible. If necessary, click the subform to select it. Place the pointer on the middle right sizing handle of the subform. When the pointer changes to ↔, click and drag the edge of the subform to the right to the 5¼-inch mark on the horizontal ruler.

3. Place the pointer on the middle bottom sizing handle of the subform. When the pointer changes to ↕, click and drag the edge of the subform down to the 2¼-inch mark on the vertical ruler.

Access

4. Right-click the label for the subform control, and then click **Cut** on the shortcut menu. See Figure 5-44.

Figure 5-44
Subform resized and label deleted

label deleted

subform resized

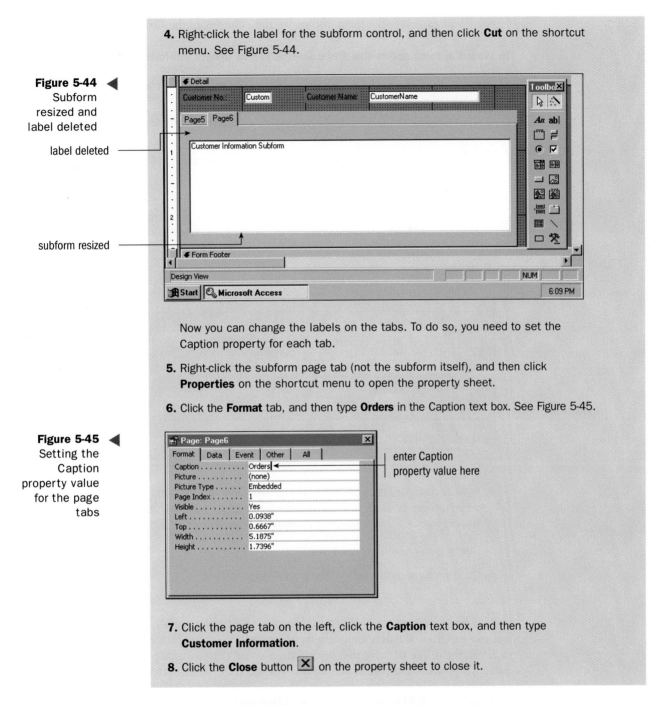

Now you can change the labels on the tabs. To do so, you need to set the Caption property for each tab.

5. Right-click the subform page tab (not the subform itself), and then click **Properties** on the shortcut menu to open the property sheet.

6. Click the **Format** tab, and then type **Orders** in the Caption text box. See Figure 5-45.

Figure 5-45
Setting the Caption property value for the page tabs

enter Caption property value here

7. Click the page tab on the left, click the **Caption** text box, and then type **Customer Information**.

8. Click the **Close** button ☒ on the property sheet to close it.

Next you'll delete the CustomerNum field from the subform. To do so, you need to open the subform in Design view.

To delete the CustomerNum field from the subform:

1. Click the **Orders** tab to display the subform.

2. Double-click the subform. Access opens the subform in Design view.

3. Right-click the **CustomerNum label**, and then click **Cut** on the shortcut menu.

4. Right-click the **CustomerNum text box**, and then click **Cut** on the shortcut menu.

5. Click the **Close** button ☒ on the Form window in Design view for the subform, and then click the **Yes** button to save the changes to the subform.

Now you can view the form and resize the columns in the Orders subform.

To view the form and resize the columns in the Orders subform:

1. Click the **View** button for Form view 🖽 on the Form Design toolbar. Access displays the first customer record, for Meadows Restaurant, in the form.

2. Click the **Orders** tab. The second page of the multi-page form displays the Order records for Meadows Restaurant.

3. Place the pointer on the column heading for the OrderNum field in the subform. When the pointer changes to ↓, click and drag the pointer to the right to highlight all of the columns in the subform.

4. Place the pointer on the line between any two columns. When the pointer changes to ↔, double-click to resize all the columns. See Figure 5-46.

Figure 5-46 ◀
Order fields
after resizing

resized fields ——————

5. Practice navigating through the Customer and Order table records using the form. When you are finished, click the **Customer Information** tab, and then click the **First Record** button 🖼 to display the customer information for Meadows Restaurant.

Now you can save the completed form.

6. Click the **Save** button 🖫 on the Form Design toolbar.

Kim has a new request. She wants to see information for all of the new customers in Indiana or Ohio. She defines a new customer as one whose first contact date was in 1996 or later. She'd like to view this information using the Customer Information Multi-page form. To produce the results she wants, you need to use a filter with the form.

Using a Filter with a Form

Recall that a **filter** is a set of criteria that describes the records you want to see in a datasheet or a form and their sequence. A filter is like a query, but it applies only to the current datasheet or form. If you want to use a filter at another time, you can save the filter as a query.

Access provides three filter tools that allow you to specify and apply filters: Filter By Selection, Filter By Form, and Advanced Filter/Sort. With Filter By Selection and Filter By Form, you specify the record selection criteria directly in the form. Filter By Selection finds records that match a particular field value. Filter By Form finds records that match multiple selection criteria using the same Access logical and comparison operators that you use in queries. After applying a filter by selection or by form, you can rearrange the records using the Sort Ascending or Sort Descending toolbar buttons, if necessary.

Advance Filter/Sort allows you to specify multiple selection criteria and to specify a sort order for the selected records in the Advanced Filter/Sort window, in the same way you specify record selection criteria and sort orders for a query in Design view.

To produce the results Kim wants, you'll use Filter By Form.

Using Filter By Form

Because the Customer Information Multi-page form already shows all of the customer information, you can use Filter By Form to display information for only the new customers in Indiana or Ohio.

REFERENCE
window

SELECTING RECORDS USING FILTER BY FORM

- Display the form in Form view.
- Click the Filter By Form button on the Form View toolbar.
- Enter a simple selection criterion or an And condition in the first form using the text boxes for the appropriate fields.
- If there is an Or condition, click the Or tab and enter the Or condition in the second form. Continue to enter Or conditions on separate forms by using the Or tab.
- Click the Apply Filter button on the Filter/Sort toolbar.

The multiple selection criteria you will enter are: Indiana *and* first contact after 12/31/95 *or* Ohio *and* first contact after 12/31/95.

To select the records using Filter By Form:

1. Click the **Filter By Form** button ▦ on the Form View toolbar. Access displays a blank form. See Figure 5-47.

Figure 5-47 ◀
Blank form for
Filter By Form

Clear Grid button

enter selection criteria
for first And condition
on blank form

Or tab

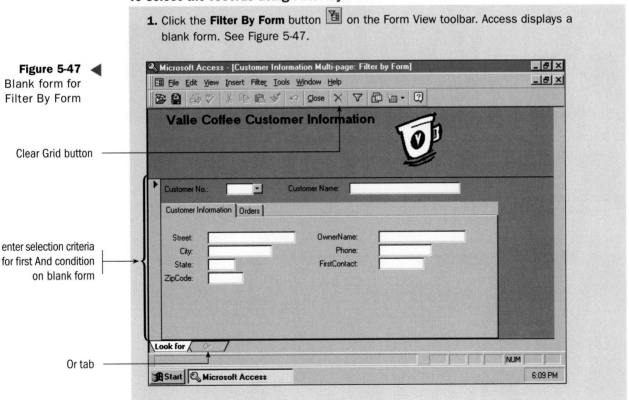

In this blank form, you specify multiple selection criteria by entering conditions in the text boxes for the fields in a record. If you enter criteria in more than one field, you create the equivalent of an And condition: Access will select any record that matches all of the criteria. To create an Or condition, you enter the criteria for the first part of the condition in the field on the first (Look for) blank form, and then click the Or tab to display a new blank form. You enter the criteria for the second part of the condition in the same field on this new blank form. Access selects any record that matches all the criteria on the Look for form *or* all the criteria on the Or form.

2. Click the **State** text box, click the list arrow, and then click **IN**.

3. Click the **FirstContact** text box, and then type **>#12/31/95#**. The number signs (#) indicate a date. If you omit them, Access adds them automatically.

   You have now specified the logical operator (And) and the comparison operator (>) for the condition Indiana *and* after 12/31/95. To add the rest of the criteria, you need to display the Or form.

4. Click the **Or** tab to display a second blank form. The insertion point is in the text box for the FirstContact field. Also, notice that a third tab, which is also labeled "Or," is now available in case you need to specify another Or condition.

5. Click the **State** text box, click the list arrow, and then click **OH**.

6. Click the **FirstContact** text box, and then type **>#12/31/95#**. The form now contains the equivalent of the second And condition: Ohio *and* after 12/31/95. See Figure 5-48.

Figure 5-48 ◀
Completed
Filter By Form

Apply Filter button

second And condition
entered on Or tab

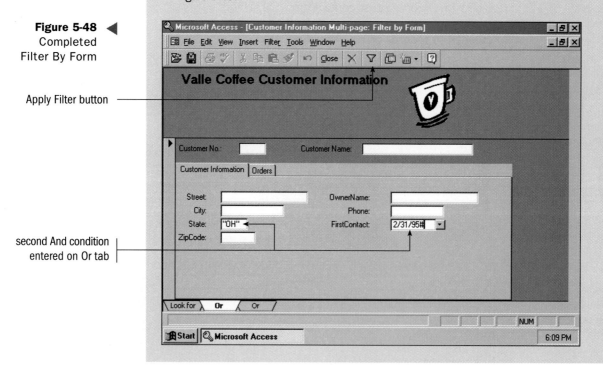

Combined with the Look for form, you now have the Or condition, and the Filter By Form conditions are complete.

7. Click the **Apply Filter** button on the Filter/Sort toolbar. Access applies the filter and displays the first record that matches the selection criteria (the Gateway Lounge in Ohio, first contacted on 3/5/96). The bottom of the screen shows that 2 records were selected. See Figure 5-49.

Figure 5-49 ◀
First record that matches the selection criteria

Remove Filter button

indicates filter applied

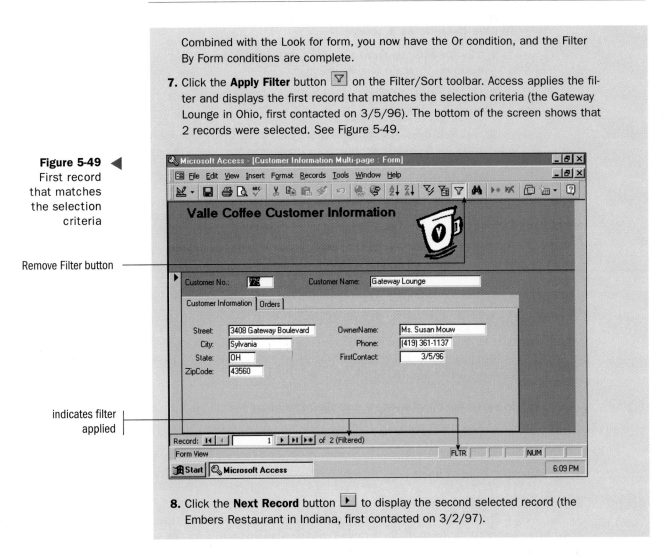

8. Click the **Next Record** button to display the second selected record (the Embers Restaurant in Indiana, first contacted on 3/2/97).

Now that you have defined the filter, you can save it as a query, so that Kim can easily view this information again in the future.

Saving a Filter as a Query

By saving a filter as a query, you can reuse the filter in the future by opening the saved query.

REFERENCE window

SAVING A FILTER AS A QUERY

- Create a filter using Filter By Selection, Filter By Form, or Advanced Filter/Sort.
- Click the Save As Query button on the toolbar to display the Save As Query dialog box.
- Type the name for the query, and then press the Enter key (or click the OK button).

You'll save the filter you just created as a query named "New Customers in Indiana and Ohio."

To save the filter as a query:

1. Click the **Filter By Form** button 🔲 on the Form View toolbar. Access displays the form with the selection criteria.

2. Click the **Save As Query** button 🔲 on the Filter/Sort toolbar. The Save As Query dialog box opens.

3. Type **New Customers in Indiana and Ohio** in the Query Name text box, and then press the **Enter** key. Access saves the filter as a query and closes the dialog box.

   Now you can clear the selection criteria, close the filter window, and return to Form view.

4. Click the **Clear Grid** button 🔲 on the Filter/Sort toolbar. Access removes the selection criteria from the forms.

5. Click the **Close** button 🔲 to close the filter window and return to Form view. The filter is still in effect in this window, so you need to remove it.

6. Click the **Remove Filter** button 🔲 on the Form View toolbar. The bottom of the screen shows that there are 38 available records.

Next, to check that the filter was saved as a query, you'll close the Form window and view the list of queries on the Queries tab.

To close the Form window and view the query list:

1. Click the **Close** button 🔲 on the Form View toolbar.

2. Click the **Queries** tab to display the Queries list box. The query "New Customers in Indiana and Ohio" is now listed.

The next time Kim wants to view the records selected by this query, she can apply the query to the form. If she simply runs the query, she will see the selected records, but they will not be shown in the Customer Information Multi-page form. Instead, she can open the form and apply the saved query to select the records she wants to view in the form.

Applying a Filter that Was Saved as a Query

To see how to apply a query as a filter to a form, you will open the Customer Information Multi-page form and apply the New Customers in Indiana and Ohio query as a filter.

REFERENCE
window

APPLYING A FILTER THAT WAS SAVED AS A QUERY

- Open the form to which you want to apply the filter.
- Click the Filter By Form button on the Form View toolbar.
- Click the Load from Query button on the Filter/Sort toolbar.
- Select the query you want to apply. Access loads the saved query into the Filter grid.
- Click the Apply Filter button on the Filter/Sort toolbar.

To apply the filter that you saved as a query:

1. Click the **Forms** tab in the Database window, and then double-click **Customer Information Multi-page** to display this form in Form view.

2. Click the **Filter By Form** button 🔳 on the Form View toolbar.

3. Click the **Load from Query** button 🔳 on the Filter/Sort toolbar. Access displays the Applicable Filter dialog box. See Figure 5-50.

Figure 5-50 ◀
Applicable
Filter dialog
box

click to select filter
saved as query

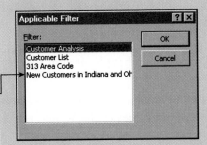

4. Click **New Customers in Indiana and Ohio** in the Filter list box, and then click the **OK** button. Access loads the saved query into the Filter grid.

5. Click the **Apply Filter** button 🔳 on the Filter/Sort toolbar. Access applies the filter and displays the first record in the form.

6. Click the **Close** button 🔳 on the Form window to close it and return to the Database window.

You can now close the Restaurant database and exit Access.

7. Click the **Close** button 🔳 on the Access window to close the database and exit Access.

Quick **Check**

1. Describe how you would use a Control Wizard to add a tab control to a form.

2. How do you right-align a group of labels?

3. How do you open a subform in Design view to edit it?

4. What is the purpose of Filter By Form?

5. How do you reuse a filter in the future?

6. What is the difference between opening a query and applying a query to a form?

The new queries and forms that you created will make it much easier for Leonard, Barbara, and Kim to enter, retrieve, and view information in the Restaurant database.

Tutorial Assignments

The Products database in the TAssign folder on your Student Disk contains information about Valle Coffee products. The Coffee table in the database contains records of the various types of coffee that Valle Coffee sells. The Product table contains pricing information and the Weight table contains packaging information. The database contains several other objects including queries, forms, and reports. Barbara wants you to make a change to the design of the Product table, create some new queries, and create a custom form. Complete the following:

1. Make sure your Student Disk is in the appropriate disk drive, start Access, and then open the Products database located in the TAssign folder on your Student Disk.

2. Open the Product table in Design view. Change the WeightCode field data type to Lookup Wizard. Look up values in the Weight table, select all fields from the Weight table, and accept all other Lookup Wizard default choices.

3. Create a query to find all records in the Coffee table where the CoffeeName field begins with "Colombian." Include all fields in the query results. Run the query, save it as Colombian Coffees, and then close the query.

4. Create a query to find all records in the Product table where the WeightCode value is A, B, or G. Use a list-of-values match for the selection criterion. Include all fields in the query results. Print the query results. Keep the query open, but do not save the query.

5. Modify the previous query to find all records in the Product table where the WeightCode is not A, B, or G. Print the query results, and then close the query without saving it.

6. Create a query to select all the records from the Coffee table for Decaffeinated coffees that are African or Special Import. Display the CoffeeName and CoffeeType fields in the query results. Print the query results, and then close the query without saving it.

7. Create a parameter query to select the Product table records for a WeightCode that the user specifies. Include all fields in the query results. Save the query as Weight Code Parameter. Run the query and enter the WeightCode A. Print the query results, and then close the query.

8. Create a custom form based on the Special Imports query. Use the design in Figure 5-51 as a guide. Save the form as Special Imports. Open the form and print the first record.

Figure 5-51 ◀

```
                    Valle Coffee Special Imports


      Coffee Name: XXXXXXXXXXX           Price: $XXX.XX


      Product Code: XXXX                 Weight/Size: XXXXXXX
```

9. Use Filter By Form with the Special Imports form to select all records where the CoffeeName field value starts with "Hawaiian" or "Yemen" and the price is over $50.00. Apply the filter. How many records are selected? Print the first selected record. Save the filter as a query named Expensive Hawaiian And Yemen Products.

Access

10. Using Figure 5-52 as a guide, create a multi-page form based on the Coffee and Product tables.

Figure 5-52 ◄

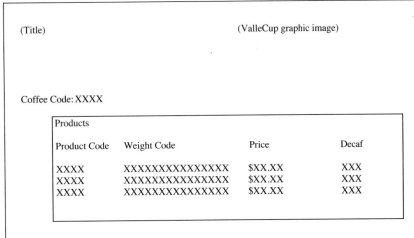

a. Place the CoffeeCode field at the top of the Detail section. Change the caption for the CoffeeCode control to Coffee Code:.

b. Insert a Form Header section in the form. Place a title label in the Form Header section. Enter the title Valle Coffee Products.

c. Place the ValleCup picture in the Form Header section to the right of the title. The file containing this picture is located in the TAssign folder on your Student Disk.

d. Place a tab control below the Coffee Code label in the Detail section. On the first page of the tab control, place the remaining fields from the Coffee table.

e. On the second page of the tab control, place a subform based on the Product table.

 f. Change the Caption property for each tab and for the necessary fields on the first page. Then change the Caption property for the necessary fields on the subform.

g. Save the form as Coffee Multi-page.

h. View the form, print both pages for the last record, and then close the form.

 11. Open the Coffee Multi-page form and then save it as Enhanced Coffee Multi-page. Make the following changes to the form design and save the changes:

a. Use the Font/Fore Color button to change the color of the text in the title label to red.

b. Add a Form Footer section. In the center of the Form Footer section, place a label with the text "Valle Gourmet Coffees are the Midwest's favorite." Change the font to 12-point italic and make the color of the text red.

c. Print both pages for the first record, and then close the form.

12. Close the Products database.

Case Problems

1. Ashbrook Mall Information Desk The Mall Operations Office is responsible for everything that happens in the Ashbrook Mall in Phoenix, Arizona. To maintain a catalog of job openings at the mall stores, Sam Bullard, director of the Mall Operations Office, has created an Access database called MallJobs. Sam asks you to create several new queries and a new form for this database. You'll do so by completing the following:

1. Make sure your Student Disk is in the appropriate disk drive, start Access, and then open the MallJobs database located in the Cases folder on your Student Disk.

2. Open the Job table in Design view. Change the Store field data type to Lookup Wizard. Look up values in the Store table, select the Store and Store Name fields from the Store table, and accept all other Lookup Wizard default choices.

3. Create a query to find all records in the Store table where the Location field begins with "B." Include all fields from the Store table in the query results. Print the query results. Save the query as B Locations, and then close the query.

4. Create a query to find all records in the Job table where the Position value is Clerk, Salesclerk, or Stock Clerk. Use a list-of-values match for the selection criterion. Display the Position and Hours/Week fields in the query results. Print the query results. Keep the query open, but do not save the query.

5. Modify the previous query to find all records in the Job table where the Position value is not Clerk, Salesclerk, or Stock Clerk. Print the query results. Close the query without saving it.

6. Create a query to select all the records for jobs where the Position value is Clerk and the Location value is A3 or B5. Display the Job, StoreName, and Contact fields in the query results. Print the query results, and then close the query without saving it.

7. Create a parameter query to select the Job table records for a Location that the user specifies. Include all the fields in the query results. Save the query as Job Location Parameter. Run the query and enter the Location B5. Print the query results, and then close the query.

8. Create a custom form based on the Store Jobs query. Display all fields in the form. Use your own design for the form. Save the form as Store Jobs. Open the form and print the first record.

9. Use Filter By Form with the Store Jobs form to select all records where the Position value is Clerk or the StoreName value is Pinson Shoes. Apply the filter. How many records are selected? Print the first record. Save the filter as a query named Clerks Or Shoe Stores.

10. Create a multi-page custom form based on the Job and Store tables by completing the following:
    a. Place the Position field in the Detail section of the form.
    b. On the first page of the tab control, display the fields from the Job table.
    c. On the second page of the tab control, display the Store information in a subform.

d. Insert a Form Header section in the form. Place a title label in the Form Header section. Enter the title Ashbrook Mall Jobs.
   e. Select the title and use the Special Effect button on the Form Design toolbar to apply the raised special effect to the title.
   f. View the form, and then print both pages for the first record.

11. Close the form and save it as Job Information Multi-page.

12. Close the MallJobs database.

2. Professional Litigation User Services Professional Litigation User Services (PLUS) creates all types of visual aids for judicial proceedings. To track daily payments received from the firm's clients, Raj Jawahir has created the Payments database. To make the database easier to use, Raj wants several new queries and forms created, which you'll do by completing the following:

1. Make sure your Student Disk is in the appropriate disk drive, start Access, and then open the Payments database located in the Cases folder on your Student Disk.

2. Open the Payment table in Design view. Change the Firm# field data type to Lookup Wizard. Look up values in the Firm table, select the Firm# and FirmName fields from the Firm table, and accept all other Lookup Wizard default choices.

3. Create a query to find all records in the Firm table where the PLUSAcctRep field begins with "Tyler." Display all fields in the query results. Print the query results. Save the query as Tyler Accounts, and then close the query.

4. Create a query to find all records in the Payment table where the Firm# value is 1111, 1115, or 1152. Use a list-of-values match for the selection criterion. Display the Payment#, Firm#, AmountPaid, and DatePaid fields in the query results. Print the query results. Keep the query open, but do not save the query.

5. Modify the previous query to find all records in the Payment table where the Firm# value is not 1111, 1115, or 1152. Print the query results, and then close the query without saving it.

6. Modify the June 2 Payments query to select all the records where the PLUSAcctRep field is Abelson, David or Martinez, Nancy. Display all the fields in the query results. Print the query results, and then close the query without saving it.

7. Create a parameter query to select the Payment table records for a Deposit# that the user specifies. Select only records where the AmountPaid is greater than $1,000.00. Include all the fields in the query results. Save the query as Deposits Parameter. Run the query and enter the Deposit# 102. Print the query results, and then close the query.

8. Create a custom form based on the Payment Statistics by Date query. Display all fields in the form. Use your own design for the form. Save the form as Payment Statistics by Date. Open the form, print the first record, and then close the form.

9. Create a custom form based on the Payment Statistics by Date by Deposit query. Display all fields in the form. Use your own design for the form. Change the Deposit# label and text box format so that the label and field value are displayed with 12-point bold text on a red background. Open the form and print the first record. Save the form as Payment Statistics by Date by Deposit.

10. Use Filter By Form with the Payment Statistics by Date by Deposit form to select all deposits made after June 10 where the Highest Payment was greater than $1800.00 or the Average Payment was greater than $1200.00. Apply the filter. How many records are selected? Print the first selected record. Do not save the filter as a query.

11. Create a multi-page custom form based on the Firm and Payment tables by completing the following:
    a. Place the Firm# and FirmName fields in the Detail section of the form.
    b. On the first page of the tab control, display the other fields from the Firm table.
    c. On the second page of the tab control, display the Payment information in a subform.

    d. Change the Firm# and FirmName label and text box formats so that the label and field values are displayed with 12-point bold text in red letters.
    e. Save the form as Firm Multi-page.
    f. View the form, print both pages for the first record, and then close the form.

12. Open the Firm Multi-page form and save it as Enhanced Firm Multi-page. Make the following changes to the form design and save the changes:
    a. Change the background color of all sections of the form (except the sub-form) to light blue.
    b. Use the Line/Border Width button to place a border (weight 2) around the Title label. Change the font size and weight for the Title label so that it stands out more on the form. Resize the label control, if necessary.
    c. Use the Font/Fore Color button to change the color of the Title value to red.
    d. Print both pages of the finished form for the first record.

13. Close the Payments database.

3. Best Friends Best Friends is a not-for-profit organization that trains hearing and service dogs for people with disabilities. To raise funds, Best Friends periodically sponsors Walk-A-Thons. These fundraisers have been so popular that Noah and Sheila Warnick, the founders of Best Friends, have created the Walks database to keep track of walkers and their pledges. The Walks database has been a useful tool for Noah and Sheila. Now, they need several new queries and new forms to provide them with better information. You'll help them create these queries and forms by completing the following:

1. Make sure your Student Disk is in the appropriate disk drive, start Access, and then open the Walks database located in the Cases folder on your Student Disk.

2. Open the Pledge table in Design view. Change the WalkerID field data type to Lookup Wizard. Look up values in the Walker table, select the WalkerID, LastName, and FirstName fields from the Walker table, and accept all other Lookup Wizard default choices.

3. Create a query to find all records in the Walker table where the Distance value is 2.4, 2.7, or 2.8. Use a list-of-values match for the selection criterion. Display all fields in the query results. Print the query results. Keep the query open, but do not save the query.

4. Modify the previous query to find all records in the Walker table where the Distance value is not 2.4, 2.7, or 2.8. Print the query results, and then close the query without saving it.

5. Modify the Pledge Statistics by Walker query to select all records where the TotalPledge is greater than 20 and the AveragePledge is greater than 10 or the #Pledges is greater than 1. Display all the fields in the query results. Print the query results, and then close the query without saving it.

6. Create a parameter query to select the Walker table records for a Distance that the user specifies. Display the LastName, FirstName, and Distance fields in the query results. Save the query as Distance Parameter. Run the query and enter the Distance 2.3. Print the query results, and then close the query.

7. Create a custom form based on the Walker table. Display all fields in the form. Use your own design for the form. Save the form as Walker. Open the form, print the first record, and then close the form.

8. Create a custom form based on the Difference query. Display all fields in the form. Use your own design for the form. Change the Pledger label and text box format so that the label and field value are displayed with 12-point bold text on a yellow background. Save the form as Difference.

9. Use Filter By Form with the Difference form to select all records where the PledgeAmt is less than $10.00. Apply the filter. How many records are selected? Print the first selected record. Save the filter as a query named Small Pledges.

10. Create a multi-page custom form based on the Walker and Pledge tables by completing the following:
   a. Place the WalkerID, LastName, and FirstName fields in the Detail section of the form.
   b. On the first page, display the other fields from the Walker table.
   c. On the second page, display the Pledge information in a subform.
   d. Save the form as Walker Information Multi-page.
   e. View the form, print both pages for the first record, and then close the form.

11. Open the Walker Information Multi-page form and save it as Enhanced Walker Information Multi-page. Make the following changes to the form design and save the changes:
   a. Change the background color of all sections of the form (except the subform) to light yellow.
   b. Use the Line/Border Width button to place a border (weight 2) around the WalkerID, LastName, and FirstName text boxes. Change the font size and weight for these labels and text boxes so that they stand out more on the form. Resize the label and text box controls, if necessary.
   c. Use the Font/Fore Color button to change the color of the LastName and FirstName values to red.
   d. Use the Special Effect button on the Form Design toolbar to display the Pledge subform with a shadow.
   e. Print the finished form for the first record.

12. Close the Walks database.

4. Lopez Lexus Dealerships Maria and Hector Lopez own a chain of Lexus dealerships throughout Texas. To keep track of the cars at their various dealerships, they have created the Lexus database. Maria and Hector want you to create several queries and forms to make the Lexus database easier to use. To create the queries and forms, complete the following:

1. Make sure your Student Disk is in the appropriate disk drive, start Access, and then open the Lexus database located in the Cases folder on your Student Disk.

2. Open the Cars table in Design view. Change the LocationCode field data type to Lookup Wizard. Look up values in the Locations table, select the LocationCode and LocationName fields from the Locations table, and accept all other Lookup Wizard default choices.

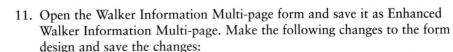

3. Create a query to find all records in the Cars table where the Class value is S1, S3, or S4. Use a list-of-values match for the selection criterion. Display all fields in the query results. Print the query results. Keep the query open, but do not save the query.

4. Modify the previous query to find all records in the Cars table where the Class value is not S1, S3, or S4. Print the query results, and then close the query without saving it.

5. Create a query to select all Cars records for cars with 5-speed manual transmissions (Transmission field value M5) in Location E1 or L1. Display the Model, Class, Year, and Selling Price fields in the query results. Print the query results, and then close the query without saving it.

6. Create a parameter query to select the Cars table records for a Transmission that the user specifies. Save the query as Transmission Parameter. Run the query and enter the Transmission A4. Print the query results, and then close the query.

7. Create a custom form based on the Cars table. Display all fields in the form. Use your own design for the form. Save the form as Car Data. Open the form, print the first record, and then close the form.

8. Create a custom form based on the 1998 Cars query. Display all fields in the form. Use your own design for the form, but place the title "1998 Lexus Automobiles" in the Form Header section. Change the Model label and text box format so that the label and field value are displayed with 12-point bold text on a light blue background. Save the form as 1998 Cars, and then close it.

9. Use Filter By Form with the 1998 Cars form to select all records for cars over $50,000 in price or located in Houston. Apply the filter. Print the first record. How many records are selected? Do not save the filter as a query.

10. Create a multi-page custom form based on the Cars and Locations tables by completing the following:
    a. Place the LocationName field in the Detail section of the form.
    b. On the first page, display the other fields from the Locations table.
    c. On the second page, display the Cars information in a subform.
    d. Save the form as Locations Information Multi-page.
    e. View the form, print both pages for the first record, and then close the form.

11. Open the Locations Information Multi-page form and save it as Enhanced Locations Information Multi-page. Make the following changes to the form design and save the changes:
    a. Change the background color of all sections of the form (except the subform) to light blue.
    b. Use the Line/Border Width button to place a border (weight 2) around the LocationName text box. Change the font size and weight for this label and text box so that they stand out more on the form. Resize the label and text box controls, if necessary.
    c. Use the Font/Fore Color button to change the color of the ManagerName value to red.
    d. Use the Raised Special Effect button on the Form Design toolbar to change the display of the Cars subform.
    e. Print the finished form for the first record.

12. Close the Lexus database.

TUTORIAL 6

Customizing Reports and Integrating Access with Other Programs

Creating a Custom Invoices Report and a Report with an Embedded Chart and a Linked Text Document

CASE

Valle Coffee

At a recent staff meeting, Leonard indicated that he would like new reports created for the Restaurant database. In the first report, he wants to see a printed list of all orders placed by Valle Coffee customers. He also wants monthly subtotals of billing amounts and a grand total for all billing amounts. The second report Leonard would like is a customer report with an embedded chart that graphically summarizes monthly billing activity. He can use both of these reports to monitor customer orders and monthly billing.

In this tutorial, you will create the reports for Leonard. In building the reports, you will use many of the Access report customization features—such as grouping data, calculating totals, and adding lines to separate report sections. These features enhance a report and make it easier to read.

You will also integrate Access with other programs to include the chart that Leonard requested to graphically summarize monthly billing activity. Finally, you will link a report to a word-processing document that describes the report's contents, and you'll export the records from an Access table to a spreadsheet for further analysis.

OBJECTIVES

In this tutorial you will:

- Design and create a custom report

- Modify report controls and properties

- Sort and group data

- Calculate group and overall totals

- Hide duplicate values

- Embed and link objects in a report

- Export Access data to other programs

SESSION

6.1

In this session you will create a custom report. You will add and modify fields in the report; create a page header with a page number and date; sort and group data; and calculate group and report totals.

Creating a Custom Report

A **report** is a formatted hardcopy of the contents of one or more tables from a database. Although you can format and print data using datasheets, queries, and forms, reports allow you greater flexibility and provide a more professional, custom appearance. Reports can be used, for example, to print billing statements and mailing labels.

An Access report is divided into sections. Each report can have seven different sections, which are described in Figure 6-1.

Figure 6-1 ◀
Descriptions of
Access report
sections

Report Section	Description
Report Header	Appears once at the beginning of a report. Use it for report titles, company logos, report introductions, and cover pages.
Page Header	Appears at the top of each page of a report. Use it for column headings, report titles, page numbers, and report dates. If your report has a Report Header section, it precedes the first Page Header section.
Group Header	Appears once at the beginning of a new group of records. Use it to print the group name and the field value that all records in the group have in common. A report can have up to 10 grouping levels.
Detail	Appears once for each record in the underlying table or query. Use it to print selected fields from the table or query and to print calculated values.
Group Footer	Appears once at the end of a group of records. It is usually used to print totals for the group.
Report Footer	Appears once at the end of the report. Use it for report totals and other summary information.
Page Footer	Appears at the bottom of each page of a report. Use it for page numbers and brief explanations of symbols or abbreviations. If your report has a Report Footer section, it precedes the Page Footer section on the last page of the report.

You don't have to include all seven sections in a report. When you design your report, you determine which sections to include and what information to place in each section. Figure 6-2 shows a sample report produced from the Restaurant database.

Figure 6-2
Sample report
showing the
seven sections
of a report

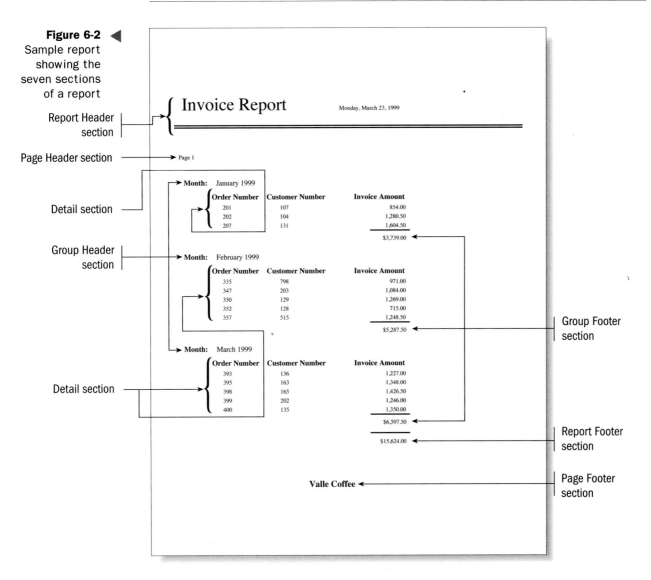

The first report you need to create will list the records for all orders in the Order table. Leonard wants the report to group the invoices by the value in the BillingDate field. The report should also contain the following five sections:

- A Report Header section will contain the report title.

- A Page Header section will show the current date, page number, and column headings for each field.

- A Detail section will list the billing date, order number, customer name, invoice amount, and whether the invoice has been paid. Records in each group will appear in ascending order by customer name.

- A Group Footer section will print subtotals of the InvoiceAmt field for each BillingDate group.

- A Report Footer section will print the grand total of the InvoiceAmt field.

From your work with AutoReport and the Report Wizard, you know that, by default, Access places the report title in the Report Header section and the date and page number in the Page Footer section. Leonard prefers the date and page number to appear at the top of each page, so you need to place this information in the Page Header section.

You could use the Report Wizard to create the report, and then modify the report to match the report design. However, because you need to make several customizations, you will create the report in Design view. If you modify a report created by AutoReport or the Report Wizard, or if you design and create your own report, you produce a **custom report**. You should create a custom report whenever AutoReport or the Report Wizard cannot automatically create the specific report you need.

Designing a Custom Report

Before you create a custom report, you should first plan the report's contents and appearance. Figure 6-3 shows the design of the report you will create for Leonard.

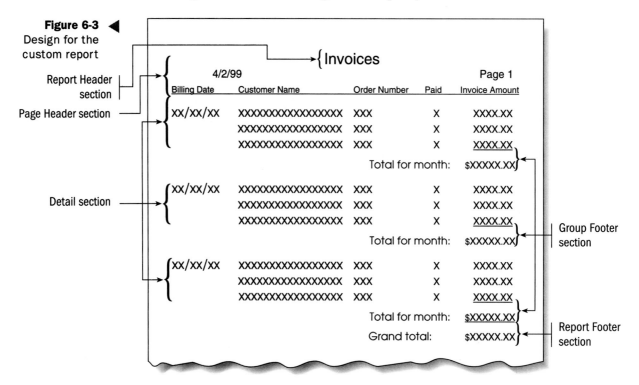

Figure 6-3 ◀
Design for the custom report

Report Header section

Page Header section

Detail section

Group Footer section

Report Footer section

The Report Header section contains the report title, Invoices. Descriptive column headings appear at the bottom of the Page Header section, which also contains the current date and page number.

In the Detail section, the locations and lengths of the field values are indicated by a series of Xs. For example, the three Xs below the Order Number field indicate that the field value will be three characters long.

The subtotals for each group will appear in the Group Footer section, and an overall total will appear in the Report Footer section. The Invoice Amount field is the only field for which totals will appear.

The data for a report can come from either a single table or from a query based on one or more tables. Your report will contain data from the Customer and Order tables. The High Invoice Amounts query contains the fields you need. You will modify the query by removing the selection criterion and deleting unnecessary fields; then you'll use the query as the basis for your report.

To modify the query:

1. Place your Student Disk in the appropriate disk drive.

2. Start Access and then open the Restaurant database located in the Tutorial folder on your Student Disk.

3. Click the **Queries** tab, click **High Invoice Amounts**, and then click the **Design** button. The query is displayed in Design view. See Figure 6-4.

Figure 6-4
Query in Design view

TROUBLE? If you do not see the High Invoice Amounts query in the Queries list box, you might need to scroll the Queries list box to the left.

4. Click the **InvoiceAmt Criteria** text box, press the **F2** key to select the criterion, and then press the **Delete** key.

   The query design also contains the State, OwnerName and Phone fields, which you do not need for this query, so you can delete them.

5. Scroll the design grid to the right until the State, OwnerName, and Phone fields are visible.

6. Position the pointer on the State field until the pointer changes to ↓, click and drag the mouse to the right until all three fields—State, OwnerName, and Phone—are selected, and then release the mouse button.

7. Click the **Cut** button ✂ on the Query Design toolbar to remove the three fields.

   The query now selects the OrderNum, Paid, InvoiceAmt, BillingDate, and CustomerName fields for all records in the Customer and Order tables. To keep the original query intact, you'll save this query as "Invoice Amounts."

8. Click **File** on the menu bar, and then click **Save As/Export**. The Save As dialog box opens.

9. Position the insertion point to the left of the query name, use the Delete key to delete the word "High" and the space following it, and then click the **OK** button. Access saves the modified query.

10. Click the **Close** button ✕ on the Query window to close it and return to the Database window.

You are now ready to create the report. To do so, you need to display the report in Design view.

Report Window in Design View

The Report window in Design view is similar to the Form window in Design view, which you used in the previous tutorial to customize forms.

REFERENCE
window

CREATING A REPORT IN DESIGN VIEW

- In the Database window, click the Reports tab to display the Reports list box.
- Click the New button to display the New Report dialog box.
- Click Design View to select it, select the table or query on which you want to base the new report, and then click the OK button.

The report you are creating will be based on the Invoice Amounts query, which you just modified. To begin, you need to create a blank report in Design view.

To create a blank report in Design view:

1. Click the **Reports** tab to display the Reports list box, and then click the **New** button to open the New Report dialog box.

2. Click **Design View** (if necessary), and then click the list arrow to display the list of tables and queries in the Restaurant database.

3. Click **Invoice Amounts** to select this query as the basis for your report, and then click the **OK** button. Access displays the Report window in Design view.

4. Click the **Maximize** button 🔲 on the Report window. See Figure 6-5.

Figure 6-5 ◀
Report window
in Design view

Toolbox button

Field List button

Page Header section

Detail section

Page Footer section

TROUBLE? If the rulers or grid do not appear, click View on the menu bar, and then click Ruler or Grid to display the missing component. A check mark appears to the left of these components when they are displayed in the Report window. If the grid is still not displayed, see your instructor or technical support person for assistance. If the toolbox is open, click the Close button ☒ on the toolbox to close it.

Notice that the Report window in Design view has many of the same components as the Form window in Design view. For example, the Report Design toolbar includes a Properties button, a Field List button, and a Toolbox button. Both windows also have horizontal and vertical rulers, a grid, and a Formatting toolbar.

Unlike the Form window in Design view, which initially displays only the Detail section on a blank form, the Report window also displays a Page Header section and a Page Footer section. Reports often contain these sections, so Access automatically includes them in a blank report.

Adding Fields to a Report

Your first task is to add bound controls to the Detail section for all the fields from the Invoice Amounts query. Recall that a bound control displays field values from the table or query on which a form or report is based. You add bound controls to a report in the same way that you add them to a form.

REFERENCE
window

ADDING FIELDS TO A REPORT

- Display the report in Design view.
- Click the Field List button on the Report Design toolbar to display the field list.
- To place all fields in the report, double-click the field list title bar to highlight all the fields. Then click anywhere in the highlighted area of the field list and drag the fields to the report. Release the mouse button when the pointer is correctly positioned.
- To place a single field in the report, position the pointer on the field name in the field list, and then click and drag the field name to the report. Release the mouse button when the pointer is correctly positioned.

You need to add a bound control for each field in the Invoice Amounts query. You can add all of these bound controls at once by dragging them as a group from the field list to the Detail section.

To add bound controls for all the fields in the field list:

1. Click the **Field List** button 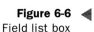 on the Report Design toolbar. The field list box opens. See Figure 6-6.

Figure 6-6 ◄
Field list box

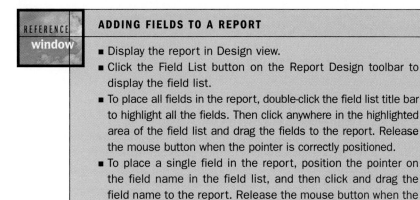

2. Double-click the field list title bar to highlight all the fields in the Invoice Amounts field list.

3. Click anywhere in the highlighted area of the field list (but not on the title bar), and then drag the fields to the Detail section. Release the mouse button when the pointer is positioned at the top of the Detail section and at the 1¼-inch mark on the horizontal ruler. Access adds bound controls for the five selected fields. Each bound control consists of a text box and an attached label. The attached labels are positioned to the left of the text boxes, except for the label for the Paid check box. See Figure 6-7. Notice that the text boxes are aligned at the 1¼-inch mark.

Figure 6-7
Adding bound
controls to
the report

one check box

attached labels

four text boxes

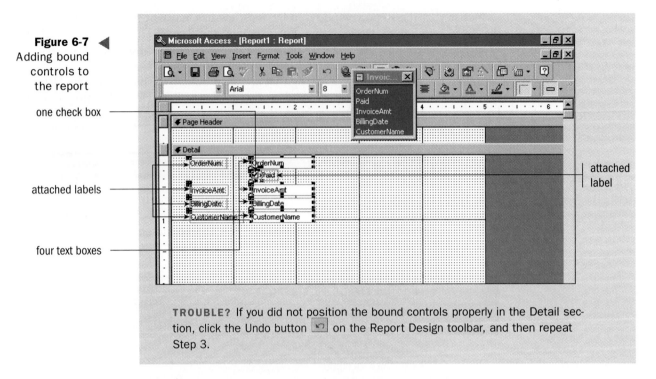

attached
label

TROUBLE? If you did not position the bound controls properly in the Detail section, click the Undo button ⟲ on the Report Design toolbar, and then repeat Step 3.

Performing operations in the Report window in Design view will become easier with practice. Remember, you can always click the Undo button immediately after you make a report design change that produces unsatisfactory results. You can also click the Print Preview button at any time to view your progress on the report.

Working with Controls

Four text boxes and one check box now appear in a column in the Detail section. Each of these boxes is a bound control linked to a field in the underlying query and has an attached label box. The label boxes appear to the left of the text boxes and to the right of the check box. The labels identify the contents of the text boxes and the check box, which will display the field values from the database. According to Leonard's plan for the report (see Figure 6-3), you need to move all the label boxes to the Page Header section, where they will serve as column headings for the field values. You then need to reposition the label boxes, text boxes, and the check box so that they are aligned properly. Before you begin working with the controls in the Report window, you'll close the field list because you no longer need it.

To close the field list and then move all the label boxes to the Page Header section:

1. Click the **Close** button ☒ on the field list box to close it.

2. Click anywhere in the Page Header section to deselect the four text boxes, the check box, and their attached label boxes.

3. While pressing and holding down the **Shift** key, click each of the five label boxes in the Detail section, and then release the Shift key. This action selects all the label boxes in preparation for cutting them from the Detail section and pasting them in the Page Header section.

4. Position the pointer in any one of the selected label boxes. The pointer changes to ✋ .

5. Click the right mouse button to display the shortcut menu.

6. Click **Cut** on the shortcut menu to delete the label boxes from the Detail section. See Figure 6-8.

Access

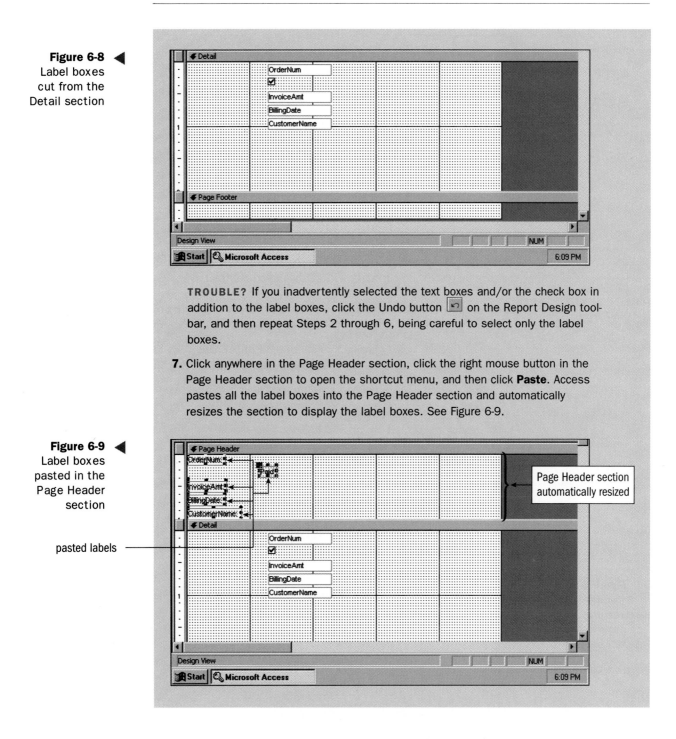

Figure 6-8 ◀
Label boxes
cut from the
Detail section

Figure 6-9 ◀
Label boxes
pasted in the
Page Header
section

pasted labels

TROUBLE? If you inadvertently selected the text boxes and/or the check box in addition to the label boxes, click the Undo button 🔄 on the Report Design toolbar, and then repeat Steps 2 through 6, being careful to select only the label boxes.

7. Click anywhere in the Page Header section, click the right mouse button in the Page Header section to open the shortcut menu, and then click **Paste**. Access pastes all the label boxes into the Page Header section and automatically resizes the section to display the label boxes. See Figure 6-9.

Cutting and pasting the label boxes has unlinked them from their attached text boxes and check box. You can now select and move either a label box or a text box (or check box), but not both at once.

Moving and Resizing Controls

You can move or resize any individual control or multiple selected controls in the Report window. When you select a control, a move handle appears in the top-left corner of the control. This is the handle you use to reposition the control. A selected control also displays sizing handles around its border, which you can use to resize a control in different directions.

REFERENCE
window

MOVING AND RESIZING CONTROLS

- In Design view, click the control to select it.
- To move a control, position the pointer on the control's move handle, click and drag the control to its new location, and then release the mouse button.
- To resize a control, position the pointer on one of the control's sizing handles, click and drag the sizing handle until the control is the proper size, and then release the mouse button.

You need to reposition the text boxes, check box, and label boxes to match the report's design. You'll begin by repositioning the text boxes and check box in the Detail section, which should appear in a row beginning with the BillingDate field. You will also resize the text boxes so the contents will be displayed completely.

To move the text boxes and check box and resize the text boxes:

1. Click the **BillingDate text box** in the Detail section, position the pointer on the move handle in the upper-left corner of the text box, and then click and drag the text box to the upper-left corner of the Detail section.

   Now you will resize the BillingDate text box so it is just large enough to display a date.

2. Position the pointer on the middle right sizing handle of the BillingDate text box. When the pointer changes to ↔, click and drag the right border to the left, to the ½-inch mark (approximately) on the horizontal ruler.

3. Refer to Figure 6-10 and use the procedures noted in Steps 1 and 2 to move the other four controls and resize the remaining text boxes in the Detail section to match the figure as closely as possible. Note that you need to increase the size of the CustomerName text box and decrease the size of both the OrderNum and InvoiceAmt text boxes. See Figure 6-10.

Figure 6-10 ◄
After moving
and resizing the
controls in the
Detail section

check box moved ─

The Detail section is now much taller than necessary to display these controls. The extra space below the text boxes and check box will show as white space between records in the printed report. The report will be more readable and require fewer pages if the records in the Detail section are printed without a large space between them. You can resize the Detail section so that the records will be printed without spacing between them.

To resize the Detail section:

1. If necessary, scroll down to display the bottom edge of the Detail section.

2. Position the pointer on the bottom edge of the Detail section. When the pointer changes to ✛ , click and drag the bottom edge up to align with the bottom of the controls. If necessary, scroll up to display the top of the report. See Figure 6-11.

Figure 6-11 ◀
After resizing
the Detail
section

Detail section resized ——

You've made many modifications to the report design and should save the report before proceeding.

To save the report design:

1. Click the **Save** button 🖫 on the Report Design toolbar. The Save As dialog box opens.

2. Type **Invoices** in the Report Name text box, and then press the **Enter** key. The dialog box closes and Access saves the report in the Restaurant database.

The report design shows column headings different from the text currently displayed in the label boxes in the Page Header section. Next, you need to change the text of the labels by changing each label's Caption property.

Changing the Caption Property

Each label has a Caption property that controls the text displayed in the label. The default Caption property value for a bound control is the field name followed by a colon. Other controls, such as buttons and tab controls, have Caption properties as well. You can change the value of a Caption property for an object by using the property sheet for that object. You should change the Caption property value for an object if the default value is difficult to read or understand.

REFERENCE
window

CHANGING THE CAPTION PROPERTY FOR A LABEL BOX

- Right-click the label box to select it and display the shortcut menu, and then click Properties to display the property sheet.
- Click the Format tab, click the Caption text box, and then press the F2 key to select the current Caption property value.
- Type the new Caption property value.
- Click the Close button to close the property sheet.

The default Caption property values for the labels in the report do not match Leonard's report design. For example, the label BillingDate: should be Billing Date. You need to change the Caption property for each label except the Paid label.

To change the Caption property for the labels:

1. Right-click the **BillingDate label box** in the Page Header section, and then click **Properties** to display the property sheet for the BillingDate label.

2. If necessary, click the **Format** tab to display the Format page of the property sheet. The current Caption property value, BillingDate:, is selected. You simply need to insert a space between the words "Billing" and "Date" and delete the colon following the text.

3. Position the insertion point to the right of the letter "g," press the **spacebar**, position the insertion point to the right of the colon, and then press the **Backspace** key to delete it. See Figure 6-12.

Figure 6-12 ◀
Changing the
Caption
property value

caption entered for
the BillingDate field

4. If necessary, drag the property sheet to the right until the OrderNum label box is visible. Click the **OrderNum label box** to select it. The property sheet changes to show the properties for the OrderNum label.

5. Edit the text of the Caption property so that it displays the value **Order Number**.

6. Click the **InvoiceAmt label box** to select it, and then edit the text of the Caption property so that it displays the value **Invoice Amount**.

7. Click the **CustomerName label box** to select it, and then edit the text of the Caption property so that it displays the value **Customer Name**.

8. Click the **Close** button ☒ on the property sheet to close it.

Next, you need to resize the Order Number and Invoice Amount label boxes so that the captions fit. You can resize both boxes at the same time.

To resize the label boxes:

1. Click an empty area of the grid to deselect any selected label boxes.

2. While pressing and holding down the **Shift** key, click the **Order Number label box** and then click the **Invoice Amount label box** to select both of them.

3. Click **Format** on the menu bar, point to **Size**, and then click **To Fit**. Access resizes the two label boxes to fit the captions.

Now you need to align the label boxes with the corresponding text boxes in the Detail section.

Access

Aligning Controls

You can align controls in a report or form using the **Align** command. This command provides options for aligning controls in different ways. For example, if you select objects in a column, you can use the Align Left option to align the left edges of the objects. Similarly, if you select objects in a row, you can use the Align Top option to align the top edges of the objects. The Align Right and Align Bottom options work in the same way. A fifth option, Align To Grid, aligns selected objects with the grid dots in the Report window. You will use the Align Right and Align Top options to align the labels in the Page Header section with their corresponding text boxes in the Detail section. Recall that the labels will serve as column headings in the report, so they must be aligned correctly with the text boxes, which will display the field values from the database.

To align the labels in the Page Header section with the text boxes in the Detail section:

1. Click the **Customer Name label** to select it. Position the pointer on the Customer Name label. When the pointer changes to 🖐, click and drag the Customer Name label to the right above the CustomerName text box.

2. Press and hold down the **Shift** key, and then click the **CustomerName text box** to select it. Both the label box and the text box are selected. You can now align them on their left edges.

3. Click **Format** on the menu bar, point to **Align**, and then click **Left** to left-align the label with the text box. See Figure 6-13.

Figure 6-13 ◄
After aligning
the Customer
Name label and
CustomerName
text box

label and text box
are left-aligned

4. Repeat Steps 1 through 3 to left-align the remaining labels with their respective text boxes.

   Now you can align the tops of all the labels. This will ensure that the column headings in the report appear in a straight row.

5. Click an empty area of the Page Header section to deselect all objects, click the **Billing Date label** to select it, press and hold down the **Shift** key, and then click the remaining labels. All of the labels are now selected.

6. Click **Format** on the menu bar, point to **Align**, and then click **Top** to top-align the labels.

7. Position the pointer on any of the selected labels. When the pointer changes to 🖐, click and drag the labels up or down as necessary until they are positioned like the labels in Figure 6-14. Leave two lines of grid dots visible below the labels to visually separate the labels from the field values when the report is printed.

Figure 6-14 ◄
Label boxes
aligned above
text boxes and
check box

Print Preview button

Now you'll save the modified report and preview it to see what it will look like when printed.

To save and preview the report:

1. Click the **Save** button 🖫 on the Report Design toolbar.

2. Click the **Print Preview** button 🔍 on the Report Design toolbar. Access displays the report in Print Preview.

3. Scroll the Print Preview window so that you can see more of the report on the screen. See Figure 6-15.

Figure 6-15 ◄
Report
displayed in
Print Preview

Zoom button

column headings in
Page Header section

records in Detail
section

TROUBLE? If your report shows a larger gap between the records in the Detail section, you need to reduce the height of the Detail section. The bottom of the Detail section should align with the bottom of the text boxes in that section. Click the Close button on the Print Preview toolbar to return to Design view, and then drag the bottom of the Detail section up until it aligns with the bottom of the text boxes in that section. Then redisplay the report in Print Preview.

You can use the Zoom button to view the entire page on the screen. This will give you a sense of how the final printed page will look.

4. Click the **Zoom** button 🔍 on the Print Preview toolbar. Access displays the full report page on the screen. See Figure 6-16.

Figure 6-16 ◄
Full report page
displayed

Print Preview
Close button

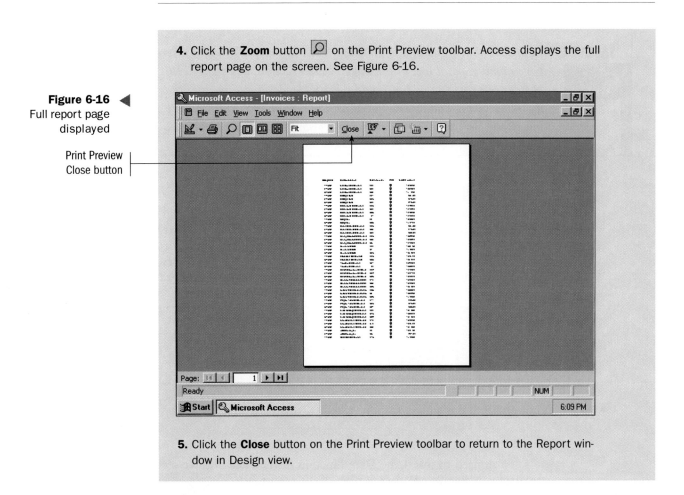

5. Click the **Close** button on the Print Preview toolbar to return to the Report window in Design view.

Quick Check

1. Describe the seven sections in an Access report.

2. What is a custom report?

3. What does the Report window in Design view have in common with the Form window in Design view? How do the two windows differ?

4. What is the Caption property for an object and when would you change it?

5. How do you left-align objects in a column?

6. What is the purpose of the Zoom button in Print Preview?

You have completed the Detail section of the report and started to work on the Page Header section. In the next session, you will complete the report according to Leonard's design.

In this session, you will complete the Invoices report. You will insert the date and page number and a line in the Page Header section, and place a title in the Report Header section. You will also add Group Header and Group Footer sections and specify the grouping and sorting fields for the records. Finally, you will add group subtotals to the Group Footer section and a grand total to the Report Footer section.

Adding the Date to a Report

According to Leonard's design, the report must include the date in the Page Header section. To add the date to a report, you insert the Date function in a text box. The **Date function** is a type of calculated control that prints the current date on a report. The format of the Date function is =Date(). The equals sign (=) indicates that this is a calculated control; Date is the name of the function; and the parentheses () indicate a function rather than simple text.

REFERENCE window

ADDING THE DATE TO A REPORT
■ Display the Report in Design view.
■ Click the Text Box tool on the toolbox.
■ Position the pointer where you want the date to appear, and then click to place the text box in the report.
■ Click the text box, type =Date(), and then press the Enter key.

You need to insert the Date function in the Page Header section so that the current date will be printed on each page of the report.

To add the Date function to the Page Header section:

1. If you took a break after the previous session, make sure your Student Disk is in the appropriate drive. Open the Restaurant database and then open the Invoices report in Design view. If necessary, maximize the Report window.

2. If necessary, click the **Toolbox** button 🔨 on the Report Design toolbar to display the toolbox.

   TROUBLE? If the toolbox is in the way of your report design, drag the toolbox to the far right side of the Report window.

3. Click the **Text Box** tool 🔲 on the toolbox.

4. Position the pointer in the Page Header section. The pointer changes to ⁺🔲.

5. When the pointer's plus symbol (+) is positioned at the top of the Page Header section at approximately the ¾-inch mark on the horizontal ruler (see Figure 6-17), click the mouse button. Access adds a text box with an attached label box to its left. Inside the text box is the description Unbound. Recall that an unbound control is a control that is not linked to a database table field.

6. Click the **Unbound text box** to position the insertion point and remove the word "Unbound," type **=Date()**, and then press the **Enter** key. See Figure 6-17.

Figure 6-17 ◀
Adding the
current date to
the report

label for the
Date function

Date function

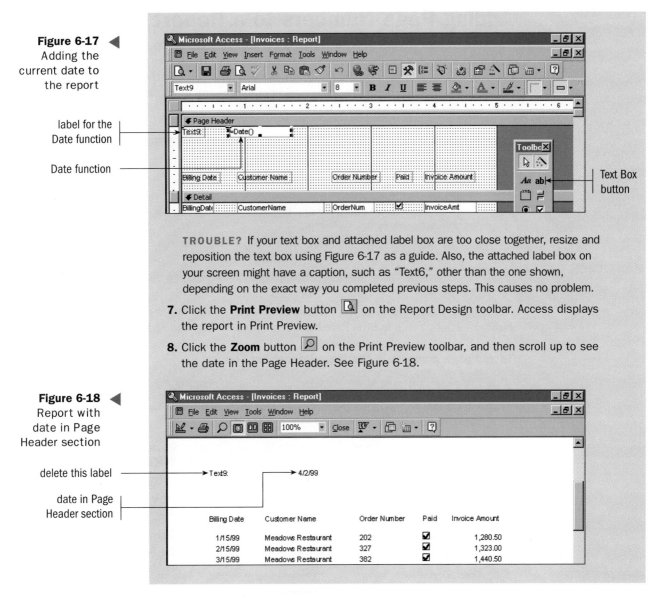

Text Box
button

TROUBLE? If your text box and attached label box are too close together, resize and reposition the text box using Figure 6-17 as a guide. Also, the attached label box on your screen might have a caption, such as "Text6," other than the one shown, depending on the exact way you completed previous steps. This causes no problem.

7. Click the **Print Preview** button 🔍 on the Report Design toolbar. Access displays the report in Print Preview.

8. Click the **Zoom** button 🔎 on the Print Preview toolbar, and then scroll up to see the date in the Page Header. See Figure 6-18.

Figure 6-18 ◀
Report with
date in Page
Header section

delete this label

date in Page
Header section

When Access prints your report, the current date appears instead of the Date function you entered in the Unbound text box. Notice that the label for the date is unnecessary, so you can delete the label box. To make the date more prominent in the Page Header, you'll increase the font size of text in the Date text box to 10 and then move the text box to the upper-left corner of the Page Header section.

To delete the Date label box and modify the Date text box:

1. Click the **Close** button on the Print Preview toolbar to return to Design view.

2. Position the pointer on the Date label box, which is located in the upper-left corner of the Page Header section.

3. Click the right mouse button to select the label box and open the shortcut menu, and then click **Cut** to delete the label.

4. Click the **Date text box**, and then drag its move handle to the upper-left corner of the Page Header section.

5. Click the **Font Size** list arrow on the Formatting toolbar, and then click **10** to change the font size of the Date text box.

You are now ready to complete the report's Page Header section by adding page numbers.

Adding Page Numbers to a Report

You can instruct Access to print the page number in a report by including an expression in the Page Header or Page Footer section. You can type the expression in an unbound control, just as you did for the Date function, or you can use the Page Numbers option on the Insert menu. The inserted page number expression automatically prints the correct page number on each page of a report.

REFERENCE window

ADDING PAGE NUMBERS TO A REPORT

- Display the report in Design view.
- Click the section where you want to place the page numbers.
- Click Insert on the menu bar, and then click Page Numbers.
- Select the formatting, position, and alignment options you want.
- Click the OK button to place the page number expression in the report.

Leonard wants the page number to be printed in the upper-right corner of the Page Header section. You'll use the Page Numbers option to insert the page number in the report.

To add page numbers in the Page Header section:

1. Click an empty area of the Page Header section to deselect the Date text box.

2. Click **Insert** on the menu bar, and then click **Page Numbers**. The Page Numbers dialog box opens.

   The Format options allow you to specify the format of the page number. Leonard wants the page numbers to appear as Page 1, Page 2, etc. This is the Page N format option. The Position options allow you to place the page numbers at the top of the page in the Page Header section or at the bottom of the page in the Page Footer section. Leonard's design shows the page numbers at the top of the page.

3. Make sure that the **Page N** option button is selected in the Format section and that the **Top of Page [Header]** option button is selected in the Position section.

   The report design shows the page numbers at the right side of the page. You can specify this placement in the Alignment list box.

4. Click the **Alignment** list arrow, and then click **Right**.

5. Make sure that the **Show Number on First Page** check box is checked so that Access prints the page number on the first page as well as all other pages. See Figure 6-19.

Figure 6-19 ◀
Completed
Page Numbers
dialog box

click to select format

click to select
position on page

indicates page
number will be
printed on all pages

6. Click the **OK** button. Access adds a text box in the upper-right corner of the Page Header section. See Figure 6-20. The expression ="Page" & [Page] in the text box means that the report will show the word "Page" followed by the page number when the report is printed.

Figure 6-20 ◄
Page number
expression
added to the
Report window

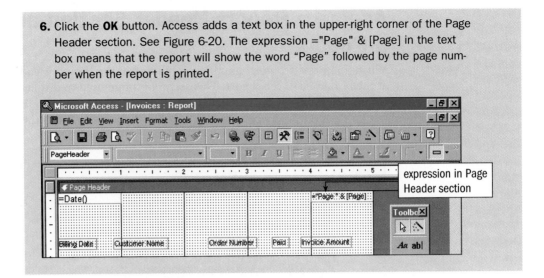

Leonard wants the text of the page number to be the same size as the text of the date. So, you need to change the font size of the Page Number text box to 10. To duplicate the formatting of the Date text box, you can use the Format Painter. The **Format Painter** allows you to copy the format of an object to other objects in the report. This makes it easy to create several objects with the same font style and size, the same color, and the same special effect applied.

To use the Format Painter to format the Page Number text box:

1. Click the **Date text box** to select it.

2. Click the **Format Painter** button ⬚ on the Report Design toolbar.

3. Click the **Page Number text box**. The Format Painter automatically formats the Page Number text box like the Date text box (with a font size of 10). The label ="Page" & [Page] is larger than the text box. Also, notice that the letter "g" in the word "Page" is not completely visible, so you need to resize the text box to fit.

4. Click the **Page Number text box**, click **Format** on the menu bar, point to **Size**, and then click **To Fit**. Access resizes the text box, and the "g" in Page is now visible. The page number expression still does not fit the text box, but the actual page number will fit when the report is printed.

5. Click the **Print Preview** button ⬚ on the Report Design toolbar. Access displays the report in Print Preview. See Figure 6-21.

Figure 6-21 ◄
Completed
Page Header
section

date ⟶ 4/2/99 → Page 1

page number ⟶

Billing Date   Customer Name   Order Number   Paid   Invoice Amount

Now that you have completed the Page Header section of the report, you are ready to add the title in the Report Header section.

Adding a Report Header Section and a Title to a Report

When you print a report, anything contained in the Report Header section appears once at the beginning of the report. This section is often used to display the report title or other identifying information. To include information in the Report Header, you must first add both a Report Header section and a Report Footer section to the report.

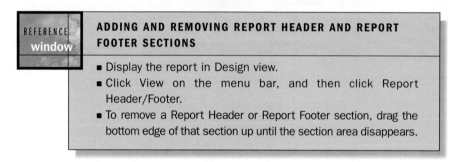

REFERENCE window

ADDING AND REMOVING REPORT HEADER AND REPORT FOOTER SECTIONS

- Display the report in Design view.
- Click View on the menu bar, and then click Report Header/Footer.
- To remove a Report Header or Report Footer section, drag the bottom edge of that section up until the section area disappears.

The report design includes the title Invoices, which you'll add to the Report Header section. To make the report title stand out, Leonard asks you to increase the report title font size from 8, the default, to 14. You'll begin by adding Report Header and Report Footer sections to the report.

To add Report Header and Report Footer sections and then add the title:

1. Click the **Close** button on the Print Preview toolbar to return to Design view.

2. Click **View** on the menu bar, and then click **Report Header/Footer**. Access places a Report Header section at the top of the Report window and a Report Footer section at the bottom. See Figure 6-22.

Figure 6-22 ◀
Report Header and Report Footer sections added

Report Header section

Report Footer section

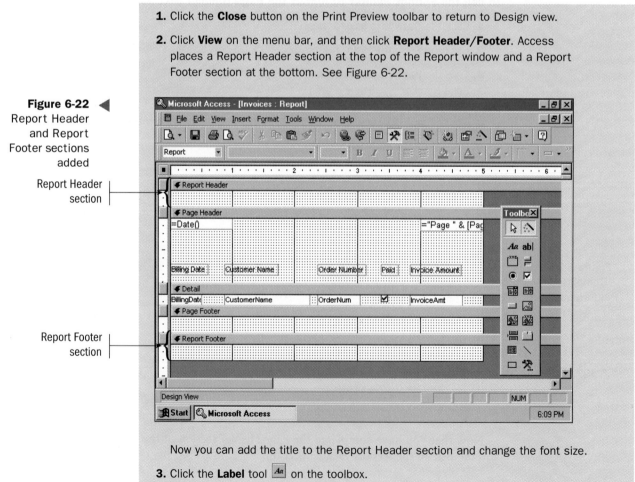

Now you can add the title to the Report Header section and change the font size.

3. Click the **Label** tool *Aa* on the toolbox.

Access

4. Position the pointer in the Report Header section. The pointer changes to ^+A.

5. Click the left mouse button when the pointer's plus symbol (+) is positioned at the top of the Report Header section at the 2-inch mark on the horizontal ruler. Access places a very narrow text box in the Page Header section. When you start typing in this text box, it will expand to accommodate the text.

6. Type **Invoices** and then press the **Enter** key. See Figure 6-23.

Figure 6-23 ◀
Adding a label
for the report
title

default font size

report title

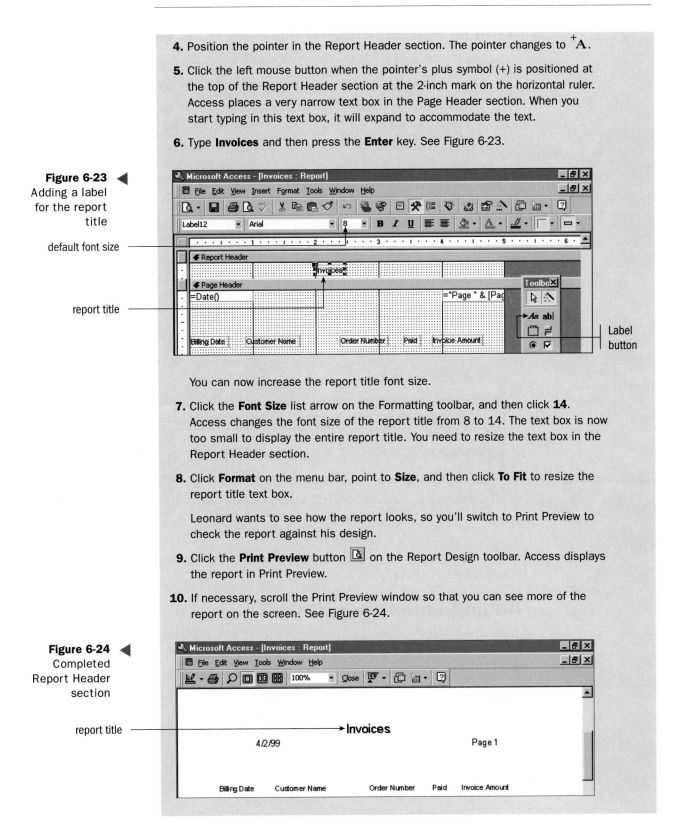

Label
button

You can now increase the report title font size.

7. Click the **Font Size** list arrow on the Formatting toolbar, and then click **14**. Access changes the font size of the report title from 8 to 14. The text box is now too small to display the entire report title. You need to resize the text box in the Report Header section.

8. Click **Format** on the menu bar, point to **Size**, and then click **To Fit** to resize the report title text box.

Leonard wants to see how the report looks, so you'll switch to Print Preview to check the report against his design.

9. Click the **Print Preview** button on the Report Design toolbar. Access displays the report in Print Preview.

10. If necessary, scroll the Print Preview window so that you can see more of the report on the screen. See Figure 6-24.

Figure 6-24 ◀
Completed
Report Header
section

report title

To make your report look more like the report design, you will reposition the column heading labels to just below the date and page number, and you'll decrease the height of the Page Header section to reduce the white space around it.

To move the labels and decrease the Page Header section height:

1. Click the **Close** button on the Print Preview toolbar to return to Design view.

2. Click an empty area of the Page Header section to deselect any selected objects.

3. While pressing and holding down the **Shift** key, click each of the five label boxes (for the report's column headings) in the Page Header section to select them.

4. Position the pointer on one of the selected labels, and when the pointer changes to ✋, click and drag the label boxes up so that they are positioned just below the date and page number. Release the mouse button when the labels are positioned one row of grid dots below the date and page number (see Figure 6-25).

   TROUBLE? If the label boxes do not move, the Page Number text box or Date text box is probably selected along with the label boxes. Repeat Steps 2 through 4.

5. Position the pointer at the bottom edge of the Page Header section. When the pointer changes to ✛, click and drag the bottom edge up to reduce the height of the Page Header section. Align the bottom edge of the section at approximately the ½-inch mark on the vertical ruler. See Figure 6-25.

Figure 6-25 ◀
Labels moved
and Page
Header section
resized

labels in new position ——————

Page
Header
section
is now
smaller

Now you can add a line beneath the column headings to separate them from the text boxes in the Detail section.

Adding Lines to a Report

You can use lines in a report to improve the report's readability and to group related information together. The Line tool on the toolbox allows you to add a line to a report or form.

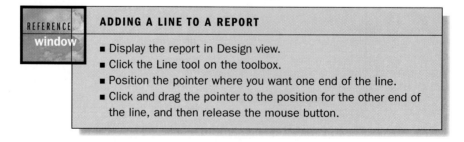

REFERENCE
window

ADDING A LINE TO A REPORT

- Display the report in Design view.
- Click the Line tool on the toolbox.
- Position the pointer where you want one end of the line.
- Click and drag the pointer to the position for the other end of the line, and then release the mouse button.

You will add a horizontal line to the bottom of the Page Header section to visually separate it from the Detail section when the report is printed.

To add a line to the report:

1. Click the **Line** tool ⬛ on the toolbox.

2. Position the pointer in the Page Header section. The pointer changes to ⁺⬛ .

3. Position the pointer's plus symbol (+) at the left edge of the Page Header section, just below the column headings.

4. Click and drag a horizontal line from left to right, ending at the right edge of the Page Header section, and then release the mouse button.

   TROUBLE? If the line is not straight, click the Undo button ⬛ on the Report Design toolbar, and then repeat Steps 1 through 4.

   Leonard wants the line to stand out more, so he asks you to increase the line's thickness.

5. Click the **Properties** button ⬛ on the Report Design toolbar to display the property sheet. The Border Width property controls the width, or thickness, of lines in a report.

6. Click the right side of the **Border Width** text box in the property sheet to display the list of border width options, and then click **3 pt**. The line's width increases. See Figure 6-26.

Figure 6-26 ◀
Changing
the width of
the line

thicker line

click to
display
list of
options

new line
width

7. Click the **Close** button ⬛ on the property sheet to close it.

8. Click the **Save** button ⬛ on the Report Design toolbar to save your changes to the report.

Leonard would like the report to print records in ascending order based on the BillingDate field and to print subtotals for each set of BillingDate field values. He also wants the records for each BillingDate group to be printed with the unpaid invoices first and in descending order by InvoiceAmt. That way, he can review the monthly billings more easily and monitor the invoices that have not been paid. To make these changes, you need to sort and group data in the report.

Sorting and Grouping Data in a Report

Access allows you to organize the records in a report by sorting the records using one or more sort keys. Each sort key can also be a grouping field. If you specify a sort key as a grouping field, you can include a Group Header section and a Group Footer section for the group. A Group Header section will typically include the name of the group, and a Group Footer section will typically include a count or subtotal for records in that group.

You use the Sorting and Grouping button on the Report Design toolbar to select sort keys and grouping fields for a report. Each report can have up to 10 sort fields, and any of the sort fields can also be grouping fields.

REFERENCE window	**SORTING AND GROUPING DATA IN A REPORT**
	■ Display the report in Design view.
	■ Click the Sorting and Grouping button on the Report Design toolbar.
	■ Click the first Field/Expression list arrow in the Sorting and Grouping dialog box, and select the field to use as the primary sort key. In the Sort Order text box, select the sort order.
	■ Repeat the previous step to select subsorting keys and their sort orders.
	■ To group data, click the field in the Field/Expression text box by which you want to group records. In the Group Properties section, select the grouping option for the field.
	■ Click the Close button on the Sorting and Grouping dialog box to close it.

Because Leonard wants records listed in ascending order based on the BillingDate field and subtotals printed for each BillingDate group, you need to specify the BillingDate field as both the primary sort key and the grouping field. Leonard also wants unpaid invoices listed first and all invoices to be sorted in descending order by InvoiceAmt. So, you need to specify the Paid field as the secondary sort key and the InvoiceAmt field as the tertiary (third) sort key.

To select the sort keys and grouping field:

1. Click the **Sorting and Grouping** button [icon] on the Report Design toolbar. The Sorting and Grouping dialog box opens.

   The top section of the Sorting and Grouping dialog box allows you to specify the sort keys for the records in the Detail section. For each sort key, the bottom section of the dialog box allows you to designate the sort key as a grouping field and to specify whether you want a Group Header section, a Group Footer section, or other options for the group.

2. Click the list arrow in the first **Field/Expression** text box to display the list of available fields, and then click **BillingDate**. Ascending is the default sort order in the Sort Order text box, so you do not need to change this setting.

   You can now designate BillingDate as a grouping field and specify that you want a Group Footer section for this group. This section will contain the subtotals for the invoices by BillingDate.

3. Click the right side of the **Group Footer** text box, and then click **Yes**. Access adds a Group Footer section called BillingDate Footer to the Report window. See Figure 6-27.

Access

Figure 6-27 ◀
Adding a Group
Footer section

primary sort key

indicates grouping
field

grouping options

Group Footer
section added

sort
order

creates
Group
Footer
section

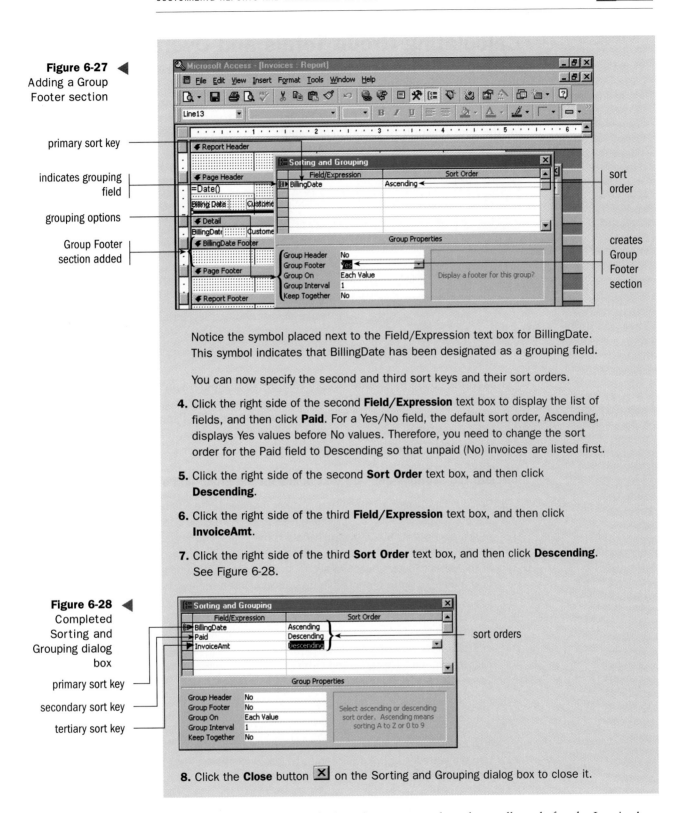

Notice the symbol placed next to the Field/Expression text box for BillingDate. This symbol indicates that BillingDate has been designated as a grouping field.

You can now specify the second and third sort keys and their sort orders.

4. Click the right side of the second **Field/Expression** text box to display the list of fields, and then click **Paid**. For a Yes/No field, the default sort order, Ascending, displays Yes values before No values. Therefore, you need to change the sort order for the Paid field to Descending so that unpaid (No) invoices are listed first.

5. Click the right side of the second **Sort Order** text box, and then click **Descending**.

6. Click the right side of the third **Field/Expression** text box, and then click **InvoiceAmt**.

7. Click the right side of the third **Sort Order** text box, and then click **Descending**. See Figure 6-28.

Figure 6-28 ◀
Completed
Sorting and
Grouping dialog
box

sort orders

primary sort key

secondary sort key

tertiary sort key

8. Click the **Close** button ☒ on the Sorting and Grouping dialog box to close it.

You are now ready to calculate the group totals and overall totals for the InvoiceAmt field values.

Calculating Group Totals and Overall Totals

Leonard wants the report to print subtotals for each BillingDate group, as well as an overall total, based on the InvoiceAmt field. To calculate these totals for the InvoiceAmt field, you use the **Sum function**. You place the Sum function in a Group Footer section to print each group's total and in the Report Footer section to print the overall total. The format for the Sum function is =Sum([*fieldname*]). To create the appropriate text boxes in the footer sections, you use the Text Box tool on the toolbox.

REFERENCE window	**CALCULATING TOTALS IN A REPORT**
	■ Display the report in Design view.
	■ Click the Text Box tool on the toolbox.
	■ Click the report section for the total—Group Footer for a group total, Page Footer for a page total, or Report Footer for an overall report total.
	■ In the displayed text box, type =Sum([*fieldname*]) where *fieldname* is the name of the field to total, and then press the Enter key.

To add the group totals and overall total to your report, you need to increase the size of the BillingDate Footer and Report Footer sections to make room for the control that will contain the Sum function. Because you will not use the Page Footer section, you can also decrease its size to zero now. Then you need to add text boxes for the Sum function in both the BillingDate Footer section and the Report Footer section.

To resize the sections and add text boxes for the group and overall totals:

1. Position the pointer on the bottom edge of the BillingDate Footer section. When the pointer changes to ✛, click and drag the bottom edge down until six rows of grid dots are visible in the BillingDate Footer section. Use the same procedure to decrease the height of the Page Footer section to 0, and increase the height of the Report Footer section to six rows of grid dots. These heights will allow sufficient room to place the totals in these sections.

2. Click the **Text Box** tool on the toolbox.

3. Position the pointer in the BillingDate Footer section, and click when the pointer's plus symbol (+) is positioned in the second row of grid dots and vertically aligned with the left edge of the InvoiceAmt text box (see Figure 6-29). Access adds a text box with an attached label box to its left.

4. Click the **Text Box** tool on the toolbox.

5. Position the pointer in the Report Footer section, and click when the pointer's plus symbol (+) is positioned in the second row of grid dots and vertically aligned with the left edge of the InvoiceAmt text box. Access adds a text box with an attached label box to its left. See Figure 6-29.

Access

Figure 6-29 ◀
Adding text
boxes in the
footer sections

sections resized

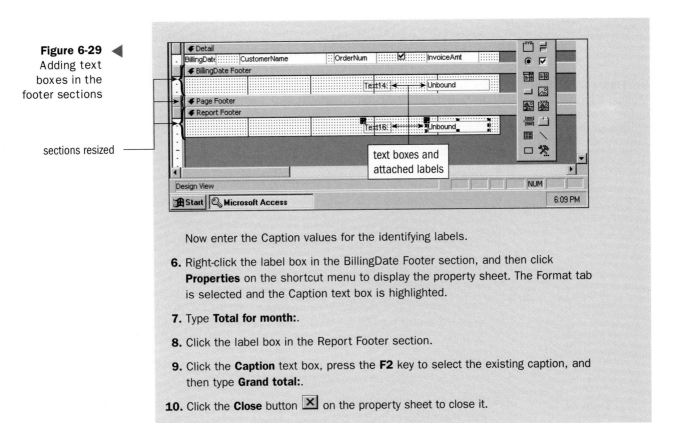

Now enter the Caption values for the identifying labels.

6. Right-click the label box in the BillingDate Footer section, and then click
Properties on the shortcut menu to display the property sheet. The Format tab
is selected and the Caption text box is highlighted.

7. Type **Total for month:**.

8. Click the label box in the Report Footer section.

9. Click the **Caption** text box, press the **F2** key to select the existing caption, and
then type **Grand total:**.

10. Click the **Close** button ☒ on the property sheet to close it.

The text box labels are not big enough to display the label values, so you need to resize
them now.

To resize the text box labels:

1. Press and hold down the **Shift** key and click the label box in the BillingDate
Footer section. Both total label boxes are now selected.

2. Click **Format** on the menu bar, point to **Size**, and then click **To Fit**. Access
resizes the label boxes to display the entire labels.

You can now add the Sum function to the two footer section text boxes. Leonard
wants the totals displayed as currency, with dollar signs and two digits after the decimal
point. You can specify this format in the Format property for the text boxes.

To add the Sum function to calculate group and overall totals:

1. Click the text box in the BillingDate Footer section to select it, click the text box
again to position the insertion point, type **=Sum([InvoiceAmt])**, and then press
the **Enter** key.

You can now resize the text box so that the total will line up with the InvoiceAmt
values in the printed report.

2. Click the middle right sizing handle of the text box and drag it to the left until the
right edge of the box is slightly to the right of the InvoiceAmt text box in the
Detail section. Refer to Figure 6-30 to help you position the right edge.

3. Click the text box in the Report Footer section to select it, click the text box
again to position the insertion point, type **=Sum([InvoiceAmt])**, and then press
the **Enter** key.

4. Resize the text box in the Report Footer section so that its right edge is slightly to the right of the InvoiceAmt text box in the Detail section. See Figure 6-30.

Figure 6-30 ◀
Adding a group
total and
overall total

labels ──

overall total ──

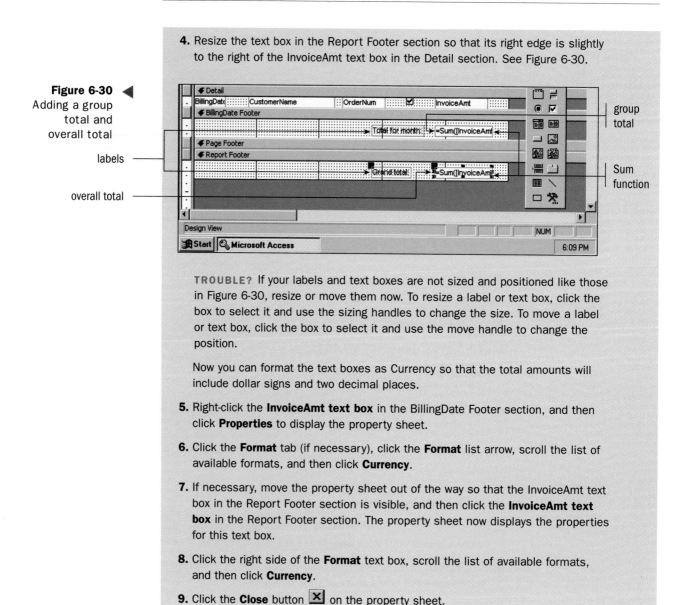

── group
total

── Sum
function

TROUBLE? If your labels and text boxes are not sized and positioned like those in Figure 6-30, resize or move them now. To resize a label or text box, click the box to select it and use the sizing handles to change the size. To move a label or text box, click the box to select it and use the move handle to change the position.

Now you can format the text boxes as Currency so that the total amounts will include dollar signs and two decimal places.

5. Right-click the **InvoiceAmt text box** in the BillingDate Footer section, and then click **Properties** to display the property sheet.

6. Click the **Format** tab (if necessary), click the **Format** list arrow, scroll the list of available formats, and then click **Currency**.

7. If necessary, move the property sheet out of the way so that the InvoiceAmt text box in the Report Footer section is visible, and then click the **InvoiceAmt text box** in the Report Footer section. The property sheet now displays the properties for this text box.

8. Click the right side of the **Format** text box, scroll the list of available formats, and then click **Currency**.

9. Click the **Close** button ☒ on the property sheet.

Leonard wants lines above both the group total and the overall total to visually separate the total amounts from the values in the Detail section. So, you'll add lines above each Sum function.

To add lines above the totals:

1. Click the **Line** tool ◥ on the toolbox.

2. Position the pointer in the BillingDate Footer section. The pointer changes to ⁺◥.

3. Position the pointer's plus symbol (+) in the first row of grid dots and vertically align it with the left edge of the InvoiceAmt text box in the Detail section above.

4. Click and drag the pointer to the right until the right end of the horizontal line is approximately above the right edge of the Sum text box (see Figure 6-31).

5. Repeat Steps 1 through 4 to add a line above the Sum function in the Report Footer section. See Figure 6-31.

Figure 6-31 ◀
Adding lines
above the
group and
overall totals

Figure 6-32 ◀
Group and
overall totals in
the report

6. Click the **Print Preview** button 🔍 on the Report Design toolbar. Access displays the first page of the report.

7. Click the **Last Page** button ▶| in the horizontal scroll bar to display the last page of the report. If necessary, scroll down to see the last BillingDate group subtotal and the overall total at the bottom of the report. See Figure 6-32.

After viewing the report, Leonard decides that the Detail section would be more readable if the BillingDate was printed only once for each group.

Hiding Duplicate Values in a Report

Your next change is to display the BillingDate value only in the first record in a group. Within a group, all BillingDate field values are the same, so if you display only the first one, you simplify the report and make it easier to read.

> **REFERENCE window**
>
> **HIDING DUPLICATE VALUES IN A REPORT**
>
> ■ Display the report in Design view.
> ■ Right-click the text box for the field whose duplicate values you want to hide, and then click Properties.
> ■ Click the right side of the Hide Duplicates text box, and then click Yes.
> ■ Click the Close button on the property sheet to close it.

To hide the duplicate BillingDate values:

1. Click the **Close** button on the Print Preview toolbar to return to Design view.

2. Right-click the **BillingDate text box** in the Detail section, and then click **Properties** to display the property sheet.

3. Click the **Format** tab (if necessary), click the right side of the **Hide Duplicates** text box, and then click **Yes**. See Figure 6-33.

Figure 6-33 ◀
Hiding the
duplicate field
values

click to display
options

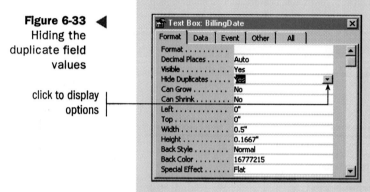

4. Click the **Close** button ☒ on the property sheet to close it.

The report is finished. You can now preview the report one more time, and then save and print the report.

To view, save, and print the report:

1. Click the **Print Preview** button ▣ on the Report Design toolbar. Access displays the first page of the report. See Figure 6-34.

Figure 6-34
The beginning
of the report in
Print Preview

duplicate values
hidden

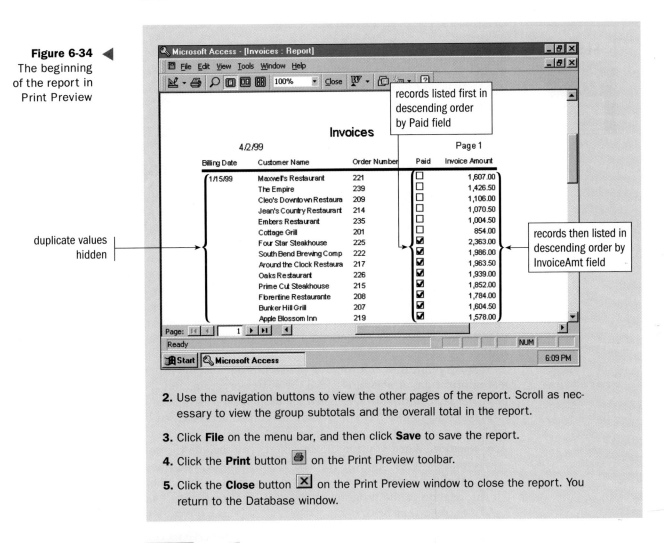

2. Use the navigation buttons to view the other pages of the report. Scroll as necessary to view the group subtotals and the overall total in the report.

3. Click **File** on the menu bar, and then click **Save** to save the report.

4. Click the **Print** button 🖨 on the Print Preview toolbar.

5. Click the **Close** button ✕ on the Print Preview window to close the report. You return to the Database window.

Quick Check

1 What is a grouping field?

2 When do you use the Text Box tool?

3 What do you type in a text box to tell Access to print the current date?

4 How do you insert a page number in a Page Header section?

5 What is the function of the Sorting and Grouping button?

6 How do you calculate group totals and overall totals?

7 Why might you want to hide duplicate values in a report that includes groups?

Leonard is very pleased with the report and feels that it will help him keep better track of outstanding invoices. In the next session, you'll use integration techniques to create another report for Leonard.

SESSION 6.3

In this session, you will integrate Access with other Windows programs. You will create an embedded chart in a report and place a linked Word document in a Report Header section, and then edit the chart and the document. Then you'll export Access data to an Excel spreadsheet.

Integrating Access with Other Programs

Leonard is so pleased with the report that you created for him that he immediately thinks of another report that would be helpful to him. He asks if you can create a report with a graph showing the total amounts for the invoices for each month.

When you create a report or form in Access, you might want to include more than just the formatted listing of records. For example, you might want to include objects such as a long text passage, a graphic image, or a chart summarizing the data. You also might want to include a graphic image or other object as a field value in a table record. Access does not allow you to create long text passages easily, nor does Access have the capability to create graphic images or charts. Instead, you can create these objects using other programs and then place them in a report or form using the appropriate integration method.

When you integrate information between programs, the program containing the original information, or **object**, is called the **source** program, and the program in which you place the same information is called the **destination** program.

Access offers three ways for you to integrate objects created by other programs:

■ **Importing.** When you import an object, you include the contents of a file in the form, report, or field. In Tutorial 5, for example, you imported a graphic image created in Microsoft Paint, a drawing program. Once an object is imported, it has no relation to the program in which it was created; it is simply an object in the form, report, or field.

■ **Embedding.** When you embed an object, you preserve its connection to the source program, which enables you to edit the object, if necessary, using the features of the source program. You can edit the object by double-clicking it, which starts the source program. Any changes you make to the object are reflected *only* in the form, report, or field in which it is embedded; the changes do not affect the original object in the file from which it was embedded. Likewise, if you start the source program outside of Access and make any changes to the original object, these changes are not reflected in the embedded object.

■ **Linking.** When you link an object to a form, report, or field, you preserve its connection to the original file. You can edit a linked object by double-clicking it, which starts the source program. Any changes you make to the object are reflected in both the original file created in the source program and the linked file in the destination program. You can also start the source program outside of Access and edit the object's original file. These changes would also be reflected in the original file and in the linked object in the Access form, report, or field.

In general, you would import an object when you simply want a copy of the object in your form, report, or field and you don't intend to make any changes to the object. You would embed or link an object when you want a copy of the object in your form, report, or field and you intend to edit the object. You embed the object if you do not want your edits to affect any other copies of the object in other programs. You link the object when you want your edits to be reflected in both the original object and the linked object.

Integrating objects among programs is made possible through the features of **Object Linking and Embedding (OLE)**. Not all programs support OLE, although most do. If you have difficulty linking or embedding objects between programs, it is possible that the program you are using does not support OLE.

The design for Leonard's report, shown in Figure 6-35, includes an embedded chart showing the totals of invoices in the report by month, and a linked text document in the Detail section. To include the chart you will use the Access Chart Wizard. The text document is a Microsoft Word file, which you will link to the report. In that way, any changes made to the original Word document will appear in the report.

Figure 6-35 ◀
Design for the
Invoice Totals
by Month
report

embedded chart

linked text document

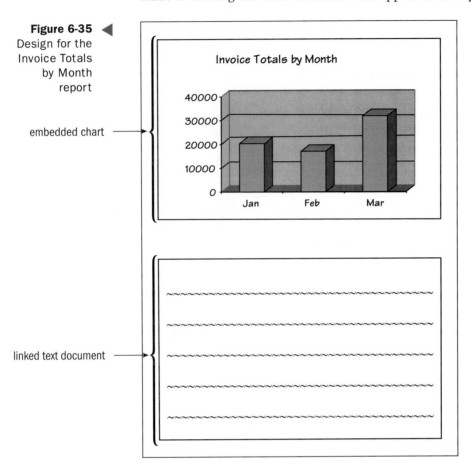

Embedding a Chart in a Report

Access provides the Chart Wizard to assist you in embedding a chart in a form or report. The chart itself is actually created by another program, Microsoft Graph, and automatically embedded by the Chart Wizard. After embedding a chart in a report, you can edit it using the Microsoft Graph program.

REFERENCE
window

EMBEDDING A CHART IN A REPORT

- In the Database window, click the Reports tab.
- Click the New button to open the New Report dialog box.
- Click Chart Wizard, select the table or query on which to base the report, and then click the OK button. Access starts the Chart Wizard.
- Follow the Chart Wizard's instructions to select the field(s) that contain the data for the chart, select the type of chart you want, specify the layout of the chart, and enter a chart title.

The Order table in the Restaurant database contains all the information necessary for the chart Leonard wants to include in his report, so you will base the report on the Order table.

To create a report with an embedded chart:

1. If you took a break after the previous session, make sure that Access is running and the Restaurant database from the Tutorial folder on your Student Disk is open. Maximize the Database window.

2. Click the **Reports** tab of the Database window, and then click the **New** button to display the New Report dialog box.

3. Click **Chart Wizard** to select it, click the list arrow for choosing the table or query on which to base the report, click **Order**, and then click the **OK** button. Access starts the Chart Wizard and displays the first Chart Wizard dialog box.

   This dialog box allows you to select the fields that contain the data for the chart. Leonard wants the chart to show the totals of the InvoiceAmt field by BillingDate, so you need to select these two fields.

4. Click **InvoiceAmt** in the Available Fields list box, and then click the ⟩ button to move the InvoiceAmt field to the Fields for Chart list.

5. Click **BillingDate** in the Available Fields list box, and then click the ⟩ button to move the BillingDate field to the Fields for Chart list.

6. Click the **Next** button. Access displays the next Chart Wizard dialog box, which allows you to select the type of chart you want.

   According to Leonard's design, the data should be represented by columns. A column chart is appropriate for showing the variation of a quantity (total of invoices) over a period of time (month). A 3-D chart adds perspective to the chart. So, you'll select a 3-D Column Chart for the report.

7. Click the **3-D Column Chart** button (second button in the first row) to select the 3-D Column Chart type. See Figure 6-36.

Figure 6-36 ◀
Selecting the type of chart

click to select 3-D Column Chart type

chart type description

The box on the right displays a brief description of the selected chart type.

8. Click the **Next** button. Access displays the next Chart Wizard dialog box. This dialog box allows you to modify the layout of the chart. You'll use the default layout and modify it later, if necessary, after seeing how the chart appears in the report.

9. Click the **Next** button to display the final dialog box, in which you enter the title that will appear at the top of the chart.

10. Type **Invoice Totals by Month** in the text box, make sure the options for displaying a legend and opening the report are selected and that the option for displaying help is not, and then click the **Finish** button. Access creates the report and displays it, with the embedded chart, in the Print Preview window.

11. Scroll the window until the entire chart is visible. See Figure 6-37.

Figure 6-37 ◄
Completed
chart in Print
Preview

chart title

3-D column chart

legend

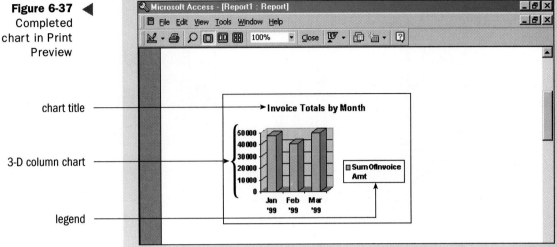

After viewing the chart, Leonard decides that it needs some modification. He'd like the chart to be larger and centered on the page. Also, he thinks that the legend is unnecessary, because the chart title is descriptive enough, and can be deleted. You can make these changes by switching to Design view and starting Microsoft Graph so that you can edit the chart.

To switch to Design view and start Microsoft Graph:

1. Click the **Close** button on the Print Preview toolbar to display the Report window in Design view. The chart appears in the Detail section of the report.

TROUBLE? If the chart appears with the incorrect legend and different columns, this is a minor Access display error and will not affect the final chart in the printed report.

2. Double-click the chart object. Microsoft Graph starts and displays the chart. See Figure 6-38.

Figure 6-38 ◄
Chart in the
Microsoft
Graph window

Report - Datasheet
window

Report - Chart
window

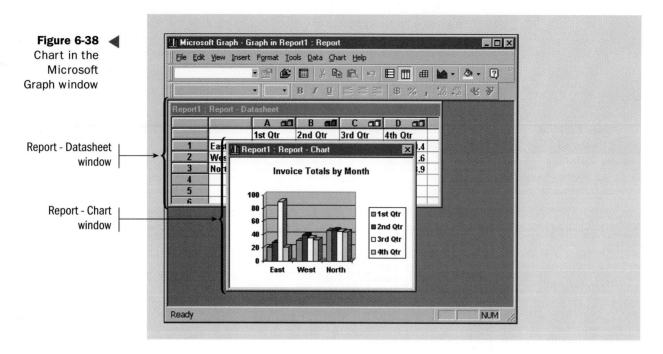

Microsoft Graph is the source program, the program in which the original chart was created by the Chart Wizard. Because the chart is embedded in the report, double-clicking the chart object starts Graph and allows you to edit the chart. The Graph window contains two smaller windows: Report - Datasheet and Report - Chart. The Report - Datasheet window displays the data on which the chart is based. The Report - Chart window displays the chart itself. All of your changes will be made in the Report - Chart window.

First, you need to enlarge the chart. Then you'll delete the legend.

To enlarge the chart and delete the legend:

1. Click the title bar of the Report - Chart window and drag the window up and to the right until it is positioned as shown in Figure 6-39. Release the mouse button.

2. Position the pointer on the lower-right corner of the Report - Chart window. When the pointer changes to ↘, click and drag the lower-right corner down and to the right until the window is the size shown in Figure 6-39. Release the mouse button.

Figure 6-39 ◀
Chart after
repositioning
and resizing
the window

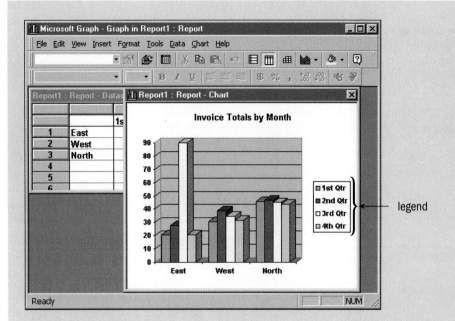

Now you can delete the legend from the chart.

3. Position the pointer on the legend object, right-click to display the shortcut menu, and then click **Clear** to remove the legend from the chart. See Figure 6-40.

Figure 6-40 ◀
Modified chart

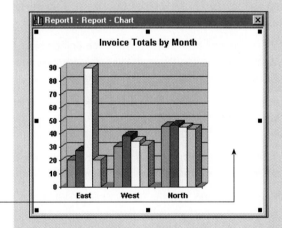

legend deleted

Finally, you'll return to the Report window in Design view and center the chart on the report page.

4. Click **File** on the menu bar, and then click **Exit & Return to Report1 : Report**. Microsoft Graph closes and the edited chart appears in the Report window. See Figure 6-41.

Figure 6-41 ◀
Edited chart in
the Report
window

resized chart ——

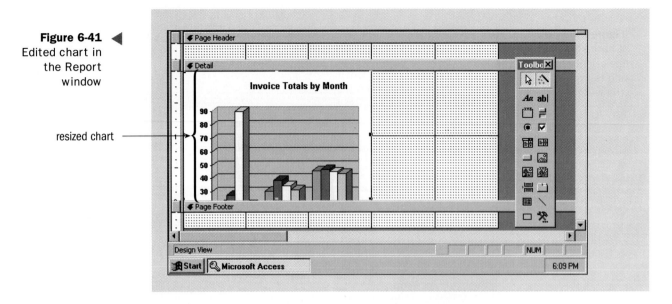

Although the chart is now larger, the box in which it appears in the Detail section is still its original size. Only a portion of the enlarged chart would show on the printed report page. So, you need to enlarge the box and center the chart in the report page.

To enlarge and center the chart in the report page:

1. Click the **Close** button ⊠ on the toolbox to close it. This will give you more room for enlarging the box containing the chart.

2. Position the pointer on the chart object. When the pointer changes to 🖑, click and drag the chart object to the right until its left edge is at the 1½-inch mark on the horizontal ruler, and then release the mouse button.

3. Position the pointer on the middle right sizing handle of the chart object. When the pointer changes to ↔, click and drag the right edge of the chart object to the 5-inch mark on the horizontal ruler, and then release the mouse button.

   Now you can make the chart object taller to accommodate the height of the resized chart. First you need to increase the height of the Detail section.

4. Move the pointer to the bottom of the Detail section. When the pointer changes to ✛, click and drag the bottom of the Detail section down a few inches, and then release the mouse button. Then adjust the bottom of the Detail section so that it is at the 3½-inch mark on the vertical ruler. Notice that the report design automatically scrolls when the pointer reaches the bottom of the screen. Use Figure 6-42 as a guide for placing the bottom of the Detail section.

   TROUBLE? If you did not position the bottom of the Detail section correctly, simply click and drag the bottom of the Detail section up or down as necessary. Then continue with the steps.

   Now you can increase the height of the chart object in the Detail section.

5. If necessary, scroll up until the bottom of the chart object is visible, click the chart object to select it, and then position the pointer on the middle bottom sizing handle of the chart object. When the pointer changes to ↕, click and drag the bottom of the chart object to the bottom of the Detail section. See Figure 6-42.

Figure 6-42 ◀
Chart object
and Detail
section resized

Figure 6-43 ◀
Chart report in
Print Preview

6. Click the **Print Preview** button [icon] on the Report Design toolbar. Access displays the first page of the report. Notice that the correct chart is displayed. Scroll to see more of the chart. See Figure 6-43.

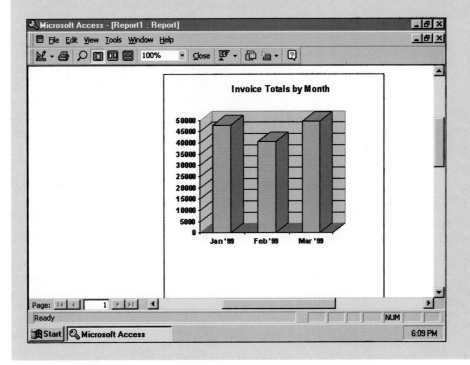

Now that the chart is properly positioned on the report page, you are ready to place the text document in the Detail section. Because you've made many changes to the report design, you'll save it first.

To save the report:

1. Click **File** on the menu bar, and then click **Save**. The Save As dialog box opens.

2. Type **Invoice Totals by Month**, and then press the **Enter** key. Access saves the report on your Student Disk.

Linking a Word Document in a Report

The report design in Figure 6-35 shows some text below the chart. This text explains the contents of the chart. You can add text to an Access report by creating a label control, but a label control is not designed to hold a large amount of text. It is inconvenient to enter and edit more than a short label in a label control. Instead, you can create a larger text document using a word-processing program, such as Microsoft Word, and then insert the document as a linked object in the report.

In the past, Barbara has created similar reports for Leonard using Microsoft Word and drawing the chart by hand. She has already created a text document that you can include in your report. You will insert this Word document as a linked object in the Detail section of your report. That way, if Barbara later changes the document in Word, the changes will be reflected automatically in the Detail section of the Invoice Totals by Month report.

REFERENCE window

INSERTING A LINKED OBJECT IN A REPORT

- Display the report in Design view.
- Click the Unbound Object Frame button on the toolbox.
- Position the pointer at the upper-left corner for the linked object, click and drag the pointer to the lower-right corner for the linked object, and then release the mouse button.
- Click the Create from File option button in the Insert Object dialog box.
- In the File text box, enter the name of the file containing the object; or click the Browse button and use the Browse dialog box to locate and select the file.
- Click the Link check box to select it.
- Click the OK button.

The Word document contains several lines of text. To make room for it in the Detail section, you need to resize the Detail section; then you'll insert the linked document.

To resize the Detail section and insert the linked text document:

1. Click the **Close** button on the Print Preview toolbar to return to Design view.

2. Scroll down until the bottom of the Detail section is visible. Position the pointer at the bottom of the Detail section. When the pointer changes to ✛ , click and drag the bottom of the Detail section down until the bottom is at the 5-inch mark on the vertical ruler. Release the mouse button.

3. Click the **Toolbox** button 🛠 on the Report Design toolbar to display the toolbox.

4. Click the **Unbound Object Frame** tool 🖼 on the toolbox.

5. Position the pointer at the 3¾-inch mark on the vertical ruler and the 1½-inch mark on the horizontal ruler. Click and drag the pointer to the bottom of the Detail section (the 5-inch mark on the vertical ruler) and the 5-inch mark on the horizontal ruler. Release the mouse button. Access inserts an unbound object frame in the Detail section and opens the Insert Object dialog box.

   The Word document is a file stored on your Student Disk, so you need to create the linked object from a file.

6. Click the **Create from File** option button to select it. The dialog box changes to display the File text box, the Browse button, and the Link check box. See Figure 6-44.

Figure 6-44 ◀
Insert Object
dialog box

click to create an
object from a file

click to locate the file

click to create a link

7. Click the **Browse** button to display the Browse dialog box. If necessary, use the Drives and Directories list boxes to display the contents of the Tutorial folder on your Student Disk.

8. In the files list box, click **ChartTxt.doc** to select the Word document file, and then click the **Open** button. The Browse dialog box closes.

Next, you must indicate that you want to link to the document file rather than embed it in the report.

9. Click the **Link** check box to select it, and then click the **OK** button. The Insert Object dialog box closes, and the text document is placed in the Detail section. See Figure 6-45.

Figure 6-45 ◀
Linked text
document in
the Detail
section

linked text document

10. Click the **Print Preview** button 🔍 on the Report Design toolbar, and then click the **Zoom** button 🔍 on the Print Preview toolbar to view the entire report page. See Figure 6-46.

Figure 6-46 ◄
Completed
report in Print
Preview

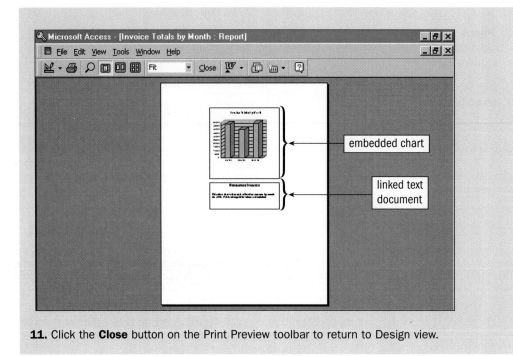

11. Click the **Close** button on the Print Preview toolbar to return to Design view.

Because you checked the Link check box, the text document is *linked* to the original Word document. Any changes made to the original document will be reflected automatically in the text document in your Access report. If you had not checked the Link check box, the text document would be *embedded*.

Barbara wants to make a change to the ChartTxt document. She wants to add a sentence indicating that the chart is updated monthly. Because the report object is linked to the Word document, you'll make this change to the original document using the Word program, and then view the results in the Report window in Access.

To edit the original document in Word:

1. Click the **Start** button on the taskbar, point to **Programs**, and then click **Microsoft Word**. The Word 97 program starts and the Word window opens. See Figure 6-47.

Figure 6-47 ◄
Word window

Open button ─────

Save button ─────

> **TROUBLE?** If you cannot locate Word on the Programs menu, it might be located in another program group on your computer. Try looking through program groups to find it. If you cannot locate Word anywhere, ask your instructor or technical support person for assistance. If the Word program is not installed on your computer, click the Access window to close the Programs menu and then skip Steps 2 through 7.

2. Click the **Open** button 🖙 on the Standard toolbar to display the Open dialog box. Use the Look in list box to open the Tutorial folder on your Student Disk, and then double-click **ChartTxt** in the file list to open the document file.

   You'll add the new sentence in its own paragraph, below the existing text.

3. Click at the end of the last sentence in the text, and then press the **Enter** key to start a new paragraph.

4. Type **This chart is updated monthly.** (Include the period.) See Figure 6-48.

Figure 6-48 ◀
Modified Word
document

new sentence added ——————→

> **TROUBLE?** If you make a typing error, use the Backspace key to erase the incorrect text and then retype the text correctly.

5. Click the **Save** button 🖫 on the Standard toolbar to save the modified document, and then click the **Close** button ✕ on the Word window title bar to exit Word. The Word window closes, and the Access Report window in Design view becomes active.

6. If necessary, scroll down to see the text object.

The text object in the Detail section does not yet reflect the change you made in the original Word document. If you were to close the Report window and return to the Database window and then reopen the report, Access would update the link and the report would show the new sentence you added. Access automatically updates any links to linked objects whenever a form or report is opened. However, you can also update a link manually to see a change reflected.

To update the link manually:

1. Click **Edit** on the menu bar, and then click **OLE/DDE Links** to display the Links dialog box. This dialog box allows you to select the linked object or objects to be updated.

2. Click **charttxt** in the Links list box to select this file. See Figure 6-49.

Figure 6-49 ◀
Updating the
link manually

click to select object
to be updated

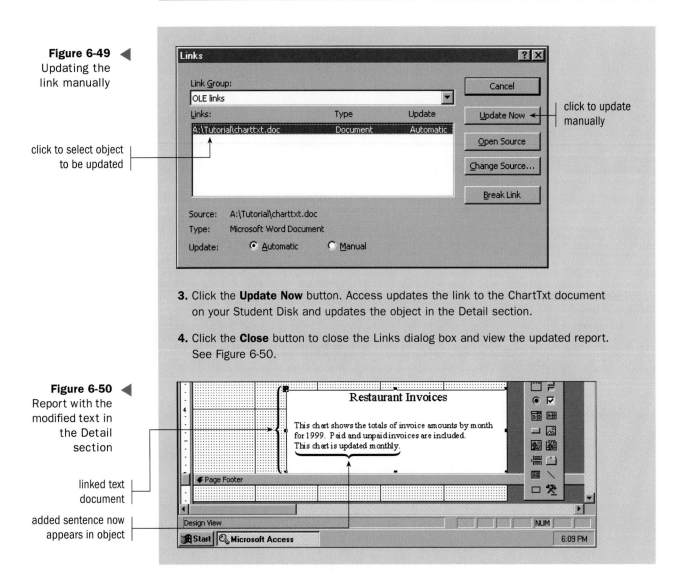

3. Click the **Update Now** button. Access updates the link to the ChartTxt document on your Student Disk and updates the object in the Detail section.

4. Click the **Close** button to close the Links dialog box and view the updated report. See Figure 6-50.

Figure 6-50 ◀
Report with the
modified text in
the Detail
section

linked text
document

added sentence now
appears in object

The report is now complete. You can save the report design, print the report for Leonard, and then close the Report window.

To save, print, and close the report:

1. Click the **Save** button 🖫 on the Report Design toolbar.

2. Click the **Print** button 🖨 on the Report Design toolbar to print the report.

3. Click the **Close** button ⊠ on the Report window to close it and return to the Database window.

Leonard views the printed report and is pleased with the results. Being able to integrate Access data with other programs, Graph and Word in this instance, makes it easier to analyze the data. Leonard has one more integration task for you to complete. He wants to perform some more detailed analysis on invoice data. To do so, he wants to work with the data in a Microsoft Excel worksheet.

Exporting an Access Table as an Excel Worksheet

A spreadsheet program, such as Microsoft Excel, is designed to assist you in analyzing data. Although a database management program provides some data analysis capabilities, it is primarily designed for storing and retrieving records. A spreadsheet program has many more powerful tools for analyzing data to create budgets, projections, and models.

You can export the contents of most Access objects, including tables, forms, and reports, to other Windows programs, including Excel.

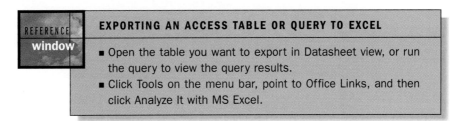

REFERENCE window

EXPORTING AN ACCESS TABLE OR QUERY TO EXCEL

- Open the table you want to export in Datasheet view, or run the query to view the query results.
- Click Tools on the menu bar, point to Office Links, and then click Analyze It with MS Excel.

Like many business managers, Leonard uses a spreadsheet program as a planning and budgeting tool for his business. He would like to use the invoice information from past months to help him project future sales. He asks you to transfer the results of the Invoice Statistics by Billing Date query to an Excel worksheet so that he can use the results to create the necessary projections. Recall that when Access runs a query, the query results are a temporary display of the records in a table. After you run the Invoice Statistics by Billing Date query, you can export the query results, just as you would any other table, directly to Excel.

To open and run the query, and then export the query results to Excel:

1. Click the **Queries** tab in the Database window to display the queries list.

2. Click **Invoice Statistics by Billing Date**, and then click the **Open** button to run the query. Access displays the query results.

3. Click **Tools** on the menu bar, point to **Office Links**, and then click **Analyze It with MS Excel**. Access automatically starts Excel and places the query results in the worksheet. See Figure 6-51.

Figure 6-51 ◀
Query results in the Excel worksheet

cell A4 ——

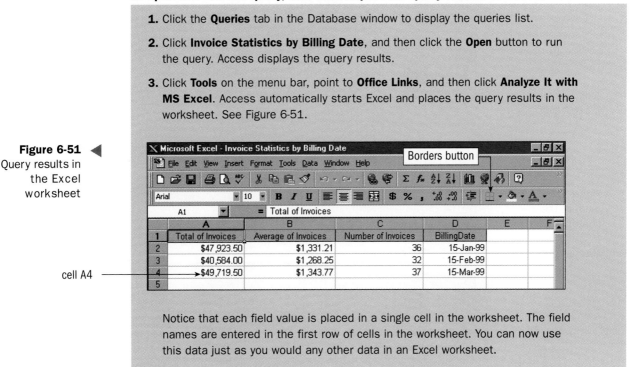

Notice that each field value is placed in a single cell in the worksheet. The field names are entered in the first row of cells in the worksheet. You can now use this data just as you would any other data in an Excel worksheet.

Leonard wants to see the total of the invoice amounts, so he asks you to create a grand total for the data in column A. You'll first create a line to separate the grand total amount from the other invoice amounts.

To create the grand total amount:

1. Click cell **A4** to select the first cell in the last row of data in column A (see Figure 6-51).

2. Click the list arrow for the **Borders** button on the Formatting toolbar to display the list of border options, and then click the heavy bottom border (the second choice in row two). See Figure 6-52. Access places a heavy border on the bottom of cell A4.

Figure 6-52 ◄
Adding a bottom border to the cell

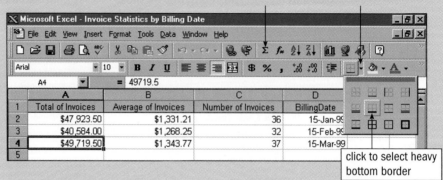

3. Click cell **A5** to select it, and then click the **AutoSum** button Σ on the Standard toolbar. Excel automatically creates the formula to sum the contents of the cells above cell A5. See Figure 6-53.

Figure 6-53 ◄
Formula to sum the contents of cells A2 through A4

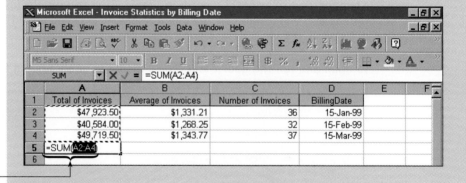

4. Press the **Enter** key to enter the formula. Excel displays the sum of the contents of cells A2 through A4 in cell A5. See Figure 6-54.

Figure 6-54 ◄
Sum of the contents of cells A2 through A4

Leonard plans on doing more work with the data in Excel later. For now, you can save the worksheet, close Excel, and return to the Database window in Access.

Saving the Worksheet and Exiting Excel

When you exported the Invoice Statistics by Billing Date query results to Excel, the worksheet was automatically saved with the name Invoice Statistics by Billing Date. Because you have made changes to the worksheet, you need to save them now before exiting Excel. Then you can exit Access.

To save the worksheet, exit Excel, and then exit Access:

1. Click the **Save** button 🖫 on the Standard toolbar. Excel saves the modified worksheet.

   TROUBLE? If Excel displays a dialog box indicating that this worksheet was created by a previous version, click the Yes button to save the worksheet.

2. Click the **Close** button ✖ on the Excel window title bar to exit Excel and return to the Database window in Access.

3. Click the **Close** button ✖ on the Access window to close Access. You return to the Windows 95 desktop.

When you exported the query results to Excel, Access placed a copy of the query results in the worksheet. The query results are not linked or embedded in the Excel worksheet, so any later changes made to the Access data will not be reflected in the Excel worksheet. Similarly, any changes made in the worksheet will not affect the Access data.

Quick Check

1. Why might you want to embed or link an object in an Access report?

2. What is the difference between embedding and linking?

3. What is OLE?

4. When you insert an object in a report or form using the Insert Object dialog box, how do you specify that the object is to be linked rather than embedded?

5. If you modify a linked object, in what program do you make the changes?

6. What are two ways to update links to linked objects in a report?

7. How do you export a table or the results of a query to Excel?

Leonard is very pleased with the new reports and the Excel worksheet you created. The reports and the integrated data will help him monitor and analyze the invoice activity of Valle Coffee's restaurant customers more easily.

Tutorial Assignments

Barbara wants you to make several changes to the Products database. She asks you to create a report based on the Coffee table. The report will contain Report Header, Page Header, Detail, Page Footer, and Report Footer sections. Barbara wants the records to be grouped on the value in the CoffeeType field, and she wants you to add a CoffeeType Header section. Barbara would also like you to embed a chart in a new report. The chart should be a pie chart showing the distribution of CoffeeType values. Finally, Barbara asks you to create an Excel worksheet based on the query results from the Pricing query.

1. Make sure your Student Disk is in the appropriate disk drive, start Access, and then open the Products database located in the TAssign folder on your Student Disk.

2. Create a new report based on the Coffee table. Figure 6-55 shows the completed report. Refer to the figure as a guide as you complete Steps 3 through 11.

Figure 6-55

14-point, bold, italic

3. Include the following sections in your report: Report Header, Page Header, Detail, and Page Footer.

4. At the top of the Report Header section, enter and format the report title. In the Page Header section, enter the current date. Position the column heading labels below the date. Add a single line below the column headings and change the necessary captions to match the figure.

5. Specify CoffeeType as the grouping field. Sort the records in ascending order by CoffeeName.

6. Create a Group Header section for the CoffeeType grouping field. Place the CoffeeType field value in the CoffeeType Header section.

7. In the Detail section, include all other field values from the Coffee table.

8. In the Page Footer section, include a right-aligned page number.

9. Use a word-processing program to create a short document describing the contents of the report. Save the document as Coffee Report Description. Link the document to your report, placing it in the Report Header section.

10. When you finish creating the report, save it as Coffee Types.

11. Print the entire report.

12. Use the Chart Wizard to create a report based on the Coffee table. Create a column chart showing the distribution of CoffeeType values. Select CoffeeType as the only field in the chart and select the Column Chart chart type. Save the report as CoffeeType Chart, and then print the report.

13. Run the Pricing query and export the query results to Excel. Save the Excel worksheet, print the worksheet, and then exit Excel.

14. Close the Products database, and then exit Access.

Case Problems

1. Ashbrook Mall Information Desk Sam Bullard needs a custom report for the MallJobs database and he wants to export the data in the Store table to an Excel worksheet. You will create the necessary report and worksheet by completing the following:

1. Make sure your Student Disk is in the appropriate disk drive, start Access, and then open the MallJobs database located in the Cases folder on your Student Disk.

2. Create a custom report based on the Store Jobs query. Figure 6-56 shows the completed report. Refer to the figure as you complete Steps 3 through 11.

Figure 6-56 ◄

3. Include the following sections in your report: Report Header, Page Header, Detail, and Page Footer.

4. At the top of the Report Header section, enter and format the report title. At the top of the Page Header section, enter the current date. Position the column heading labels below the date. Add a single line below the column headings and change the necessary captions to match the figure.

5. Specify Position as the grouping field. There is no sorting field. Create a Position Group Header section and include the Position field value in the section.

6. In the Detail section, include all other field values from the Store Jobs query.

7. In the Page Footer section, include a page number centered at the bottom of the page.

8. Use a word-processing program, such as Word, WordPad, or NotePad, to create a short document describing the contents of the report. Save the document as Store Jobs Report Description. Link the document to your report, placing it in the Report Header section.

9. Use the Special Effect button on the Report Design toolbar to create a Shadowed special effect for the report title in the Report Header section.

10. When you finish creating the report, save it as Store Jobs.

11. Print the report.

12. Export the Store table data to Excel. Save the Excel worksheet, print the worksheet, and then exit Excel.

13. Close the MallJobs database, and then exit Access.

2. Professional Litigation User Services Raj Jawahir wants you to create a custom report for the Payments database. The report will be based on the results of a query you will create using the Firm and Payments tables. Raj also asks you to export the Payments data to Excel for analysis. You will create the query, report, and worksheet by completing the following:

1. Make sure your Student Disk is in the disk drive, start Access, and then open the Payments database located in the Cases folder on your Student Disk.

2. Create a query based on the Firm and Payments tables. Select the Firm#, FirmName and PLUSAcctRep fields from the Firm table and all fields except Firm# from the Payments table. Save the query as Account Representatives.

3. Create a custom report based on the Account Representatives query. Figure 6-57 shows the completed report. Refer to the figure as a guide as you complete Steps 4 through 15.

Figure 6-57

14-point, bold

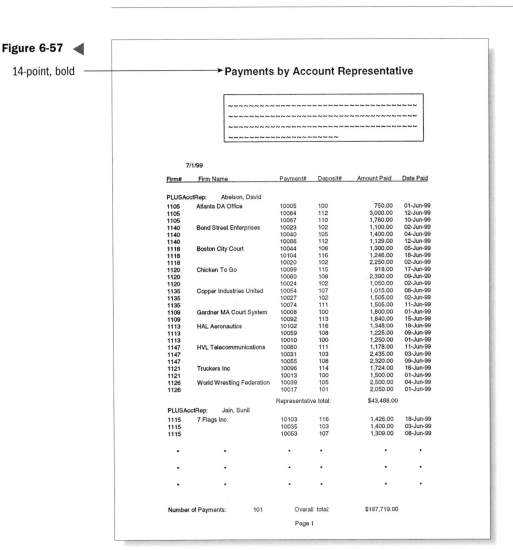

4. Include the following sections in your report: Report Header, Page Header, Detail, Page Footer, and Report Footer.

5. In the Report Header section, enter and format the report title.

6. At the top of the Page Header section, enter the current date. Position the column headings below the date. Add a single line below the column headings and change the necessary captions to match the figure.

7. Specify PLUSAcctRep as the grouping field. Sort the records in ascending order by FirmName. Create a PLUSAcctRep Group Header section and a PLUSAcctRep Group Footer section. In the PLUSAcctRep Header section, include the PLUSAcctRep field value.

8. In the Detail section, include all other field values from the Account Representatives query. Hide duplicate values for the Firm# and FirmName fields.

9. In the Page Footer section, include a centered page number.

10. In the PLUSAcctRep Footer section, include a subtotal of the AmtPaid field values.

11. In the Report Footer section, include a grand total of the AmtPaid field values.

12. In the Report Footer section, include a count of the Payment# values. Use the expression =Count([Payment#]) and enter the label shown in the figure.

13. Use a word-processing program, such as Word, WordPad, or NotePad, to create a short document describing the contents of the report. Save the document as Account Representatives Report Description. Link the document to your report, placing it in the Report Header section.

14. Save the report as Payments By Account Representative.

15. Print the report.

16. Run the Account Representatives query and export the query results to Excel. Print the Excel worksheet.

17. Modify the Excel worksheet to calculate the average payment amount. (*Hint:* Click the Paste Function button on the toolbar.) Label the cell appropriately. Save the modified worksheet, and then exit Excel.

18. Close the Payments database, and then exit Access.

3. Best Friends Noah Warnick asks you to create a custom report for the Walks database so that he can keep better track of the participants in their Walk-A-Thons. The report will be based on the Walker table. Also, Sheila Warnick needs to analyze the pledges and asks you to create a worksheet based on the Pledge Statistics by Walker query. You'll create the report and worksheet by completing the following:

1. Make sure your Student Disk is in the disk drive, start Access, and then open the Walks database located in the Cases folder on your Student Disk.

2. Create a report based on the Walker table. Figure 6-58 shows the completed report. Refer to the figure as a guide as you complete Steps 3 through 12.

Figure 6-58 ◄

16-point, bold ——————

3. Include the following sections in your report: Report Header, Page Header, Detail, and Page Footer.

4. At the top of the Report Header section, enter and format the report title.

5. Use the Special Effect button on the Report Design toolbar to apply the Raised special effect to the title label in the Report Header section.

6. At the top right of the Page Header section, enter the current date. Position the column heading labels below the date. Add a single line below the column headings and change the necessary captions to match the figure.

7. Specify Distance as the grouping field. Sort the records in ascending order by LastName. Add the Distance Group Header section and include the Distance field value and the label "Distance:" in the section. Format the Distance field value and label as 10-point italic.

8. In the Detail section, include all other field values from the Walker table.

9. In the Page Footer section, include a page number at the center of the page.

10. Use a word-processing program to create a short document describing the contents of the report. Save the document as Walkers Report Description. Link the document to your report, placing it in the Report Header section.

11. When you finish creating the report, save it as Walkers.

12. Print the report.

13. Run the Pledge Statistics by Walker query and export the query results to Excel. Save the Excel worksheet, print the worksheet, and then exit Excel.

14. Close the Walks database, and then exit Access.

4. Lopez Lexus Dealerships Maria and Hector Lopez need two new custom reports for the Lexus database. Hector asks you to create a report based on the Cars table by modifying a report you will create using the Report Wizard. Maria asks you to create a custom report based on the Cars table. The Cars records will be grouped by Model and you will include subtotals and totals for the Cost and SellingPrice fields. They also ask you to create an Excel chart based on the query results from the Cost vs Selling query. Complete the following:

1. Make sure your Student Disk is in the disk drive, start Access, and then open the Lexus database located in the Cases folder on your Student Disk.

2. Use the Report Wizard to create a report in the Corporate style based on the Cars table. Select all the fields from the table in the order in which they are stored in the table. Do not select a grouping field, use the tabular layout, and enter Cars by Year as the report title. Save the report as Cars By Year.

3. Move the day/date (Now()) and page number text fields to the Report Header section. Adjust the font size and widths in the column headings so that the entire labels are visible.

4. Preview and then print the entire report.

5. Save the report, and then return to the Database window.

6. Create a blank report based on the Cars table.

7. Sketch a design for the report based on the requirements described in Steps 8 through 13, and then create the report following these steps.

8. Include the following sections in your report: Page Header, Detail, Group Footer, and Report Footer.

9. At the top of the Page Header section, enter the report title Cars by Model and Year. Enter the current date and the page number in appropriate locations in this section. Below these elements, add a row of column headings with these labels: Manufacturer, Model, Year, Cost, and Selling Price. Add a single horizontal line below the column headings.

10. In the Detail section, include the field values for Manufacturer, Model, Year, Cost, and Selling Price. Hide duplicate values for the Manufacturer field.

11. In the Group Footer section, print the group total for the Cost and Selling Price fields. Select Model as the primary sort key and as the grouping field. Select Year as the secondary sort key, but do not use it as a grouping field. Choose ascending sort order for the sort keys.

12. Use a word-processing program, such as Word, WordPad, or NotePad, to create a short document describing the contents of the report. Save the document as Cars Report Description. Link the document to your report, placing it in the Report Header section.

13. In the Report Footer section, print the overall totals for the Cost and Selling Price fields.

14. When you finish creating the report, save it as Cars By Model And Year.

15. Print the entire report.

16. Use the Chart Wizard to create a pie chart report based on the Model field in the Cars table. Each wedge in the pie should represent the count of cars of each model. Insert percents as labels for each wedge. Save the report as Model Pie Chart. Print the report.

17. Run the Cost vs Selling query and export the query results to Excel. Print the Excel worksheet.

18. Use Excel's Chart Wizard to create a chart based on the Cost vs Selling query. Create an X-Y chart with Cost on the x-axis and Selling on the y-axis. Print the worksheet with the chart. Save the worksheet, and then exit Excel.

19. Hector has pictures of some of the cars available for sale. He asks you to include these pictures with the appropriate records in the Cars table. You'll embed the pictures as OLE objects in a new field by doing the following:
   a. Open the Cars table in Design view.
   b. Create a new field named Picture. Select OLE Object as the data type for the new field.
   c. Save the table design and switch to Datasheet view.
   d. Click the Picture field for the record for VehicleID 3N4TA (record 1). Click Insert on the menu bar, and then click Object to display the Insert Object dialog box.
   e. Click the Create from File option button, and then click the Browse button. Open the file 3N4TA.bmp. Click the OK button in the Insert Object dialog box to insert the object in the field. Notice that the value Bitmap Image appears in the Picture field for the first record.
   f. Repeat Steps d and e to enter field values for VehicleID 79XBF (record 3) and VehicleID AAEAF (record 6). The filenames are 79XBF.bmp and AAEAF.bmp, respectively.
   g. Double-click the Picture field value for the first record to view the picture. Access automatically opens the Paint application to display the picture. When you are done viewing the picture, close the Paint window.
   h. Repeat Step g to view the picture for record 3 and then for record 6.
   i. Close the Cars table.

20. Close the Lexus database, and then exit Access.

TUTORIAL 7

Using the World Wide Web and Hyperlink Fields

Creating Hypertext Documents for Valle Coffee

CASE

Valle Coffee

Leonard, Barbara, and Kim are pleased with the design and contents of the Restaurant database. Their work has been made much easier because they are able to obtain the information they need from the database quickly. Barbara feels that others in the company would benefit from access to the Restaurant database. Leonard asks whether the database can be made available to employees over the company network. That way, employees could obtain company information through their desktop computers rather than through paper forms.

Kim mentions that most employees, such as the customer representatives in the Marketing Department, do not need access to the entire database nor should they be able to make changes to the database objects. She proposes publishing the necessary Access data on the company's internal network as World Wide Web documents.

In this tutorial you will use the Access tools for publishing data to the World Wide Web to publish objects in the Restaurant database.

SESSION

7.1

In this session, you will save an Access table and an Access report in HTML format using the Publish to the Web Wizard. You will view the HTML files using a Web browser. You will also use templates to enhance the appearance of the HTML files and save your Publish to the Web Wizard choices in a profile. Then, you'll use the saved profile to create updated HTML files. Finally, you will import data from an HTML file into an Access table.

Using the World Wide Web

The **World Wide Web** (also called **WWW** or simply the **Web**) is a vast collection of linked documents that reside on computers around the world. These computers are linked together in a public worldwide network called the **Internet**. A computer that publishes documents on the World Wide Web must be running special server software. A computer running server software is called a **Web server** and it has an Internet address called a **Uniform Resource Locator (URL)**. If your computer has a telephone connection, such as a modem, and you have an account with an Internet service provider, you can connect your computer to any Web server and view the World Wide Web documents published there. You view the documents using a program called a **Web browser**. Popular Web browsers, like Microsoft Internet Explorer and Netscape Navigator, are often bundled with other application software.

A World Wide Web document contains the necessary instructions for your Web browser to display text and graphics. These instructions, called **tags**, describe how text is formatted, where graphic images are displayed, the background color, and other visual characteristics of the Web page. Certain tags, called **hyperlinks**, link one Web document to another. When you click hyperlink text, the linked document is displayed. Hyperlinks connect Web documents throughout the Internet and these connections form the World Wide Web. Hyperlinks are the primary means of navigation in the World Wide Web.

You can create a World Wide Web page by typing the necessary instructions, using the **HyperText Markup Language (HTML)**, into a word-processing document and saving the document on a disk. Some programs, such as Access, have built-in tools to convert objects to HTML documents for viewing on the Web. Figure 7-1 illustrates the process of creating a Web page using Access and viewing it with a Web browser.

Figure 7-1 ◀
Creating and
viewing a Web
page

Figure 7-2 shows a Web page and the HTML document that creates it.

Figure 7-2 ◀
A World Wide
Web page

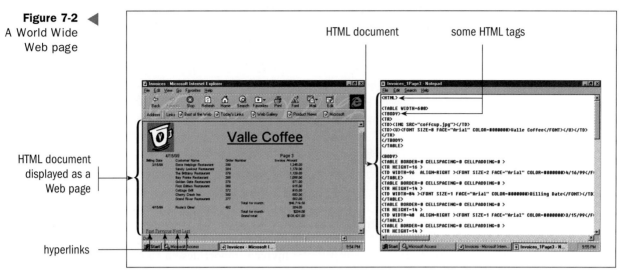

HTML document
displayed as a
Web page

hyperlinks

The HTML document in Figure 7-2 contains the necessary information to create a Web page that displays one page of the Invoices report. The words enclosed in angle brackets (<>) are HTML tags. The Web page shows how this document looks when you view it using a Web browser. Notice the words First, Previous, Next, and Last at the bottom of the Web page. These are hyperlinks to other Web pages, in this case to other pages of the Invoices report. Hyperlinks are usually displayed in a different color from other text on a Web page and are often underlined to indicate that they are hyperlinks.

Web pages that are created from an Access database can be either static or dynamic. A **static** page reflects the state of the database when the page is created. Subsequent changes to the database records are not reflected in the Web page. A **dynamic** page is updated automatically each time the page is viewed and reflects the current state of the database at that time.

To publish information in the Restaurant database to the World Wide Web, you must convert Access objects to HTML format. When you have created the HTML documents, you can place them on the company Web server where they can be viewed on any computer on the network using a Web browser. Of course, Valle Coffee does not want its private database to be available worldwide, so your documents will be placed on a Web server dedicated to the company's private network. Private networks, called **intranets**, are common in companies, schools, and other organizations. Data can be shared on an intranet in much the same way as on the Internet, but access is restricted to members of the organization.

Saving Access Objects in an HTML File

Leonard has asked you to create HTML documents for the Customer table and the Invoices report. He wants this data to be available to customer representatives working outside the office. The customer representatives will access the company's intranet from laptop computers connected to telephone lines. Leonard wants these Web pages to be static, because the customer representatives need to view them only once a month, when completing their monthly status reports. The pages will be updated monthly by Barbara. Also, Leonard decides that the Web pages don't need to include the Paid field, so he asks you to remove the Paid field from the Invoices report.

Creating the necessary HTML documents is not as difficult as it might appear at first. You will use the Publish to the Web Wizard, which can automatically convert database objects to HTML files.

> **REFERENCE window**
>
> **SAVING ACCESS OBJECTS IN AN HTML FILE**
>
> - Open the database that contains the objects you want to save in an HTML file.
> - Click File on the menu bar, and then click Save As HTML. Access opens the Publish to the Web Wizard.
> - Complete the wizard dialog boxes to select the objects you want to save as HTML files, select any templates to use, specify which objects will be static and which will be dynamic, select a folder in which to store the HTML files, and indicate whether you want to create a home page.

To complete the following steps, you need a Web browser in addition to Access. The steps in this tutorial are written for Internet Explorer, the Web browser used at Valle Coffee. If you use the Netscape Navigator browser, the steps you need to complete will be slightly different.

You will begin by modifying the Invoices report design to remove the Paid field from the report.

To remove the Paid field from the Invoices report:

1. Place your Student Disk in the appropriate disk drive.

2. Start Access and open the Restaurant database located in the Tutorial folder on your Student Disk.

3. Click the **Reports** tab to display the Reports list, click **Invoices**, and then click the **Design** button. Access opens the Invoices report in Design view. See Figure 7-3.

Figure 7-3 ◄
Invoices report
in Design view

delete Paid label ——

delete Paid
check box ——

4. Right-click the **Paid** label in the Page Header section, and then click **Cut** on the shortcut menu.

5. Right-click the **Paid** check box in the Detail section, and then click **Cut** on the shortcut menu.

6. Click the **Save** button 🖫 on the Report Design toolbar to save the changes, and then click the **Close** button ☒ on the Report window to close it and return to the Database window.

You can now use the Publish to the Web Wizard to save the Customer table and the Invoices report as HTML files.

To save the Customer table and the Invoices report as HTML files:

1. Click **File** on the menu bar, and then click **Save As HTML**. The Publish to the Web Wizard opens and displays the introductory page. See Figure 7-4.

Figure 7-4 ◀
Publish to the Web Wizard introductory page

2. Click the **Next** button. The wizard displays the list of tables in the Restaurant database. Click the check box next to the **Customer** table to select it.

3. Click the **Reports** tab, and then click the check box next to the **Invoices** report to select it. See Figure 7-5.

Figure 7-5 ◀
Selecting the database objects to publish

click to select object ─────▶

4. Click the **Next** button. This dialog box allows you to select a template for the HTML pages that will be created. For now, you don't want to select a template.

5. Click the **Next** button. This dialog box allows you to specify which objects will be displayed in static pages and which will be in dynamic pages. Make sure the **Static HTML** option button is selected, because Leonard wants the pages to be static, not dynamic.

6. Click the **Next** button. This dialog box allows you to select the folder in which the HTML files will be stored for later viewing. Make sure the text box displays the Tutorial folder on your Student Disk.

7. Click the **Next** button. This dialog box allows you to create a home page that will contain hyperlinks to each of the HTML pages created by the wizard. Click the check box for creating a home page.

   The home page will be the starting point for viewing the Customer table page and the Invoices report page. Users will be able to click either of the hyperlinks and then view the selected page.

8. Click the file name text box, select the current file name (Default), and then type **Valle Home Page**. Access will create a home page file with the name Valle Home Page.html. See Figure 7-6.

Figure 7-6 ◄
Selecting the
home page
option

click to create
a home page

name of home
page file

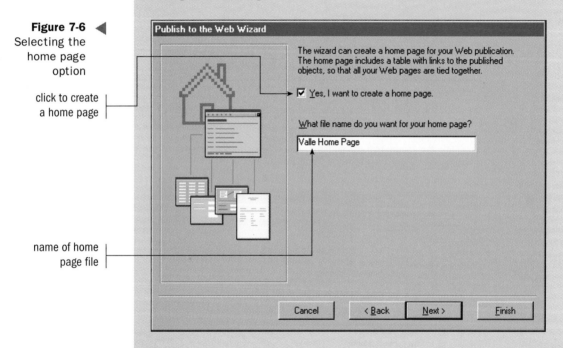

9. Click the **Next** button. The next Publish to the Web Wizard dialog box allows you to save your choices in a profile. You do not want to save a profile now; you'll learn about profiles later in the tutorial.

10. Click the **Finish** button. The Publish to the Web Wizard dialog box closes, and the wizard creates the HTML files you requested.

The Publish to the Web Wizard now has all the information necessary to create the home page and the HTML files for the Customer table and the Invoices report. The wizard creates a home page HTML file called Valle Home Page and an HTML file for the Customer table data, called Customer_1. The wizard also creates three HTML files for the Invoices report—one file for each page of the report. These files are named Invoices_1, Invoices_1Page2, and Invoices_1Page3. All of the HTML files are stored in the Tutorial folder on your Student Disk and can be viewed using the Web browser on your computer.

Viewing the HTML Files Using Internet Explorer

Leonard asks to see the Web pages you have created. The HTML files created by the Publish to the Web Wizard can be viewed using any Web browser software. You'll view these files using Microsoft Internet Explorer.

REFERENCE window

VIEWING AN HTML FILE

- Click View on the menu bar, point to Toolbars, and then click Web to display the Web toolbar (if necessary).
- Click the Go button, and then click Open.
- Use the Browse button to select the file to open, and then click the Open button.
- Click the OK button.

You'll begin by viewing the Valle Home Page file.

To view the Valle Home Page HTML file:

1. Click **View** on the menu bar, point to **Toolbars**, and then click **Web**. Access displays the Web toolbar. See Figure 7-7.

Figure 7-7 ◀
Displaying the Web toolbar

Web toolbar ⎯

Go button ⎯

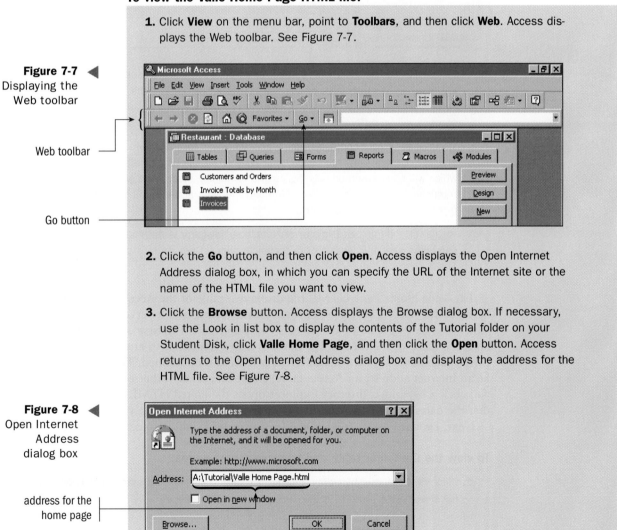

2. Click the **Go** button, and then click **Open**. Access displays the Open Internet Address dialog box, in which you can specify the URL of the Internet site or the name of the HTML file you want to view.

3. Click the **Browse** button. Access displays the Browse dialog box. If necessary, use the Look in list box to display the contents of the Tutorial folder on your Student Disk, click **Valle Home Page**, and then click the **Open** button. Access returns to the Open Internet Address dialog box and displays the address for the HTML file. See Figure 7-8.

Figure 7-8 ◀
Open Internet Address dialog box

address for the home page ⎯

4. Click the **OK** button. Access opens the Internet Explorer and displays the Valle Home Page HTML file. See Figure 7-9.

Figure 7-9
Internet Explorer displaying the Valle Home Page HTML file

page title

hyperlinks to other HTML files

Web page

TROUBLE? If Access opens another program, such as Microsoft Word, the Internet Explorer might not be installed on your computer. If the title bar on your screen displays "Microsoft Word," you can continue with the steps, but your screens will be different from those in the figures.

TROUBLE? If your computer has Netscape Navigator installed as the default browser, you can view the Valle Home Page HTML file using Netscape Navigator, which will start automatically. Follow the remaining steps, and similar steps throughout this tutorial, but keep in mind that your screens will look slightly different from those in the figures.

TROUBLE? If Internet Explorer or Netscape Navigator is not installed on your computer, see your instructor or technical support person for assistance.

The Valle Home Page HTML file displays a table of the Access objects that you published to the Web. This table is called a **switchboard**, and it serves as a home page from which you can view all of the objects you published. The first column of the table contains the name of the object. The name is also a hyperlink to another HTML file, which is why each name appears in a different color and is underlined. The linked document can be an Internet address, an Access table, a text file, or any other object. In this case, when you click a hyperlink, Internet Explorer opens the linked HTML file for the object. Note that the dates in the Last Modified column will be different on your screen.

Next, Leonard wants to view the Customer table and Invoices report pages.

To view the Customer table and Invoices report pages:

1. Click the **Customer** hyperlink. Internet Explorer displays the Customer_1 HTML file showing the records in the Customer table. See Figure 7-10.

Figure 7-10 ◀
Customer table
in the Internet
Explorer

records from the
Customer table

2. Click the **Back** button on the toolbar. Internet Explorer returns to the switchboard page.

3. Click the **Invoices** hyperlink. Internet Explorer displays the Invoices_1 HTML file, the first page of the Invoices report.

4. Scroll to the bottom of the report page. Because the report has more than one page, Access automatically included hyperlinks to the other pages of the report. These hyperlinks are named First, Previous, Next, and Last, and they are linked with the first, previous, next, and last pages of the report, respectively. Because you are viewing the first page of the report, the First and Previous hyperlinks are inactive and appear in a different color from the Next and Last hyperlinks. See Figure 7-11.

Figure 7-11 ◀
Viewing the
report page

report page

hyperlinks to other
report pages

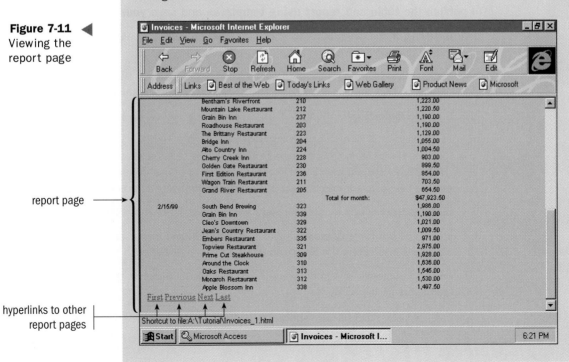

5. Click the **Next** hyperlink. Internet Explorer displays the second page of the report, contained in the Invoices_1Page2 HTML file. Notice that the Address text box displays the address for this page.

6. Scroll to the bottom of the report page, and then click the **Last** hyperlink. Internet Explorer displays the third and last page of the report, contained in the Invoices_1Page3 HTML file.

7. Click the **First** hyperlink at the bottom of the report page. Internet Explorer displays the first page of the report.

8. Click the **Close** button ❎ on the Internet Explorer window to close it.

9. Click the **Microsoft Access** button on the taskbar to return to Access.

Barbara stops by to see the Web pages you have created. She likes the pages but suggests that they would look better with a title and graphic image at the top to identify them as Valle Coffee's pages.

Using an HTML Template

You can include text, graphics, and other information in the pages created by the Publish to the Web Wizard by using a template. A **template** is a file that contains HTML instructions for creating a Web page together with special instructions that tell Access where to place the Access data on the page. Barbara has created two templates using Microsoft Word. She saved the templates in two files, Valletbl and Vallerpt. The Valletbl template includes instructions for a title and the Valle Coffee cup logo at the top of the page. You can use the Valletbl template to create an HTML file for a table (or query results). The Vallerpt template is similar, but it also contains the necessary instructions to include the First, Previous, Next, and Last hyperlinks. You can use the Vallerpt template to create an HTML file for a report.

Barbara will need to recreate these Web pages periodically as the data in the Restaurant database changes. To save her time later on, you can instruct the Publish to the Web Wizard to record your choices and save them as a **profile**. In this way, Barbara can recreate the Web pages by telling the Publish to the Web Wizard to use the saved profile.

To publish the table and report using templates and save your choices in a profile:

1. Click **File** on the menu bar, and then click **Save As HTML**. Access opens the Publish to the Web Wizard.

2. Click the **Next** button. The wizard displays the list of tables in the Restaurant database. Click the check box next to the **Customer** table to select it.

3. Click the **Reports** tab, and then click the check box next to the **Invoices** report to select it.

4. Click the **Next** button. This dialog box allows you to select a template for the HTML pages that will be created. Because you need to use different templates for each of the selected objects, click the check box for using different templates.

5. Click the **Next** button. Access displays a dialog box listing the selected objects.

6. Make sure the **Table:Customer** table is highlighted, and then click the **Browse** button. Access opens the Select an HTML Template dialog box.

   Because Customer is a table, you will use the Valletbl template that Barbara created to create the HTML file.

7. Use the Look in list box to display the contents of the Tutorial folder on your Student Disk, click **Valletbl**, and then click the **Select** button.

8. Click **Report: Invoices** to highlight it, click the **Browse** button, click **Vallerpt** to select the template for a report, and then click the **Select** button to return to the Publish to the Web Wizard. See Figure 7-12.

Figure 7-12
Selecting templates for the objects to be published

9. Click the **Next** button to display the next dialog box. Make sure the **Static HTML** option button is selected, and then click the **Next** button.

10. Click the **Next** button to place your Web publication in the Tutorial folder on your Student Disk. Click the check box for creating a home page, click the file name text box, select the Default name, and then type **Valle Home Page**. Click the **Next** button. The next dialog box allows you to save your choices in a profile.

11. Click the check box for saving your choices in a profile, click the **Profile Name** text box, select the current name, and then type **Valle Profile**. Your Web page choices will be saved in a profile named Valle Profile. See Figure 7-13.

Figure 7-13
Creating the Web publication profile

Publish to the Web Wizard

You can save all the information you have provided while using this wizard to a Web publication profile for the next time you use the wizard. This makes republishing this set of objects a snap!

☑ Yes, I want to save wizard answers to a Web publication profile.

click to save choices in a profile

Profile Name: Valle Profile

enter profile name here

That's all of the information the wizard needs to create your Web publication.

Cancel   < Back   Next >   Finish

12. Click the **Finish** button. The Publish to the Web Wizard creates the HTML files according to the profile and saves them in the Tutorial folder on your Student Disk.

When the Publish to the Web Wizard creates the new Web pages, it overwrites the pages you created before. When these pages need to be updated in the future, you can simply use the profile you saved rather than having to complete all the Publish to the Web Wizard steps again.

Barbara asks to see the new HTML files created with the templates, which display the Valle Coffee title and coffee cup logo.

To view the new HTML files:

1. Click the **Go** button on the Web toolbar, and then click **Open**.

2. Click the **Browse** button, click **Valle Home Page** in the Tutorial folder on your Student Disk, and then click the **Open** button to return to the Open Internet Address dialog box.

3. Click the **OK** button. Access opens the Internet Explorer and displays the Valle Home Page HTML file.

4. Click the **Customer** hyperlink. Internet Explorer displays the Customer_1 HTML file showing the records in the Customer table. Because you used the Valletbl template to create this page, it displays both the Valle Coffee title and coffee cup logo. See Figure 7-14.

Figure 7-14 ◀
Customer table
with title
and logo

added title ———

added picture (logo) ———

5. Click the **Back** button on the toolbar. Internet Explorer returns to the switchboard page.

6. Click the **Invoices** hyperlink. Internet Explorer displays the Invoices_1 HTML file, the first page of the Invoices report. Because you used the Vallerpt template to create this page, it displays both the Valle Coffee title and coffee cup logo.

7. Use the First, Previous, Next, and Last hyperlinks to view the other pages of the report. When you are finished, click the **Close** button ☒ on the Internet Explorer window to close it.

8. Click the **Microsoft Access** button on the taskbar to return to Access.

Barbara likes the new HTML files much better. She mentions that Valle Coffee has received an order from a new customer. The customer and order information must be entered in the Restaurant database. The new information must be put in the HTML files as well. She asks you to do this now.

Updating a Web Page

The HTML files created by the Publish to the Web Wizard are static—that is, they reflect the state of the database at the time they were created. Changes to the database are not automatically reflected in the HTML files. If database records are changed, the HTML files must be created again so that they are up to date. Because you saved a profile when you created the HTML files, you can update the HTML files easily by instructing the Publish to the Web Wizard to use the profile to recreate the files.

Figure 7-15 shows the two new records, one for the Customer table and one for the Order table.

Figure 7-15 ◄
New records for the Restaurant database

New Customer record:

CustomerNum	CustomerName	Street	City	State	ZipCode	OwnerName	Phone	FirstContact
800	Rosie's Diner	1004 Highway 99 S	Monroe	MI	48161	Ms. Rosie Finnegan	(313) 792-1834	4/1/99

New Order record:

OrderNum	CustomerName	Paid	InvoiceAmt	BillingDate
402	Rosie's Diner	No	204.00	4/15/99

First you'll enter the new records in the Restaurant database.

To enter the new records:

1. If necessary click the **Tables** tab to display the tables list in the Database window, click **Customer** to select it, and then click the **Open** button to open the table.

2. Click the **New Record** button [▶*] on the Table Datasheet toolbar, and then enter the data for the new Customer record, as shown in Figure 7-15.

3. Click the **Close** button [✕] on the Table window to close the Customer table datasheet.

4. Click **Order**, and then click the **Open** button to open the Order table.

5. Click the **New Record** button [▶*] on the Table Datasheet toolbar, and then enter the data for the new Order record, as shown in Figure 7-15.

6. Click the **Close** button [✕] on the Table window to close the Order table datasheet.

Now you can create the HTML files again using the profile you saved earlier.

To create the HTML files using the saved profile:

1. Click **File** on the menu bar, and then click **Save As HTML**. Access starts the Publish to the Web Wizard. The first dialog box shows the Valle Profile in the profiles list. See Figure 7-16.

Figure 7-16 ◀
Selecting
the profile

click to use a profile ——

click to select
Valle Profile ——

2. Click the check box for using an existing profile.

3. Click **Valle Profile** to select the profile. Because you don't need to change any of the choices you made before, you are finished with the wizard.

4. Click the **Finish** button. The Publish to the Web Wizard creates a Valle Home Page HTML file and HTML files for the Customer table and the Invoices report. The new files include the information in the new records you just added.

5. Click the **Go** button on the Web toolbar, and then click **Open**.

6. Click the **Browse** button, click the **Valle Home Page** file in the Tutorial folder on your Student Disk, and then click the **Open** button to return to the Open Internet Address dialog box.

7. Click the **OK** button. Access opens the Internet Explorer and displays the Valle Home Page HTML file.

8. Click the **Customer** hyperlink. Internet Explorer displays the Customer_1 HTML file showing the records in the Customer table. Scroll down to see that the new customer record, CustomerNum 800, has been added to the customer list. See Figure 7-17.

Figure 7-17 ◀
Customer table
with the new
customer
record

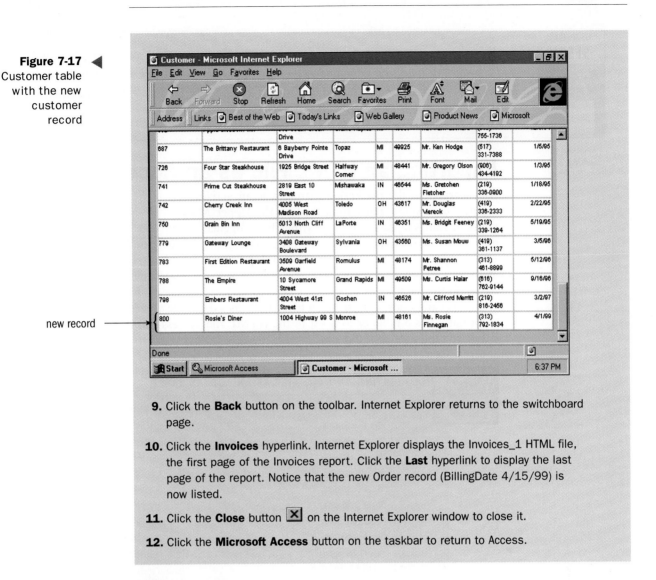

new record ──→

9. Click the **Back** button on the toolbar. Internet Explorer returns to the switchboard page.

10. Click the **Invoices** hyperlink. Internet Explorer displays the Invoices_1 HTML file, the first page of the Invoices report. Click the **Last** hyperlink to display the last page of the report. Notice that the new Order record (BillingDate 4/15/99) is now listed.

11. Click the **Close** button ☒ on the Internet Explorer window to close it.

12. Click the **Microsoft Access** button on the taskbar to return to Access.

Quick Check

1. What is HTML?

2. What is the World Wide Web?

3. What is the purpose of a Web browser?

4. What is a hyperlink?

5. What is an HTML template?

6. What is the purpose of saving a profile for the Publish to the Web Wizard?

Leonard and Barbara are pleased with the HTML files that you created. The files will make it easy to distribute important Restaurant database information on the company's intranet. In the next session, you will continue to work with HTML files to further enhance the database.

SESSION

7.2

In this session you will import data from an HTML file into an Access table. You will add a hyperlink field to a table and enter hyperlink values that link records to bookmarks in a Word document. You will also add a hyperlink field to a table and enter hyperlink values that link records to HTML files.

Importing an HTML File as an Access Table

Kim Carpenter, the marketing manager, is an active user of the World Wide Web. She recently discovered a site published by the Upper Midwest Tourism Office. One of the pages at that site lists restaurants that have opened recently in Valle Coffee's customer area. Each of these new restaurants is a potential customer for Valle Coffee. Kim asks whether you can import the restaurant information from that page into an Access table. With the data in an Access table, she will be able to create queries, forms, and reports based on the data.

Access can import data from an HTML file as a database object. Provided that the data is formatted as a table or as a list in the HTML file, Access can import it directly into a database table.

REFERENCE
window

IMPORTING AN HTML FILE AS AN ACCESS TABLE

- Click File on the menu bar, point to Get External Data, and then click Import.
- Click the Files of type list arrow, and then click HTML Documents.
- Use the Look in list box to select the HTML file to import.
- Click the Import button. Access displays the first Import HTML Wizard dialog box.
- Complete the wizard dialog boxes to specify whether the first row of data should be used for column headings; specify whether records should be imported to a new table or appended to an existing table; specify the field names, data types, and indexing options for the fields; specify a primary key; and enter the table name.
- Click the OK button to confirm that the data has been imported.

The HTML file containing the information Kim wants is stored in the Tutorial folder on your Student Disk with the name NewRest. You will use the Access Import HTML Wizard to import the data into a new table in the Restaurant database. First, you'll begin by viewing the HTML file using Internet Explorer.

To view the NewRest HTML file:

1. If you took a break after the previous session, make sure that Access is running and the Restaurant database from the Tutorial folder on your Student Disk is open.

2. Click the **Go** button on the Web toolbar, and then click **Open**.

3. Click the **Browse** button.

4. Make sure the Look in list box displays the Tutorial folder on your Student Disk, click **NewRest**, and then click the **Open** button to select the file and return to the Open Internet Address dialog box.

5. Click the **OK** button. Access opens the Internet Explorer and displays the NewRest HTML file. See Figure 7-18.

Figure 7-18
NewRest
HTML file

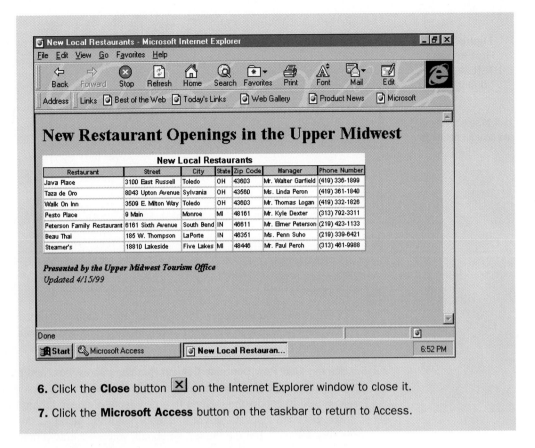

6. Click the **Close** button ☒ on the Internet Explorer window to close it.

7. Click the **Microsoft Access** button on the taskbar to return to Access.

Now you will import the NewRest HTML file as an Access database table using the Import HTML Wizard.

To import the HTML file as an Access table:

1. Click **File** on the menu bar, point to **Get External Data**, and then click **Import**. The Import dialog box opens.

2. Click the **Files of type** list arrow, and then click **HTML Documents**.

3. Make sure the Look in list box displays the Tutorial folder on your Student Disk, and then click **NewRest** to select the HTML file.

4. Click the **Import** button. Access displays the first Import HTML Wizard dialog box. This dialog box displays the first few rows of data read from the HTML file. See Figure 7-19.

Figure 7-19 ◄
First Import
HTML Wizard
dialog box

click to select first row
as column headings

Access allows you to specify that the first row of data contains column headings (field names). Because the first row of this data contains column headings, you will specify that the first row should be used as field names in the new table.

5. Click the **First Row Contains Column Headings** check box, and then click the **Next** button. Access displays the next Import HTML Wizard dialog box, which allows you to import the records to a new table or append them to an existing table. Because the structure of this table is not the same as the structure of any existing tables in the Restaurant database, you will create a new table.

6. Make sure the **In a New Table** option button is selected, and then click the **Next** button to display the next dialog box. See Figure 7-20.

Figure 7-20 ◄
Specifying field
names, data
types, and
indexing
options

In this dialog box you can change the field name, data type, and indexing option for each of the fields in the new table. If you do not make any choices, Access will assign an appropriate field name, data type, and indexing option for each field. You can also choose not to import selected fields. You will change the name of the Zip Code field to ZipCode and the name of the Phone Number field to PhoneNumber to be consistent with the field naming style in other Restaurant database tables.

7. Scroll the field list to the right to display the Zip Code and Phone Number fields. Click the **Zip Code** field to select it, and then delete the space between Zip and Code in the Field Name text box.

Access

8. Click the **Phone Number** field to select it, and then delete the space between Phone and Number in the Field Name text box. See Figure 7-21.

Figure 7-21 ◄
After changing the ZipCode and PhoneNumber field names

edit field name here

edited field names

9. Click the **Next** button. The next dialog box allows you to specify a primary key field for the table or let Access add an AutoNumber field as a primary key field. See Figure 7-22.

Figure 7-22 ◄
Specifying the primary key field

indicates that Access will create an AutoNumber field as the primary key

column for AutoNumber field

Because the table does not contain a field that would be appropriate as a primary key, you'll let Access assign a primary key field. Access will create a field with the AutoNumber data type as the primary key field for the new table.

10. Make sure the **Let Access add Primary Key** option button is selected, and then click the **Next** button. This dialog box allows you to enter the name of the new table.

11. In the Import to Table text box, type **Potential Customers**, and then click the **Finish** button. Access imports the HTML file and saves the data in a table called Potential Customers. When the wizard is finished creating the file, it displays a dialog box confirming that it has finished.

12. Click the **OK** button to end the importing process and return to the Database window.

The HTML file has been imported and the data has been saved in a new table called Potential Customers. This table is now listed on the Tables tab of the Database window. Kim asks you to view the data and then print a copy of the records for her.

To view the Potential Customers table and print the records:

1. Click **Potential Customers** in the tables list (if necessary), and then click the **Open** button. Access opens the Potential Customers table in Datasheet view. See Figure 7-23.

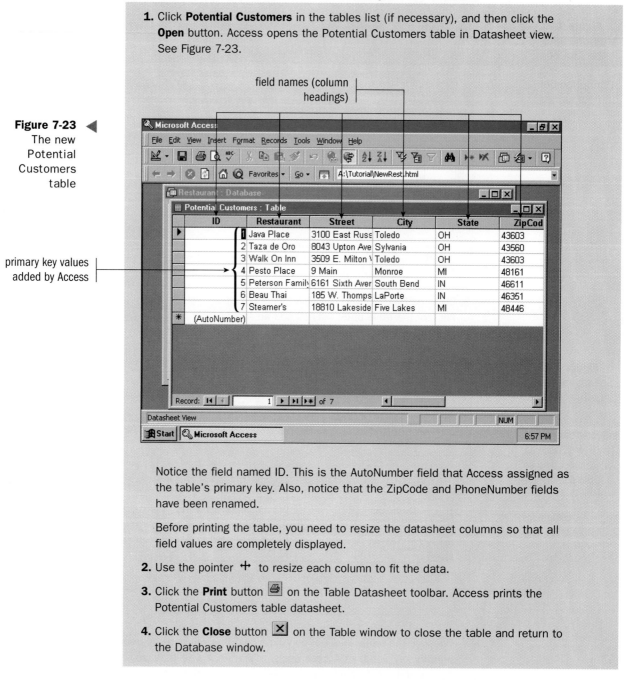

Figure 7-23
The new
Potential
Customers
table

primary key values
added by Access

Notice the field named ID. This is the AutoNumber field that Access assigned as the table's primary key. Also, notice that the ZipCode and PhoneNumber fields have been renamed.

Before printing the table, you need to resize the datasheet columns so that all field values are completely displayed.

2. Use the pointer ⟷ to resize each column to fit the data.

3. Click the **Print** button 🖨 on the Table Datasheet toolbar. Access prints the Potential Customers table datasheet.

4. Click the **Close** button ⊠ on the Table window to close the table and return to the Database window.

Kim reviews and approves the printed output. In the future, when the Upper Midwest Tourism Office publishes new lists of recently opened restaurants, she can add them to the Potential Customers table.

Creating Hyperlinks to Documents in Other Office 97 Programs

Kim has used the Potential Customers list to set up meetings with the new restaurants' managers. She visited several of the restaurants and returned with notes about the visits. Kim saved her field notes in a Word document named Fldnotes. Now she would like some way of connecting these notes with the corresponding records in the Potential Customers table. This would allow her to review her notes when she views the records in the table.

Each restaurant's set of notes in the Fldnotes file is identified with a bookmark. A **bookmark** is a section of text in a Word document that is identified with a name. For example, Kim has placed a bookmark named Java to mark her notes on the new Java Place restaurant. Similarly, her notes on Taza de Oro are marked with the bookmark Taza, and the bookmark for Peterson Family Restaurant is named Peterson. To connect Kim's notes with the corresponding records in the Potential Customers table, you need to create a hyperlink field in the table.

Creating a Hyperlink Field

Access allows you to create a hyperlink field in a table. The field value in a hyperlink field is a hyperlink to another object. These objects can be database objects (such as tables or forms), a bookmark in a Word document, a named range in an Excel worksheet, or even a World Wide Web page. When you click a hyperlink field value, Access starts the associated program and opens the linked object.

REFERENCE window

CREATING A HYPERLINK FIELD

- Display the table in Design view.
- In a blank Field Name text box, type the name of the new field, and then press the Tab key.
- Click the Data Type list arrow, and then click Hyperlink.

You will create a hyperlink field in the Potential Customers table. The hyperlink field value will be a hyperlink to a bookmark in Kim's Fldnotes document. When Kim clicks a hyperlink, Access will start Word and display the bookmarked text.

To add a hyperlink field to the table:

1. In the Database window tables list, click **Potential Customers** (if necessary), and then click the **Design** button. The table is displayed in Design view.

2. Scroll down the field list to display a blank row, click the Field Name text box, type **FieldNotes**, and then press the **Tab** key.

3. Click the **Data Type** list arrow, and then click **Hyperlink**. See Figure 7-24.

Figure 7-24 ◀
Adding a
hyperlink field

new field ——————

selected data type ——————

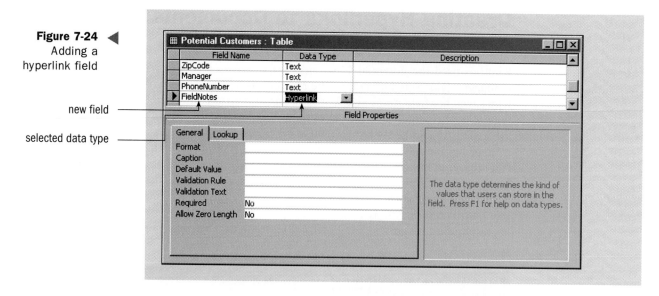

Now you can add the hyperlink field values to the Potential Customers table. These field values will be hyperlinks to the bookmarked text in the Fldnotes document.

Entering a Hyperlink Field Value

When you add a field value in a hyperlink field, you can enter the name of an object, such as a table, form, worksheet or document, or a URL. You can type the field value directly into the field or you can use the Insert Hyperlink dialog box to enter it. If you use the Insert Hyperlink dialog box, you can also specify a named location in the object. For example, in a Word document, a named location is any bookmark. If you are hyperlinking to an Access database, a named location could be a table, query, form, or any other database object.

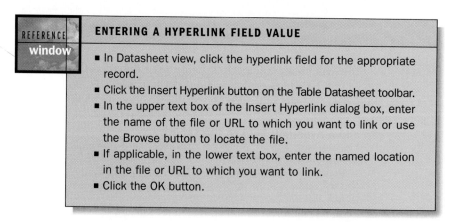

REFERENCE window

ENTERING A HYPERLINK FIELD VALUE

- In Datasheet view, click the hyperlink field for the appropriate record.
- Click the Insert Hyperlink button on the Table Datasheet toolbar.
- In the upper text box of the Insert Hyperlink dialog box, enter the name of the file or URL to which you want to link or use the Browse button to locate the file.
- If applicable, in the lower text box, enter the named location in the file or URL to which you want to link.
- Click the OK button.

You will use the Insert Hyperlink dialog box to enter the necessary hyperlink field values and specify the relevant bookmarks in the Fldnotes document.

To enter field values in the hyperlink field:

1. Click the **View** button for Datasheet view ▦ on the Table Design toolbar. Access opens a dialog box asking if you want to save the table.

2. Click the **Yes** button. The table is displayed in Datasheet view.

3. Scroll right until the FieldNotes field is visible, and then click the **FieldNotes** text box for the Java Place record (record 1).

4. Click the **Insert Hyperlink** button 🔗 on the Table Datasheet toolbar. The Insert Hyperlink dialog box opens. See Figure 7-25.

Figure 7-25 ◀
Insert Hyperlink dialog box

enter bookmark name here

click to select file or URL

The Insert Hyperlink dialog box contains two text boxes. The upper text box allows you to enter the name of the file or URL to which you want to link, and the lower text box allows you to enter the named location in that file or URL to which you want to link (if applicable). Notice that the insertion point is already in the Link to file or URL text box.

5. Click the **Browse** button. The Link to File dialog box opens.

6. Make sure the Look in list box displays the contents of the Tutorial folder on your Student Disk, click **Fldnotes**, and then click the **OK** button. The Link to File dialog box closes and the name of the Fldnotes file appears in the Link to file or URL text box.

The named location for Kim's notes on the Java Place restaurant is a bookmark called Java. You will specify the bookmark as a named location in the Fldnotes file, so that Access will display the text at this location when the user clicks the hyperlink field value.

7. Click the **Named location in file** text box, and then type **Java**. See Figure 7-26.

Figure 7-26 ◀
Entering a hyperlink field value and named location

hyperlinked file

bookmark in Word document

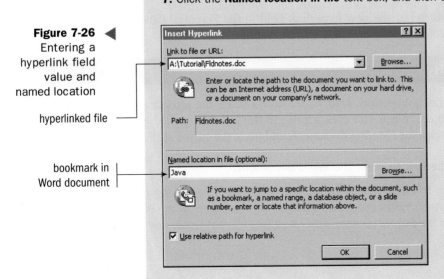

TROUBLE? The Fldnotes filename on your screen might be displayed in all uppercase letters or some other variation of uppercase and lowercase letters. This will not affect the final results; simply proceed with the steps.

8. Click the **OK** button to close the Insert Hyperlink dialog box. The hyperlink field value appears in the FieldNotes field for the first record. See Figure 7-27.

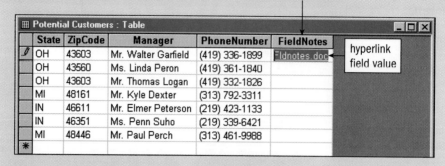

Figure 7-27
Hyperlink field
value entered

9. Use the same procedure to enter hyperlink field values for the records for Taza de Oro (record 2) and Peterson Family Restaurant (record 5). Enter **Taza** as the named location in the Fldnotes file for the Taza de Oro record and **Peterson** as the named location in the Fldnotes file for the Peterson record. When you are finished, the Datasheet window should look like Figure 7-28.

Figure 7-28
Hyperlink field
values entered
for the three
records

Notice that the hyperlink field values have a different appearance from the other field values. The hyperlink field values are shown in a different color and are underlined. This indicates that they are hyperlinks.

Kim wants to test the new hyperlink field in the Potential Customers table. You'll use the hyperlinks to view the corresponding notes.

Using a Hyperlink

When you click a hyperlink field value, Access starts the associated program and displays the linked object. When you click a value in the FieldNotes field, for example, Access will start Word, open the Fldnotes document, and place the cursor at the appropriate bookmark.

To use a hyperlink to open the Word document:

1. Click the **Peterson Family Restaurant FieldNotes** hyperlink. Access starts Word, opens the Fldnotes document, and positions the cursor at the Peterson bookmark at the beginning of the field notes for Peterson Family Restaurant. See Figure 7-29.

Figure 7-29 ◀
Field notes for
Peterson
Family
Restaurant in
the Fldnotes
file

Word opens
Fldnotes file

Peterson bookmark

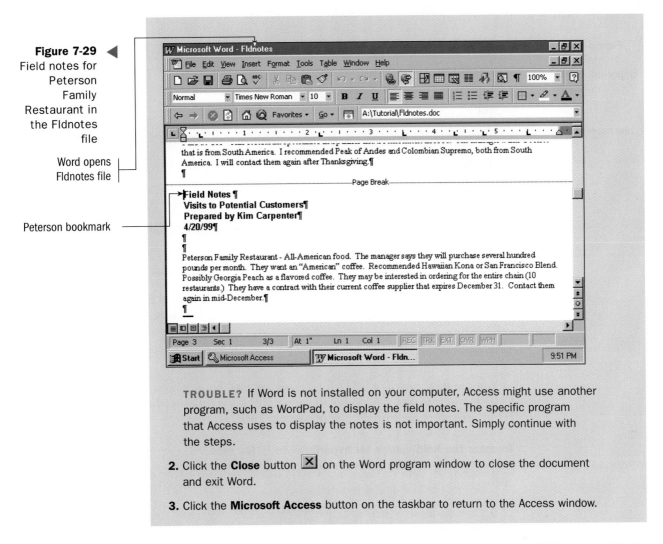

TROUBLE? If Word is not installed on your computer, Access might use another program, such as WordPad, to display the field notes. The specific program that Access uses to display the notes is not important. Simply continue with the steps.

2. Click the **Close** button [X] on the Word program window to close the document and exit Word.

3. Click the **Microsoft Access** button on the taskbar to return to the Access window.

Kim reviews the notes and is satisfied that she can now link her field notes with the Potential Customers data. She asks you to add one more hyperlink field to the Potential Customers table. This new field will contain hyperlinks to World Wide Web pages.

Creating Hyperlinks to World Wide Web Pages

When Kim visited the potential new customers, she learned that some of the restaurants have home pages on the World Wide Web. These pages serve as advertisements for the restaurants. Kim wants you to add a hyperlink field to the Potential Customers table. The field value for each record will be a hyperlink to the particular restaurant's home page.

The field value for the hyperlink is the URL for that Web site. When you click a field value for a record, Access starts the Web browser on your computer and opens the HTML document at that site.

Before you can enter the field values, you must add a new hyperlink field to the Potential Customers table.

To add a new hyperlink field:

1. Click the **View** button for Design view [icon] on the Table Datasheet toolbar.

2. Scroll down the field list to the first blank row, click the **Field Name** text box for the blank row, type **HomePage**, and then press the **Tab** key.

3. Click the **Data Type** list arrow, and then click **Hyperlink**. See Figure 7-30.

Figure 7-30
HomePage
hyperlink field
defined

new hyperlink field

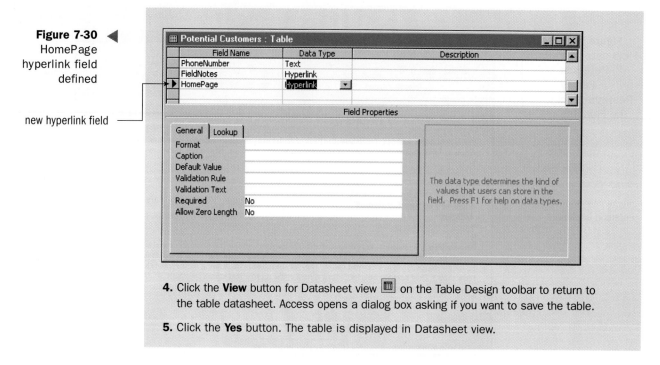

4. Click the **View** button for Datasheet view on the Table Design toolbar to return to the table datasheet. Access opens a dialog box asking if you want to save the table.

5. Click the **Yes** button. The table is displayed in Datasheet view.

You can now enter the URLs for the restaurants' home pages. You will not enter actual URLs; instead you will simulate using URLs by entering the names of appropriate HTML files that are stored on your Student Disk.

To enter the field values for hyperlinks to HTML files:

1. Scroll right until the HomePage field is visible, and then click the **HomePage** text box for the Taza de Oro record (record 2).

2. Click the **Insert Hyperlink** button on the Table Datasheet toolbar. The Insert Hyperlink dialog box opens.

3. Click the upper **Browse** button. The Link to File dialog box opens.

4. Make sure the Look in list box displays the contents of the Tutorial folder on your Student Disk, click **Taza**, and then click the **OK** button. The Link to File dialog box closes and the name of the Taza file appears in the Link to file or URL text box. See Figure 7-31.

Figure 7-31
Entering a
hyperlink field
value for the
HTML file

hyperlinked file

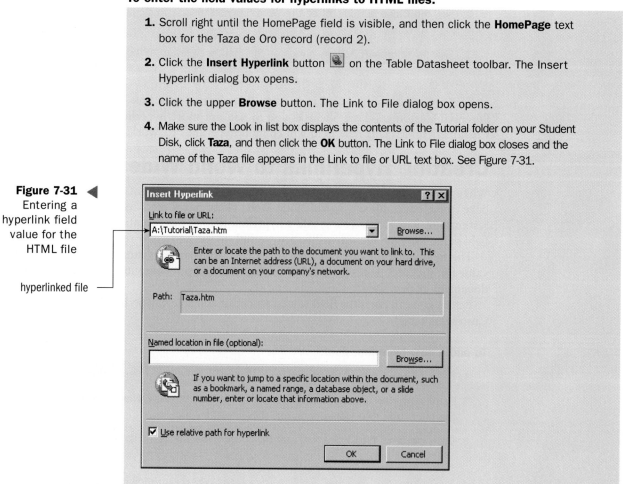

Because you want to view the entire Taza file, not a named location in the file, you do not need to specify a named location.

5. Click the **OK** button to close the Insert Hyperlink dialog box. The hyperlink field value appears in the HomePage field for the second record. See Figure 7-32.

Figure 7-32 ◀
Hyperlink field value entered for the restaurant's home page

6. Use the same procedure to enter a hyperlink field value for the record for Pesto Place (record 4). Select the HTML file named Pesto as the file to link to.

You can now view the restaurant home pages by clicking the hyperlinks in the HomePage field.

To view the home pages:

1. Click **Pesto.htm** in the HomePage field for record 4. Access starts Internet Explorer and displays the HTML file for Pesto Place's home page. See Figure 7-33.

Figure 7-33 ◀
Home page for Pesto Place

2. Click the **Close** button ⊠ on the Internet Explorer window to close it.

3. Click the **Microsoft Access** button on the taskbar to return to the Access window.

4. Click **Taza.htm** in the HomePage field for record 2. Access starts Internet Explorer and displays the HTML file for Taza de Oro's home page.

5. Click the **Close** button ⊠ on the Internet Explorer window to close it.

6. Click the **Microsoft Access** button on the taskbar to return to the Access window.

You can now close the Restaurant database and exit Access. First you'll close the Web toolbar.

7. Click **View** on the menu bar, point to **Toolbars**, and then click **Web**. Access closes the Web toolbar.

8. Click the **Close** button ☒ on the Access program window to close the Restaurant database and to exit Access. You return to the Windows 95 desktop.

Quick Check

1 What types of HTML formats can Access import as table data?

2 How do you specify a named location in a hyperlinked file?

3 What is a bookmark?

4 What is one difference between typing a hyperlink value directly into a field and using the Insert Hyperlink dialog box?

5 What is a URL?

6 How do you view a hyperlink that is named in a hyperlink field?

Kim is pleased with the finished Potential Customers table. She is certain that the link from the table to the document containing her notes will make it much easier for her and others in the Marketing Department to identify and track potential new customers for Valle Coffee.

Tutorial Assignments

Barbara wants you to publish parts of the Products database on the company intranet. She wants to make the Product table data and the Coffee Types report available to company employees on the World Wide Web. She asks you to do the following:

1. Make sure your Student Disk is in the appropriate disk drive, start Access, and then open the Products database located in the TAssign folder on your Student Disk.

2. Use the Publish to the Web Wizard to create a home page:
   a. Save the Product table and the Coffee Types report as HTML files.
   b. Do not use a template for the files.
   c. Choose the static page format for the files.
   d. Publish the files in the TAssign folder on your Student Disk.
   e. Use the Default name for the home page.
   f. Do not save your choices in a profile.

3. Use Internet Explorer to do the following:
   a. Open the Default home page, and then view both the Product table and the Coffee Types report.
   b. Print the Product table HTML file from Internet Explorer.

4. Use the Publish to the Web Wizard to create a home page again:
   a. Save the Special Imports query and the Coffee Types report as HTML files.
   b. Use the Valletbl template for the Special Imports query and the Vallerpt template for the Coffee Types report. Both templates are located in the TAssign folder on your Student Disk.
   c. Choose the static page format for the files.
   d. Publish the files in the TAssign folder on your Student Disk.
   e. Use the name Products for the home page.
   f. Save your choices as a profile named Products Profile.

5. Use Internet Explorer to open the Products home page, and then view both the Special Imports data and the Coffee Types report.

6. Add the record shown in Figure 7-34 to the Product table in the Products database.

Figure 7-34 ◀

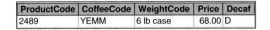

ProductCode	CoffeeCode	WeightCode	Price	Decaf
2489	YEMM	6 lb case	68.00	D

7. Use the Publish to the Web Wizard to update the Products home page:
   a. Use the Products Profile to recreate the HTML files.
   b. Use Internet Explorer to open the Products home page, and then view the Special Imports data. Verify that the new record (for ProductCode 2489) has been included in the query results.
   c. Print the Special Imports HTML file from Internet Explorer.

8. View and then print the Coffee Types report HTML file from Internet Explorer.

9. The Importers HTML file on your Student Disk contains a table of coffee importers in the local area. Import the Importers HTML file into the Products database as a new table:
   a. Choose the option for using the column headings as field names in the table.
   b. Let Access assign the primary key.
   c. Name the new table Coffee Importers.
   d. Open the Coffee Importers table, resize all datasheet columns to fit the data, and then print the table.
   e. Close and save the table.

10. Some of the importers have home pages on the World Wide Web. Two of the HTML files for the home pages are stored on your Student Disk. These files are called Wwfoods (the home page for World-Wide Foods) and Johnson (the home page for Johnson Restaurant Supply). Add a hyperlink field called Home Page to the Coffee Importers table. Add hyperlink values for World-Wide Foods (record 3) and Johnson Restaurant Supply (record 5).

11. View the World-Wide Foods home page, and then print the page. View the Johnson Restaurant Supply home page, and then print the page.

12. Close the Products database, and then exit Access.

Case Problems

1. Ashbrook Mall Information Desk Sam Bullard wants to use the mall's computer intranet to publicize job openings at the mall. He wants to put the Job table and Store Jobs report on the intranet as Web pages. He asks you to make the following changes to the MallJobs database:

1. Make sure your Student Disk is in the appropriate disk drive, start Access, and then open the MallJobs database located in the Cases folder on your Student Disk.

2. Use the Publish to the Web Wizard to create a home page:
   a. Save the Job table and the Store Jobs report as HTML files.
   b. Do not use a template for the files.
   c. Choose the static page format for the files.
   d. Publish the files in the Cases folder on your Student Disk.
   e. Use the name MallJobs for the home page.
   f. Do not save your choices in a profile.

3. Use Internet Explorer to do the following:
   a. Open the MallJobs home page, and then view both the Job table and the Store Jobs report.
   b. Print the Job HTML file from Internet Explorer.

4. Use the Publish to the Web Wizard to create a home page again:
   a. Save the Job table and the Store Jobs report as HTML files.
   b. Use the Jobtbl template for the Job table and the Jobsrpt template for the Store Jobs report. Both templates are located in the Cases folder on your Student Disk.
   c. Choose the static page format for the files.
   d. Publish the files in the Cases folder on your Student Disk.
   e. Use the name MallJobs for the home page.
   f. Save your choices as a profile named MallJobs Profile.

5. Use Internet Explorer to open the MallJobs home page, and then view both the Job table and the Store Jobs report.

6. Add the record shown in Figure 7-35 to the Job table in the MallJobs database.

Figure 7-35 ◀

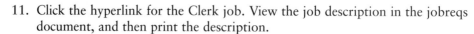

Job	Store	Position	Hours/Week
10010	Big Cookies	Clerk	20-30

7. Use the Publish to the Web Wizard to update the MallJobs home page:
   a. Use the MallJobs Profile to recreate the HTML files.
   b. Use Internet Explorer to open the MallJobs home page, and then view the Job data. Verify that the new record (for Job 10010) has been included in the table.
   c. Print the Job HTML file from Internet Explorer.

8. View and then print the Store Jobs report HTML file from Internet Explorer.

9. The HTML file Wages on your Student Disk contains information about the minimum allowable wages for positions offered by Ashbrook Mall stores. Import the Wages HTML file as an Access table:
   a. Choose the option for using the column headings as field names in the table.
   b. Let Access assign the primary key.
   c. Name the new table Minimum Wages.
   d. Open the Minimum Wages table, resize all datasheet columns to fit the data, and then print the table.
   e. Close and save the table.

10. The file Jobreqs is a Word document containing details about various mall jobs, with bookmarks for each of the jobs. Add a hyperlink field to the Minimum Wages table. Add hyperlink field values for the Baker, Cashier, Clerk and Fry Cook records. The bookmarks are the names of the positions; for example, the bookmark for the Fry Cook position is FryCook.

11. Click the hyperlink for the Clerk job. View the job description in the jobreqs document, and then print the description.

12. Close the MallJobs database, and then exit Access.

2. Professional Litigation User Services Raj Jawahir wants you to integrate the Payments database with the company intranet. He wants to publish the Firm table and the Payments By Account Representative report as Web pages. He asks you to complete the following:

1. Make sure your Student Disk is in the appropriate disk drive, start Access, and then open the Payments database located in the Cases folder on your Student Disk.

2. Use the Publish to the Web Wizard to create a home page:
   a. Save the Firm table and the Payments By Account Representative report as HTML files.
   b. Do not use a template for the files.
   c. Choose the static page format for the files.
   d. Publish the files in the Cases folder on your Student Disk.
   e. Use the Default name for the home page.
   f. Do not save your choices in a profile.

3. Use Internet Explorer to do the following:
   a. Open the Default home page, and then view both the Firm table and the Payments By Account Representative report.
   b. Print the Firm HTML file from Internet Explorer.

EXPLORE

4. Use the Publish to the Web Wizard to create a home page again:
   a. Save the Payment Statistics by Date query and the Payments By Account Representative report as HTML files.
   b. Use the PLUStbl template for the Payment Statistics by Date query and the PLUSrpt template for the Payments By Account Representative report. Both templates are located in the Cases folder on your Student Disk.
   c. Choose the static page format for the files.
   d. Publish the files in the Cases folder on your Student Disk.
   e. Use PLUS as the name for the home page.
   f. Save your choices as a profile named PLUS Profile.

5. Use Internet Explorer to open the PLUS home page, and then view both the Payment Statistics by Date data and the Payments By Account Representative report.

6. Add the record shown in Figure 7-36 to the Payment table in the Payments database.

Figure 7-36 ◀

Payment#	Deposit#	FirmName	AmtPaid	DatePaid
10106	117	Ling, Bingham, & Boyer	850.00	20-Jun-99

7. Use the Publish to the Web Wizard to update the PLUS home page:
   a. Use the PLUS Profile to recreate the HTML files.
   b. Use Internet Explorer to open the PLUS home page, and then view the Payment Statistics by Date data. Verify that the new record (for Payment# 10106) has been included in the statistics shown in the query results.
   c. Print the Payment Statistics by Date HTML file from Internet Explorer.

EXPLORE

EXPLORE

8. View and then print the Payments By Account Representative report HTML file from Internet Explorer.

9. The local bar association maintains a Web site that lists the new legal firms opening in the area. The HTML file Newfirms, which is located in the Cases folder on your Student Disk, contains this data. Import the Newfirms HTML file as an Access table:
   a. Choose the option for using the column headings as field names in the table.
   b. Let Access assign the primary key.
   c. Name the new table Prospects.
   d. Open the Prospects table, resize all datasheet columns to fit the data, and then print the table.
   e. Close and save the table.

10. The firm Dupont Investments has a Web site it uses to advertise its practice. The firm's home page HTML file is named Dupont and is stored in the Cases folder on your Student Disk. Add a hyperlink field to the Prospects table.

Name the field Website. Enter a hyperlink for the Dupont Investments record to the Dupont HTML file on your Student Disk.

11. Click the hyperlink for the Dupont Investments record and view the Dupont HTML file. Print the Web page.

12. Close and save the Payments database, and then exit Access.

3. Best Friends Noah and Sheila Warnick want to publish some of the Walks database data on the office intranet. Specifically, they want to publish the Walker table and the Walkers report as Web pages. They ask you to complete the following:

1. Make sure your Student Disk is in the appropriate disk drive, start Access, and then open the Walks database located in the Cases folder on your Student Disk.

2. Use the Publish to the Web Wizard to create a home page:
   a. Save the Walker table and the Walkers report as HTML files.
   b. Do not use a template for the files.
   c. Choose the static page format for the files.
   d. Publish the files in the Cases folder on your Student Disk.
   e. Use the Default name for the home page.
   f. Do not save your choices in a profile.

3. Use Internet Explorer to do the following:
   a. Open the Default home page, and then view both the Walker table and the Walkers report.
   b. Print the Walker HTML file from Internet Explorer.

4. Use the Publish to the Web Wizard to create a home page again:
   a. Save the Walker Distance query and the Walkers report as HTML files.
   b. Use the Walkstbl template for the Walker Distance query and the Walksrpt template for the Walkers report. Both templates are located in the Cases folder on your Student Disk.
   c. Choose the static page format for the files.
   d. Publish the files in the Cases folder on your Student Disk.
   e. Use the name Walks for the home page.
   f. Save your choices as a profile named Walks Profile.

5. Use Internet Explorer to open the Walks home page, and then view both the Walker Distance data and the Walkers report.

6. Add the record shown in Figure 7-37 to the Walker table in the Walks database.

Figure 7-37 ◀

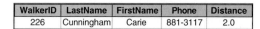

WalkerID	LastName	FirstName	Phone	Distance
226	Cunningham	Carie	881-3117	2.0

7. Use the Publish to the Web Wizard to update the Walks home page:
   a. Use the Walks Profile to recreate the HTML files.
   b. Use Internet Explorer to open the Walks home page, and then view the Walker Distance data. Verify that the new record (for WalkerID 226) has been included in the query results.
   c. Print the Walker Distance HTML file from Internet Explorer.

8. View and then print the Walkers report HTML file from Internet Explorer.

9. Noah is interested in contacting several local malls to hold "mall walk" events as fundraisers. The file Malls, which is stored in the Cases folder on your Student Disk, is the HTML file from a Web site that publishes a list of local malls and their managers. Import the Malls HTML file as an Access table:
   a. Choose the option for using the column headings as field names in the table.
   b. Let Access assign the primary key.

c. Name the new table Malls.

d. Open the Malls table, resize all datasheet columns to fit the data, and then print the table.

e. Close and save the table.

10. The file Southgat is the HTML file from a Web site for the Southgate Mall. Add a hyperlink field to the Malls table. Name the field Home Pages. Add a hyperlink for the Southgate Mall record to the Southgat HTML file in the Cases folder on your Student Disk.

11. Click the Southgate Mall hyperlink to view the Southgate Mall home page. Print the home page.

12. Close the Walks database, and then exit Access.

4. Lopez Lexus Dealerships Maria and Hector Lopez have established an intranet for their dealerships. They want you to publish some of the Lexus database data as HTML files for their dealers to view. Complete the following:

1. Make sure your Student Disk is in the appropriate disk drive, start Access, and then open the Lexus database located in the Cases folder on your Student Disk.

2. Use the Publish to the Web Wizard to create a home page:
   a. Save the Cars table and the Cars by Model and Year report as HTML files.
   b. Do not use a template for the files.
   c. Choose the static page format for the files.
   d. Publish the files in the Cases folder on your Student Disk.
   e. Use Cars as the name for the home page.
   f. Do not save your choices in a profile.

3. Use Internet Explorer to do the following:
   a. Open the Cars home page, and then view both the Cars table and the Cars by Model and Year report.

   b. Print the Cars HTML file from Internet Explorer.

4. Use the Publish to the Web Wizard to create a home page again:
   a. Save the Car Statistics by Location query and the Cars by Model and Year report as HTML files.
   b. Use the Lopeztbl template for the Car Statistics by Location query and the Lopezrpt template for the Cars by Model and Year report. Both templates are located in the Cases folder on your Student Disk.
   c. Choose the static page format for the files.
   d. Publish the files in the Cases folder on your Student Disk.
   e. Use the name Cars for the home page.
   f. Save your choices as a profile named Lexus Profile.

5. Use Internet Explorer to open the Cars home page, and then view both the Car Statistics by Location data and the Cars by Model and Year report.

6. Add the record shown in Figure 7-38 to the Cars table in the Lexus database.

Figure 7-38 ◀

VehicleID	Manufacturer	Model	Class	Transmission	Year	LocationCode	Cost	SellingPrice
PAJ9B	Lexus	SC400	S3	A4	1999	Amarillo	$37,600.00	$43,000.00

7. Use the Publish to the Web Wizard to update the Cars home page:
   a. Use the Lexus Profile to recreate the HTML files.
   b. Use Internet Explorer to open the Cars home page, and then view the Cars by Model and Year data. Verify that the new record has been included in the report.
   c. Print the Cars by Model and Year HTML file from Internet Explorer.

8. View and then print the Car Statistics by Location HTML file from Internet Explorer.

9. The Mileage HTML file on your Student Disk contains fuel mileage data for Lexus models. Import the Mileage HTML file as a new table in the Lexus database:
   a. Choose the option for using the column headings as field names in the table.
   b. Let Access assign the primary key.
   c. Name the new table Mileage.
   d. Open the Mileage table, resize all datasheet columns to fit the data, and then print the table.
   e. Close and save the table.

10. The Word document named Reviews, which is stored in the Cases folder on your Student Disk, contains a bookmark for each Lexus model. Add a hyperlink field named Reviews to the Mileage table. Add hyperlink field values for each of the records in the table, using the bookmarks to link to the named locations in the Reviews document.

11. Click the hyperlink for the LS400 model. Use the pointer to select the comments for just that model, and then print the selected text. (*Hint:* Use the Print command on the File menu.)

12. Close the Lexus database, and then exit Access.

Answers to Quick Check Questions

SESSION 5.1

1 A Lookup Wizard field lets you select a value from a list of possible values, making data entry easier.

2 the Like comparison operator

3 The asterisk is a wildcard that represents any string of characters in a pattern match query.

4 Use the In comparison operator to define a condition with two or more values.

5 Use the Not logical operator to negate a criterion.

6 when you want the user to be prompted to enter the selection criteria when the query runs

SESSION 5.2

1 A bound control is linked to a field in the underlying table or query; an unbound control is not.

2 Position the pointer anywhere on the border of the control, then drag the control and its attached label box.

3 Right-click the label, click Properties on the shortcut menu, click the Format tab, edit the existing label in the Caption text box or double-click it to select the current value and then type a new caption.

4 Select the control, position the pointer on a sizing handle, and then click and drag the pointer.

5 The Form Header section allows you to add titles, instructions, command buttons, and other information to the top of your form.

6 Open the form in Design view, click the Image button on the toolbox, position the pointer at the location for the upper-left corner of the picture, click the left mouse button, select the picture file, click OK.

SESSION 5.3

1 Open the form in Design view, click the Tab Control button on the toolbox, position the pointer in the form at the location for the upper-left corner of the tab control, click the left mouse button.

2 Click a label, press and hold down the Shift key and click the other labels, click Format, point to Align, click Right.

3 Double-click the subform object.

4 Filter By Form finds records that match multiple selection criteria using the same Access logical and comparison operators that you use in queries.

5 Save the filter as a query, and then apply the query to a form.

6 Opening a query runs the query and displays the results in Datasheet view. Applying a query to a form opens the query and displays the results in the form.

SESSION 6.1

1 The Report Header section appears once at the beginning of a report. The Page Header section appears at the top of each page of a report. The Group Header section appears once at the beginning of a new group of records. The Detail section appears once for each record in the underlying table or query. The Group Footer section appears once at the end of a group of records. The Report Footer section appears once at the end of the report. The Page Footer section appears at the bottom of each page of a report.

2 A custom report is a report you make by modifying a report created by AutoReport or the Report Wizard, or by creating a report from scratch in Design view.

3 The Report window in Design view has many of the same components as the Form window in Design view, including a Properties button, a Field List button, and a Toolbox button on the toolbar. Both windows also have horizontal and vertical rulers, a grid, and a Formatting toolbar. Unlike the Form window in Design view, which initially displays only the Detail section on a blank form, the Report window also displays a Page Header section and a Page Footer section.

4 The Caption property for an object determines the text displayed in the object. You would change the Caption property value for an object if the default value is difficult to read or understand.

5 Click an object, hold down Shift and click the other objects, click Format, point to Align, click Left.

6 Clicking the Zoom button changes the size of the page displayed in Print Preview.

SESSION 6.2

1 a field from the underlying table or query by which records are grouped in a report.

2 Use the Text Box tool to create a text box in a form or report.

3 Type =Date() in the text box.

4 Click Insert, click Page Numbers, specify the format, position, and alignment of the page number, click OK.

5 The Sorting and Grouping button displays the Sorting and Grouping dialog box, which allows you to specify sorting and grouping fields for a report.

6 Place a text box in the Group Footer or Report Footer section. In the text box, enter the expression =Sum([*fieldname*]) where *fieldname* is the name of the field you want to total.

7 Hiding duplicate values makes the report easier to read; duplicate values clutter up the report.

SESSION 6.3

1 You embed or link objects in an Access report to include objects created by other programs, including objects that you cannot create in Access (for example, charts).

2 An embedded object preserves its connection to the program in which it was created. Any changes you make in the object are reflected in the Access embedded file, not in the original file. A linked object preserves its connection to the original source file. Any changes you make in the object are reflected in both the linked file in Access and the original file.

3 OLE stands for Object Linking and Embedding; a program that supports OLE can create objects that can be embedded or linked in another program.

4 Insert the object from a file and select the Link check box.

5 You use the source program in which the object was originally created.

6 Each linked object is updated automatically when the report is opened. To update links manually, click Edit, click OLE/DDE Links, select the link (or links) to update, click Update Now, click Close.

7 Select the table or query in the Database window or open the table or query in Datasheet view, click Tools, point to Office Links, click Analyze It with MS Excel.

SESSION 7.1

1 HTML stands for HyperText Markup Language, the language used to create World Wide Web documents.

2 the collection of HTML documents stored on Web servers linked through the Internet

3 A Web browser is a program used to view HTML documents.

4 A hyperlink links one Web document to another.

5 A template is a file that contains HTML instructions for creating a Web page together with special instructions that tell Access where to place the Access data on the page.

6 You can use a saved profile to recreate HTML documents without having to reenter your choices.

SESSION 7.2

1 Access can import HTML data that is formatted as a table or as a list.

2 In the Insert Hyperlink dialog box, enter the name of the location in the Named location in file text box.

3 A bookmark is a named location in a Microsoft Word document.

4 Typing a hyperlink value directly into a field allows you to specify only the hyperlink address. The Insert Hyperlink dialog box also allows you to specify a named location in the hyperlinked file.

5 URL stands for uniform resource locator; a URL is an Internet address.

6 Click the hyperlink field value to open the hyperlinked document or object.

Microsoft Access 97 **Index**

If you are using this text as part of our Custom Edition Program, you will find entries in the Index and Task Reference that do not apply to your custom tutorials.

Microsoft Access 97 **Task Reference**

TASK	PAGE #	RECOMMENDED METHOD
Access, exit	A 1.13	Click ❎ on the program window
Access, start	A 1.7	Click Start, point to Programs, click Microsoft Access
Aggregate functions, use	A 3.31	Display the query in Design view, click Σ
And operator, enter in selection criteria	A 5.12	Enter selection criteria in the same Criteria row in the design grid
AutoForm, create	A 1.16	Click the Forms tab, click New, click an AutoForm Wizard, choose the table or query for the form, click OK
AutoFormat, change	A 4.4	See Reference Window: Changing a Form's AutoFormat
AutoReport, create	A 1.21	Click the Reports tab, click New, click an AutoReport Wizard, choose the table or query for the form, click OK
Calculated field, add to a query	A 3.28	See Reference Window: Using Expression Builder
Caption, change for a label	A 5.24	Right-click the label, click Properties, click the Format tab, edit the label in the Caption text box
Chart, edit	A 6.35	Double-click the chart object
Chart, embed in a report	A 6.33	See Reference Window: Embedding a Chart in a Report
Chart Wizard, activate	A 6.34	Click the Reports tab, click New, click Chart Wizard, select the table or query, click OK
Color, add to a form control	A 5.32	Select the control, click the Fill/Back Color list arrow, click the color box you want
Column, adjust width of	A 3.21	Double-click the right border of the column heading
Control, move	A 5.23	Select the control, click the control's move handle, drag the control to its new position
Control, resize	A 5.26	Select the control, click and drag a sizing handle, release the mouse button
Data, find	A 4.7	See Reference Window: Finding Data
Data, group in a report	A 6.24	See Reference Window: Sorting and Grouping Data in a Report
Data, sort in a report	A 6.24	See Reference Window: Sorting and Grouping Data in a Report
Database, compact	A 4.28	See Reference Window: Compacting a Database
Datasheet view, switch to	A 2.14	Click 🖽
Date, add to a report	A 6.16	See Reference Window: Adding the Date to a Report
Design view, switch to	A 2.18	Click 📐

Microsoft Access 97 **Task Reference**

TASK	PAGE #	RECOMMENDED METHOD
Duplicate values, hide	A 6.30	Right-click the field's text box, click Properties, click the right side of the Hide Duplicates text box, click Yes
Field, add	A 2.19	See Reference Window: Adding a Field Between Two Existing Fields
Field, add to a form or report	A 5.21	Drag the field from the field list to the form or report in Design view
Field, define	A 2.8	See Reference Window: Defining a Field in a Table
Field, delete	A 2.18	Display the table in Design view, right-click the field's row selector, click Delete Rows
Field, move	A 2.19	Display the table in Design view, click the field's row selector, drag the field with the pointer
Filter, save as a query	A 5.46	Click ![save icon], enter the query name
Filter, saved as a query, apply	A 5.46	See Reference Window: Applying a Filter that Was Saved as a Query
Filter By Form, activate	A 5.43	Click ![filter icon]
Filter By Form, create	A 5.43	See Reference Window: Selecting Records Using Filter By Form
Filter By Selection, activate	A 3.16	Select the field value, click ![filter by selection icon]
Form, custom, create	A 5.18	See Reference Window: Creating a Form in Design View
Form Footer, add	A 5.28	Click View, click Form Header/Footer
Form Footer, remove	A 5.28	Click and drag the bottom edge of the footer up until the section area disappears
Form Header, add	A 5.28	Click View, click Form Header/Footer
Form Header, remove	A 5.28	Click and drag the bottom edge of the header up until the section area disappears
Form Wizard, activate	A 4.2	Click the Forms tab, click New, click Form Wizard, choose the table or query for the form, click OK
Group totals, calculate in a report	A 6.26	See Reference Window: Calculating Totals in a Report
HTML file, import as a table	A 7.16	See Reference Window: Importing an HTML File as an Access Table
HTML file, view	A 7.7	Click the Go button on the Web toolbar, click Open, select the file to open, click the Open button, click OK
Hyperlink, use	A 7.24	Click the hyperlink field value

Microsoft Access 97 **Task Reference**

TASK	PAGE #	RECOMMENDED METHOD
Hyperlink field, create	A 7.21	In Design view, type the field name in a blank Field Name text box, press Tab, click the Data Type list arrow, click Hyperlink
Hyperlink field value, enter	A 7.22	In Datasheet view, click the hyperlink field, click [icon], enter the name of the file or URL, enter the named location in the file or URL (if any), click OK
Label, add to a form	A 5.29	Click [icon], click and drag the pointer to create the label box, type the label in the box
Line, add to a report	A 6.23	Click [icon], click and drag the pointer to create the line
Object, embedded or linked, edit	A 6.35	Double-click the object
Object, embedded or linked, update manually	A 6.43	Click Edit, click OLE/DDE Links, select the object, click Update Now
Object, link in a report	A 6.40	Click [icon], click and drag the pointer to create a box for the linked object, click Create from File, specify the file containing the object, click Link, click OK
Objects, align	A 5.36	Select the objects, right-click a selected object, point to Align, and then click the alignment you want
Objects, save in an HTML file	A 7.4	See Reference Window: Saving Access Objects in an HTML File
Office Assistant, use to get Help	A 1.18	See Reference Window: Using the Office Assistant
Or operator, enter in selection criteria	A 5.12	Enter selection criteria in the Criteria and or rows in the design grid
Overall totals, calculate in a report	A 6.26	See Reference Window: Calculating Totals in a Report
Page numbers, add to a report	A 6.18	Click the section to contain page numbers, click Insert, click Page Numbers, select formatting options, click OK
Parameter query, create	A 5.14	See Reference Window: Creating a Parameter Query
Picture, add to a form	A 5.30	Click [icon], click the left mouse button to place an outline in the form, click the name of the picture file, click OK
Picture, insert on a report	A 4.24	Click Insert on the menu bar, click Picture, select the picture file, click OK
Primary key, specify	A 2.12	See Reference Window: Specifying a Primary Key for a Table
Profile, create	A 7.11	In the final Publish to the Web Wizard dialog box, click the check box to save a profile, enter a name for the profile
Profile, use	A 7.14	In the first Publish to the Web Wizard dialog box, select the profile to use
Publish to the Web Wizard, activate	A 7.5	Click File, click Save As HTML

Microsoft Access 97 **Task Reference**

TASK	PAGE #	RECOMMENDED METHOD
Query, define	A 3.3	Click the Queries tab, click New, click Design View, click OK
Query, export as an Excel worksheet	A 6.45	Click Tools, point to Office Links, click Analyze It with MS Excel
Query, run	A 3.5	Click ▣
Query results, sort	A 3.14	See Reference Window: Sorting a Query Datasheet
Record, add a new one	A 1.12	Click ▶✳
Record, delete	A 2.25	Right-click the record's row selector, click Delete Record, click Yes
Record, move to first	A 1.12	Click ◄◄
Record, move to last	A 1.12	Click ►►
Record, move to next	A 1.12	Click ►
Record, move to previous	A 1.12	Click ◄
Record, move to a specific one	A 1.12	Type the record number in the Specific Record box, press Enter
Records, redisplay all after filter	A 3.17	Click ▼
Relationship, define between two tables	A 3.8	Click ▣
Report, custom, create	A 6.6	Click the Reports tab, click New, click Design View, select the table or query for the report, click OK
Report, preview	A 6.14	Click ▣
Report Footer, add	A 6.20	Click View, click Report Header/Footer
Report Footer, remove	A 6.20	Click and drag the bottom edge of the footer up until the section area disappears
Report Header, add	A 6.20	Click View, click Report Header/Footer
Report Header, remove	A 6.20	Click and drag the bottom edge of the header up until the section area disappears
Report Wizard, activate	A 4.17	Click the Reports tab, click New, click Report Wizard, choose the table or query for the report, click OK
Sort, specify ascending	A 3.12	Click ▣
Sort, specify descending	A 3.12	Click ▣

TASK	PAGE #	RECOMMENDED METHOD
Subform/Subreport Wizard, activate	A 5.38	Make sure is selected, click , click at the upper-left corner for the subform
Tab control, add to a form	A 5.35	Click , click at the upper-left corner for the tab control
Table, create	A 2.6	Click the Tables tab, click New, click Design View, click OK
Table, export as an Excel worksheet	A 6.45	Click Tools, point to Office Links, click Analyze It with MS Excel
Table, open	A 1.11	Click the Tables tab, click the table name, click Open
Table, print	A 1.13	Click
Table structure, save	A 2.13	See Reference Window: Saving a Table Structure
Template, use	A 7.10	Select HTML template in the Publish to the Web Wizard dialog box